No Regrets

Gene Lassers

ISBN # 9780962078415

Library of Congress # 2013934248

Publication date August, 2013

Author/Publisher contact steamtrn@aol..com

Printed by   Minuteman Press
                    Long Beach, CA

Cover Photo   Helen the cook and Gene looking in the
                    neighborhood grocery store window (circa 1938)

Contents

FOREWARD

There is no doubt that the decision of the Lassers family to leave Europe and immigrate to America has had a profound impact on my life. The exciting escape from Lithuania (or Russia as the border was constantly changing back and forth), as described by my distant cousin Arthur in Chapter 1 remains very memorable. Imagine if they had not persevered, our name could have been inscribed in the Gulag of the Pogroms.

If the Lilienfeld, and Silberman patriarchs had stayed in Germany rather than leaving in the 1860's for America, the family might have been part of "The Final Solution," *Die Endloung,* the Holocaust! Of course we were not alone as people immigrated from all over Europe, and other parts of the world, and considered America as the land of opportunity, and they were right.

So to say that I am lucky there is no doubt, and double lucky to be born a fourth generation red, white, and blue baby to a wealthy family in the land of the brave and the free. I have fulfilled my family obligation of renewal by siring three sons, and they in turn have married, and fathered six wonderful grandchildren who can look forward to a life of wonder challenge, and adventure.

My reason for publishing this book is to make sure that the family and future generations are aware of the history of their heritage, and the special and wonderful life that I was privileged to lead. I am the pivot point, the last responder to document our past or it will be lost forever. That said, I hope others will find this book an interesting read.

No Regrets

On a Sunday morning, at the finish of *Meet The Press*, my wife Linda began channel surfing as I gathered the discarded morning papers for disposal. She stopped abruptly to view a motivational pastor, Joel Osteen, a strange selection because this is not our normal viewing pattern. He was a white Pentecostal minister that never missed a beat and was pouring out devotional words at machine gun velocity. He was preaching to a full house at his mega-church based in Houston, Texas that attracts 16,000 people weekly to hear his sermons, and I can see why, he is good.

Every time he mentioned God, if the word Ford had been substituted, I am sure their sales would have doubled. During the twenty minutes we tuned in, his sermon repeatedly emphasized that a strong belief will produce positive results in one's life.

So I thought, why has my life turned around in so many ways? The dots lead to a belief in a supreme being, and a daily acknowledgement of his Grace. His silent guidance has been a beacon of light leading me through good times and bad. I have been introduced to the doctrine of forgiveness, and adopted it as the best weapon I can embrace to relieve the yoke on my shoulders that was holding me back and weighting me down. It allowed me to move on.

My mother taught me to pray each night. Opel, my nanny, a future Christian missionary no doubt refined and encouraged my reverence. There is seldom a night I have not blessed my family, friends and country. Is it logical that God has cleared my path for a better life, not just luck?

This book is dedicated to generations past, present, and future. My life has been unique, interesting, challenging and has embraced perseverance, as well as bad judgment, and good intentions. I chose to call this memoir, *No Regrets*, for this illustrates in words my footsteps of the past 77 years through life. The time to write it has taken over three years, indeed a personal challenge.

The effort started with a page or two of rambling thoughts which I put aside, only to return to a day or two later with regrets, as the effort was so poor. Rewrite, rewrite, rewrite is the mantra of any author and it became mine until I had over 52,000 words devoted to my life. The thoughts flowed easily, because it was all about me, me, me, *mirror, mirror on the wall....!* .

My wife Linda read the 252 page narrative and her comments were not of a wilting pansy but more like a Panzer tank commander, yet quite valuable. I even sent the manuscript to my cousin in Florida who was in his eighties, and had the time to read and critique it. "Interesting, different, ponderous, boring, too much aviation and Howard Hughes material. It jumps around too much, but it is worth pursuing..." was his opinion. He was also interested in my accomplishments, but that is what relatives are for.

It was enough encouragement to follow up with some professional advice and the only telephone number I could think of was 1-800-Cal State Long Beach University, prompt, English Department. They were kind enough to give me the name of an instructor in the Department who read, advised, and corrected masters and doctorial thesis for aspiring candidates.

Susan returned my call and agreed to meet over coffee, and discuss the project to date. We talked, and she agreed to undertake the challenge of reading 3 envelopes containing 256 pages of my memories. Approximately 8 weeks later we met again, as she had finished the assignment. Her thoughts were that I had an interesting story which was all over the place, bouncing like a moving ball on the silver screen of another era. It was hard to follow, disorganized, rambling, and not personal enough. Her comments were not given lightly or without fervor. It is not good when you submit a manuscript to an editor, and it is returned with more writing on the pages than were originally turned in.

Huh...this is the end of the entire book???? We just had a thud of a landing....hmmmm

In my opinion too heavy a moral for such a light tale

Song lyric-copyright issue?

This comes out of nowhere! Are paragraphs missing or something?

Need details, explain all this

You are just name dropping here. What went on or lose it.

As always we need a transition rather than just lurching on.

Run on and messy sentence to open a paragraph

This was brutal. I was devastated but not defeated. Where do I go from here? Do I even want to go anywhere from here? I put it aside for a week or two, peeking at a page occasionally. Her note attached to the work said,

"I think your story has the potential to fulfill this description of a successful story. ...it draws us, believably to its action and to its people and leaves us feeling we have spent a good time in an interesting place."

I could not let it go at that point and I started over, revamping the entire structure, and putting it into definable chapters, and using Susan's notes and a pair of scissors to nip and tuck. Now I believed I was on the right track. I was fortunate to have my friend Susan Stuhlbarg complete the final editing, and to have my wife Linda's invaluable and priceless encouragement and direction.

No Regrets is a glimpse of a life nurtured in the 1940's and 50's, about a person fortunate enough to have been born during the "Lucky Generation," as I call my era.

I hope you will find it interesting and different. Maybe your name is in here, but if not I apologize for the omission. Anyway, welcome to my world.

Chapter 1

The Hyde Park Years

I was conceived during the Great Depression by Sanford and Mary Lassers. They lived in the Hyde Park area on the Southside of Chicago. It was a neighborhood known for its mansions, fine homes and the University of Chicago campus, dominating the 'Midway', once part of the Columbian Exposition Fair of 1893. My folks had resided on the Southside their entire lives, and my mother lived in the same house since birth. This is the neighborhood where President Barack Obama has his home today and it was once considered the finest area to live in South of the 'Loop' (reference to elevated rail tracks originally the street car track loop) in downtown Chicago.

The homes were palatial for the time. Although our house, owned by my widowed grandfather, was large and comfortable, I do not think it matched many of the others in the neighborhood. The finer properties were north of Hyde Park boulevard, and nearer the University, but that is not to say that ours was a 'tear-down,' far from it.

As the 'Black Migration' escalated from the Southern states, at the turn of the 20th century, the demographics of this area changed from all white to a creeping black residency. All of the Negroes were escaping the prejudice and poverty of the south for the higher wages and a chance, not a promise, for a better life in the north. Train loads of black southerners crowded into the near Southside of Chicago, and it eventually turned into a bitterly contested turf resulting in racial tension and riots as it did in other cities. The blacks exploded further south as their numbers swelled, and the neighborhoods up to 47th street were turning color, and change was coming. It would take World War II to come and go for the area to become integrated.

As I lay in the nursery at the hospital, I was not dressed in swaddling clothes although I am sure that nearby there was a pile of Coulter infant ready to wear for my departure home, to be raised in the lap of luxury. The changing neighborhood never would have occurred to me. My folks received over fifty telegrams and more letters than can be imagined heralding my arrival with nothing but good wishes. Unto them '*a prince was born*' and I still have the evidence of the tributes that my mother saved.

This correspondence regarding my introduction into the world on March 7, 1936 commanded almost as much attention in my folks circle as world events. There were stacks of letters and telegrams of congratulations for the happy couple on the birth of their son Eugene William Lassers. The Eugene William was in honor of my grandfather who had the same first two names and the same three initials. Everything in our house had initials. I suspect it was the expected thing to brand your belongings. Towels, handkerchiefs, doilies, silverware, sweaters, stockings and blouses were a few of the items that come to mind. It was a Woman's fetish forced on the men in most cases. In our house, the men could have cared less about being branded like a cow as to who they were.

"To the manor born" may be an appropriate term here for I entered the comfortable world to live in a large house, stocked with servants and financial stability. I was raised by the help (servants) from the beginning as my parents continued their vast social life without interruption and the need of local baby sitters. Miss Angel took care of me for a year or so and then there were others in between while Opel, who I will discuss later, finished the nanny roster as I was approaching seven years of silver spoon treatment. Then the job was taken over by Helen (I called her HaHa), our cook, a person who no doubt influenced my life as did Opel. My future would be one of a separate path and numerous second chances.

The Great Depression began with the collapse of the stock market in 1929 and in 1936 it was still a major economic factor in the country's well being and attitude. Soup kitchens, hoboes and the unemployed were an overwhelming factor for the Franklin Roosevelt Administration to deal with. FDR was now into his second term of what would be four in total, and was popular to the poor majority and disdained by the rich minority. Objectively speaking we were the rich minority during a period when the country was on the dole, and people were desperate and homeless, selling apples on street corners and begging at back doors for food. Hyde Park was still in the money and isolated.

I can remember men knocking on our back door, and Helen our cook would answer and generously feed the wanting hands, stretched out in front of empty stomachs. I can remember the blind man on the corner with his flea bitten scrawny dog begging which made me cry, possibly the last real good cry I've had, and the tattered organ grinder with the monkey on a leash, where the little fellow would take your penny and put it in to his cup.

Americans were looking for a second chance to recoup their normal way of life and it would come, but they had to be patient. I too would take advantage of second chances throughout my life, and they played a significant part in the twists and turns of a course I would follow, a different path.

My Dad was what today would be called a 'Bluedog Democrat', a semi conservative right winger if you will, where the rest of the extended family were kennel-bred Republican blue bloods dating back to the American Civil War. They asked dad at a family dinner why he voted for the Roosevelt ticket? His answer was "...that his business," a small chain of three furniture stores outside the Chicago area, "was doing financially better." That was enough to put the Republican blood hounds back in the bottle, probably the only answer that would since business was everything to them. Just to back this up, my mother's grandfather, Sigmund Silberman, was a registered Republican in 1860, and probably voted for Abraham Lincoln! Of course at that time the GOP was the liberal party and also home to Progressives, and Abolitionists who wanted to end slavery in America.

As mentioned, I was born at Michael Reese Hospital, a noted medical facility of the time as it is today. Mother would not return for a second go at the same procedure of having a baby for reasons I can only speculate on. My dad had wanted another child but it takes two persons to agree, and it never did happen. From a letter in 1930 (their courting days) to my dad, mailed from New York City, shows a hesitancy of the heart regarding the prospects of children from my Mother.

"I am going to buy some dresses for (?). I am just thrilled over the idea, one would think it is my own child. Maybe in a few years from now I will be buying my own some clothes, who knows?"

There is only one posed picture that I have in the family album, of mother holding me a few months down the line after birth, and she does not look comfortable, but stiff. It was taken by the professional photographer who came to the house for years to record my history. I would not have minded another sibling rather than be the third generation only child on my mother's side.

My welcome into the world did not change the news as it unfurled in distant lands. Germany continued its aggressive ways in Europe and eventually brought Italy in on their side thus creating the Axis between Berlin and Rome. Other countries joined and became our enemies in World War II.

The abdication of the British Monarch Edward the VIII for the American woman he loved, Wallace Simpson, was a first in history for the English, and it rocked the country and startled the rest of the world. Was he nuts? What a wimp he turned out to be, still it was for the best since his Brother "Bertie," a better man came to the throne, and was the right man for the historic time which lay ahead, for World War II was soon to begin. Although I was not aware of this, I of course was not going to give up my throne. In fact I am sure I was getting use to it.

A public opinion poll taken in the United States in the early 1930's showed that 41% of those polled thought the Jews had too much power and 20% wanted to rid the United States of them. There were signs to be seen that read, "No dogs, Jews or colors (sic) need apply." Apparently I was not informed, and I wasn't going anywhere. The Jews had always provoked controversy wherever they settled on our good earth. They were smart, educated, hard working people who wanted the best for their families and fought for it. Some had traditional ways that were strange to main street America, and not only did they endure being ostracized in many countries, they ignored the snubs and built and enlarged their own ethnic establishments.

In Chicago there were Gentile and Jewish country clubs, downtown business clubs, doctor groups, law firms and on and on. There was factual evidence of discrimination signs that said "No Jews need apply, Jews will enter through the back," and segregated neighborhoods that were off limits to live in. Some thought that Jews were despicable, vile, filthy people, and you should not do business with, or associate with them.

My birth did not bring such controversy, only accolades. Our household was able to keep everybody straight because everything was monogrammed that was not nailed down in the house. EWL (my grandfather's), and MLL (my mother's) initials were abundant   It was the gilded trend of the time. My only acknowledgement of this during my life was to have his and hers initials on the license plates of my wife's car and mine. It is odd that the hard to get plate, LBL, was available when Linda became my second wife, and the initials, SBL, of Sharon my first wife had to disappear.

At my home, love and attention was given in the Victorian style and more prevalent from the servants than from my parents or grandfather. That's a strong statement but as I look back it was comparable to being brought up like an English Royal, yet for the times an accepted practice among the wealthy. I can remember reciting to Helen the cook, a real companion to me, a list of household occupants whom I liked and didn't like. My mother would always come in last. Helen tried to shhh me from saying that, yet I still remember it to this day. Although I had nannies until seven, it was Helen or Opel who were my friends, my confidants, my playmates in reality.

For 10 years I lived with my grandfather (Papa), and of course my parents. He had been a widower since 1923 when his first wife died from a heart attack. In 1943 he remarried a wonderful lady of long acquaintance by the name of Ellen Williams whom I called Aunt Ellen, and we all lived in the same house. When World War II was over, my family moved into a beautiful duplex apartment located on the 16th and 17th floor at 20 E. Cedar on the ritzy near north side of town. I can remember a controversy between my mother and her father over the cost for the rent of $500.00 per month, an equivalent in 2010 dollars of $5600.00 per month but my mother prevailed and paid a large portion of it out of the separate funds held in her name.

My dad could not afford such extravagance. Mother bought another dog against the advice of her father and her husband, which I ended up walking most of the time. She was a runaway train, or maybe spoiled is a better word. She had her own wealth, left from her mother, and still depended on her father for advice and an allowance, a strain on their marriage. Dad did not rule the roost.

Our family background was a mixture of German and Lithuanian. My mother's side held trump on the genealogy card since both her grandmother and grandfather came from the cities of Rockenhausen and Hanover in Germany while my dad's parents were more recent arrivals in the late 1800's from Lithuania, by way of Canada. For those not familiar with Jewish heritage, the German Jews embraced a feeling of refinement, superior education, and adapted more easily into the main stream of American life than those from Eastern Europe. Their attitude generally speaking was the attitude of the German people as a whole, they were superior! They felt this was testified to by Germany and its numerous achievements during the past 400 years.

Years later after being discharged from the Army in 1961, my first wife, Sharon, and I returned home from a three month sojourn to Europe courtesy of Aunt Ellen. I had been reading Leon Uris' book <u>Exodus</u> as we entered Italy and was so enamored with it that we decided to turn east rather than west at the "boot," and board a Greek ship to Israel. On the spur of the moment we returned to America by ship and sailed on the Israeli Zim Line's *MS Israel* a 5,000 ton tub bound for New York City, a trip of 15 days. The Captain, a German Jew and his wife ate dinner with us every night and sought our company rather than rub shoulders with the Eastern European Jews on board who were emigrating to Canada.

Jews of German descent were professionals, industrialists, merchants and educated people and I believe many thought of other Jews as mere rag merchants or ghetto dwellers, people who practice Judaism in a different way than they did. The Lilienfelds (later changed to Lilienfield because of the intense dislike of Germans by Americans during the First World War) were merchants and manufacturers while the Silbermans became wool merchants, fur traders, manufacturers and store owners. The Eastern European Jews with nothing in their pockets and no worldly goods on their backs also came looking for a better life, freedom from oppression and gold on the street. They became peddlers and worked their way up to owning stores near or away from the large city ghettos where they had congregated.

My Lithuanian grandfather Joseph Aaron Lassers is credited with starting the "Boston Store" in Kankakee, Illinois, which eventually became Lassers Furniture Company when my father took over. It was an upgrade from the 'peddler wagon days,' working the farms and ranches, the homesteads and the villages, which he and his family did to survive in their newly adopted country.

My distant cousin, Arthur Lassers, whose acquaintance I have made in the past few years, told about my father's family background. Here is a quote from his note to me on June 18, 2007:

My grandfather's name was Aaron Liesserovitz. Or it could have been Lasserovitz. In that the family might have migrated from Russia generations before, the name might have been spelled in the Cyrillic alphabet. Or perhaps in the Hebrew alphabet since the family conversed in Yiddish. So there is of course a question as to the spelling. But it was shortened and Americanized to Lassers on arriving in America.

My father told me that we are descendents of the prophet Eliazer, but today that seems a little far fetched to me. Yet I am sure my father believed that to be true. However since Lazer is the word for reader, it could also be that we were descendents of a reader. And Readers were prized, and later in America were often hired to read aloud to workers in a factory.

At the time the family immigrated to America, they lived in Miriapol, Lithuania. My great grandfather was a Rabbi. But I'm not sure how my grandfather made his living. I remember stories about them living in a very large house, which they probably rented, and that they took in boarders. I heard many stories about how life was not easy for Jews in any place in Europe, especially a place dominated by Russia.

My Grandfather Aaron and my Grandmother Esther had five children that survived, four sons and a daughter, plus one that died either in infancy or birth. Starting from the oldest they were Isaac, Joseph, Libby, Henry (my father) and Emanuel. My grandfather's greatest worry was that his sons would be drafted into the Russian Army, surely a sorry lot for any Jewish man! Primarily because of his fear of this draft, but also because he yearned for a better life for himself and his family, he decided to move the family to America. This was probably around 1885. To this day I marvel at the courage of this man to undertake that great a change in the life of himself and the lives of his family.

The plan was that he and his oldest son, Isaac, would go first, get established, earn some money, and then send for the rest of the family, not a unique or unusual plan. But he was afraid that since Isaac was at or near draft age already the Czar's police would come looking for Isaac, and for him too for taking Isaac out of the country. So he devised a plan to outwit the Czar's police!

First of all, he coached Esther on how to act when the police came looking for him and Isaac. She was to wring her hands, and cry out that her oldest son had disappeared and her husband had deserted her. And how was she to live now that she was a woman alone trying to raise four children? She was to scream and cry hysterically, saying she thought her husband had run off to Poland, and could they find him and bring him back to her!

Let me pause in the historical dissertation. Not everyone in Russia or Russian controlled Provinces hated Jews. Some were fair minded. However there was much evidence that the Czar hated Jews with a vengeance. He also hated the English, although he admired the French. But one of the Czar's favorite epitaphs was, "An Englishman is a Jew!" But one of my father's stories was about the time a group of Russian soldiers were in town and came to my grandparents' door. Since it was a big house, they thought it would be a good place to be put up for a few nights. Well my grandmother didn't think she had much choice, but she was paid! As they were about to leave, my grandmother took the man aside who commanded the soldiers and told him that a pillow was missing and that it was filled with real goose down and had an embroidered pillow case. The soldier in command found her pillow, brought it back to her and apologized to her. My father said the man who tried to steal the pillow was punished.

Now: Back to the family history. My grandfather and my Uncle Isaac did not take passage on any ship sailing from a Russian controlled port. Instead they traveled to Hamburg, Germany, but there is some confusion in the stories as to how they got there. In one version, they traveled by night and slept in the fields during the day so as not to attract the attention of the Czar's police! It is a long way to Hamburg so it might be that they did this the first few nights, though I think they got some better means of transportation than walking.

When they arrived in Hamburg, Germany they booked passage on a steamship, but not one bound for New York. My grandfather reasoned that since everybody going to America went to New York, he was sure the Czar's police would be waiting for them on the New York dock the instant they got off the boat! So they sailed to Montreal Canada instead. Back then, locks had not yet been built around the rapids in the St. Laurence River, so Montreal was as far as ships were able to go. In Montreal they took a train to Windsor, Ontario, and then a ferry to Detroit. (There were no bridges yet.) In Detroit, they laughed, embraced, and kissed, convinced that they had finally outwitted the dreaded Czar's police and that they were safe at last in America!

Now they embarked on the next step in my grandfather's master plan. He had decided that they would go to Texas! Evidently, he had heard that everyone in Texas had come from some place else, therefore these two Jews would not stand out, but would mix easily into the general population since all the others would also be immigrant foreigners! It never occurred to him that the "someplace else" might well be Mississippi, Alabama, Louisiana or Oklahoma. Not someplace in Europe! So, "Head for Texas" they did! They took a train to Chicago, and then another train to Joplin, Missouri. Now here is where there are several versions of the story, depending on which uncle I chose to believe. It could have been somewhere else in Missouri, or some place in Arkansas. But evidently they got to the place they were lead to believe that was as far west as this (or any other) railroad went! In whatever town that was, they bought a wagon and a team of oxen. They found a wholesale hardware dealer where they bought a load of hardware. Then they set off for Texas. A short time later, they arrived in Texas and at this point the story did strain my belief even as a youngster! How could they have arrived in Texas in a "short time," in an oxen-driven wagon yet? But as I grew older, I reasoned that "a short time later," my grandfather and my uncle Isaac saw cattle grazing and probably said to each other, o.k. this has got to be Texas!" So they then started selling the hardware from farm to farm, from ranch to ranch, and from village to village.

When they had sold enough of the hardware, they were able to sleep nights in the wagon instead of under it. And when they had sold all the hardware, they then made their way back to the city where the railroad ended. In one version of the story, they also sold the wagon and the team of oxen. But if so, how did they get back? I never did learn how they made their way back, perhaps by Greyhound stage coach! Or maybe they didn't sell the wagon and oxen. I'll never know. But they bought another load of hardware, and headed for "Texas" again. They kept doing this for anywhere from one to three years until they had earned enough money to return to Chicago (where they had changed trains) and opened a store.

I believe the rest of the family embarked from Hamburg for their trip to America. I don't know where they sailed to in America, but evidently they didn't have the morbid fear that the Czar's police were hot on their trail! My father told me the story of this voyage to America, and to me, as a child it was such a thrilling story that I asked him to repeat it over and over again on many occasions. The ship they were on was not an ocean liner, but was a small freighter which also carried passengers. The fare was cheaper than on a regular liner although the trip took longer. The Captain of the freighter was evidently a skilled navigator since he understood the advantage of a great circle route to save time and fuel. I doubt that any of the passengers understood why he was sailing so far North, or even knew that he was. Enroute in the middle of the night, the ship encountered some sheet ice which sliced a hole in the hull of the freighter, right at the water line near the bow. The ship started taking on water faster than the bilge pumps could handle it and it was soon obvious that if something was not done, and soon, the ship would sink, right there in the middle of the ocean!

So the Captain woke up all of the able bodied men, (including my Uncle Joe-Gene's Grandfather) and told them (in my fathers words) "that they were going to work!" They were to move as much of the cargo as possible as far back in the ship as they could. This caused the ships stern to ride lower in the water, which in turn caused the bow to ride higher. The Captain's ingenuity saved the ship, the cargo and perhaps all the people on board. The jubilation of the passengers and crew can only be imagined. Any wonder that this was my favorite story as a little child!

Shortly after my grandmother (Gene Lassers great grandmother) my Aunt Libby, and my two uncles (Joseph being Sanford's father and Gene's grandfather) arrived in South Chicago, Emanuel, Joe, and my father (Henry) started night school while working in the store during the day. Now, I am not sure what they sold in the store when they first started, but as the business became established, it was a true general store, selling grocery items, hardware, work clothes and shoes, and even furniture. ...When my grandfather reached the point where he could no longer work, the business was divided between his four sons. Uncle Joe got the furniture part and moved it to Kankakee (Illinois). Joe did reasonably well, but the furniture store really took off and prospered when ...Sanford took over.

The German Jews left the old country with more knowledge, experience and assets and were faster out of the starting gate on the road to success in America than their eastern European cousins. They brought savings to help them start anew and in all likelihood had a business in the old country from which they had garnered street savvy to use in their new home. In Germany, Austria or Prussia they were given a longer leash to pull on to become successful. The Jews were tolerated, but never fully accepted no matter how wealthy or powerful they were. There was always an undercurrent of dislike and envy which once in awhile erupted into violence, yet only some would take note. They had fought and died for the Germanic nations in the Franco-Prussian and the First World War. In their minds they were Germans first and Jews second. It turned out they were wrong, and paid disastrously for this miscalculation with their lives and those of their children.

My great, great grandfather Sigmund Silberman and his siblings came from Rockenhausen, Bavaria, in the south of Germany. He had originally settled in Quincy, Illinois, west of Chicago in 1860, and entered the fur and wool business with his brothers, and in 10 years they were extremely successful. I imagine this was a business they were involved in while living in Rockenhausen. They were still traveling to the far west to negotiate with trappers over animal pelts to be used as furs in the manufacture of women's and men's coats and hats.

He had a large mansion in Hyde Park on the south side of Chicago. It was a grand home with 3 stories including a basement and ballroom. Apparently running water wasn't enough. His immediate family lived nearby and I remember one of his sons' having a golf driving range in his attic on Greenwood Avenue.

As the great Depression dragged out, and the 'Dust Bowl' took its toll in the Plains States, my family lived 'high on the hog', with automobiles, suburban country club, and downtown business club memberships, as well as extensive travel and a house with servants. The older generation went back and forth to Germany numerous times while the down and out Oklahoman's drove west in old jalopies with signs on them that read "California or bust." Their livelihoods had dried up with the land going from a farm with crops and animals to desolation, boll weevils, locusts, wind and dust. People migrated like refugees looking for work to the golden state of California.

The following excerpt is from a letter in my possession written to my grandmother by her mother or my great grandmother. It is an indication of the wealth of the times, and the family's blessings. The letter was addressed aboard the eastbound Lloyd-Bremen German ship *SS. Berlin* to Beulah Lilienfeld from her Mother Mary L. Silberman. The *Titanic* would leave for America on its historic voyage a little over a month after this was written, and sank on April 14, 1912.

Nordeutscher Lloyd Bremen
Dampfer "Berlin"
March 3rd, 1912.

My dear darling Beulah, Father (Sigmund) *left to join the gentlemen and I have sauntered up to the writing room. Took out your letter for the second day* (letters were given to voyagers in packets to be opened a day at a time) *and laughed aloud when I saw the next envelope. Being all strangers around me I don't know what they imagined was my ailment.*

20

Up (sic) morning at 4pm (am.?) I did finely, but was awakened then by a spell of asthma. But am o.k. this aft. Father is simply fine. He received thirty telegrams, at least fifteen letters, seven handsome baskets of fruit, one basket champagne in splits, one box of books, five boxes of flowers. The employees sent Father numerous beauties (roses), about four feet high. The box that Dave sent for Hubert & Dave (two of their sons-there were five siblings) was a dream. I am wearing flowers from it everyday. One bunch of violets, one of lilies of the valley & all the handsome productions of spring flowers small & large.

One box was from Emil Kohnstetter of N.Y., one from Mrs. Friedenthal, & one from Helen & Louise (sister, and niece). Ida Yondorf brought me prunes and filled figs to our room. But in these baskets of fruit were also boxes of dates, figs candies ginger, box of chocolates, ...milk chocolates, and all fruit one could think of, strawberries, peaches, Chinese plumbs, large hot house black grapes, pears & then the general run of fruits.

Aunt Bertha & son took a basket & Helen & Louise one, but I doubt if they got very far as Uncle Dave refused to carry it if he could get out of it.

Aunt – brought a flask of liquor to Father. The baskets were sent by Dora & Jake W., Irwin Woof & wife. .... The latter one was an enormous One. Also the one sent by Mr. Regan of the Knickerbocker (hotel) , the proprietor. He also sent ½ doz. of the prettiest squab-chickens & three dozen fresh eggs. That was such a surprise...............

The boat is quite shaky. We have had snow twice today.. ...

How can your parties be otherwise than a success. You take things so beautifully calmly that even if a few things don't turn out as planned you are in good humor any how and that is half the success of and the other parties sure to mature.

March 4th, weather warmer but fur coat is still in the ring. Left Father out in his chair, came in to attend to a couple of things. Opened your third letter Beulah & still have something to look forward to for tomorrow....

Fifth day out. This has been a corker. I went to bed with half my clothes on last eve-about nine o'clock. Got up -1am to finish undressing & then did not appear on deck until this afternoon. We have had such a dreadful storm. So far Father nor I have been sea-sick but some others! Just finish reading your last & Dear Mary's note. Mrs. Hirsch ..... told me last night –that she was so happy to hear whom my daughter married...

The remainder of the letter is lost, but I would imagine the reference to her daughter was that Beulah had married my grandfather Eugene William Lilienfeld, I am sure he was a very good catch. They had 11 year's together before she passed on. The letter illustrates how the wealthy traveled during those times. Apparently the entire family was returning to Germany for a visit. It would be easy to draw a conclusion after reading this letter that the ship's dining room was not a frequent occasion for the Silbermans with all the *bon voyage* food they received. Unfortunately I met only a few of these folks but if I could today there would be many questions!

Silberman -Lilienfield-Lassers Family Geneology

The Family Tree

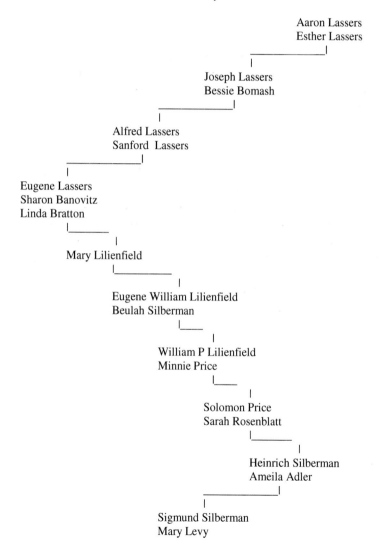

Aaron Lassers
Esther Lassers
_____|
|
Joseph Lassers
Bessie Bomash
_____|
|
Alfred Lassers
Sanford Lassers
_____|
|
Eugene Lassers
Sharon Banovitz
Linda Bratton
|_____
|
Mary Lilienfield
|_____
|
Eugene William Lilienfield
Beulah Silberman
|____
|
William P Lilienfield
Minnie Price
|____
|
Solomon Price
Sarah Rosenblatt
|_____
|
Heinrich Silberman
Ameila Adler
_____|
|
Sigmund Silberman
Mary Levy

Questions like how was Beulah involved with Sinclair Lewis who autographed a first edition of his classic book <u>Main Street</u>, a work that changed the way novels were written. Lewis was the first American to win the Nobel Prize, and also was nominated for a Pulitzer Prize. It changed the view of small town America. The insertion reads:

To Beulah Lilienfield with memories of
Milwaukee, E. Braitow,
Wilmette, Down Town Club, Drexel Boulevard,
Sinai, & ? ? ?

Sinclair Lewis March 21, 1921

In addition he has made a drawing of a decanter of water with H^2O written on it, + a bottle with the inscription *Ole Crow* on its side, and a stick figure with the 'willies." I never thought to ask my mother about this and she had the book on her bedroom shelf until she passed. What was the relationship here, what do the???'s mean in the inscription, I'll never know.

My grandmother played the piano, but it was never talked about. Why did she own a concert Steinway in the living room, and nothing was ever said about her musical abilities?

Why was my grandfather's sister who lived but a few months, buried in the family mausoleum without recognition, no headstone in the floor, and nothing was ever mentioned about this? It was only recently that I knew she existed at all. Big Gene was always said to be an only child. Was the grief too much to bear for her life to be remembered?

One person, who knew the family well, told me that my mother only read from light novels and insinuated her intellect was not "inquiring" to put it nicely. Her Father traveled extensively to promote and build his business after he was widowed and she was left at 13 years of age to be raised by her aunts, and probably suffered emotionally from this. Although mother loved her father as no one else, I have the feeling he enjoyed the company of various other women and that is why he was a widower for such a long period of time. Apparently after a 12 year protracted relationship, Aunt Ellen told him that he should marry her now or forget about it, they were getting too old. When they 'tied the knot' she was 40 and he was 62 years of age. Of course there were no birth certificates in the days grandfather was born, and he always fudged a year or two on his age.

One of the few times I saw mother cry was when her father passed. I never witnessed my dad cry or express emotion aside from an occasional temper outburst at my mother because she pushed him too far, and he had internalized it to the point of breaking.

When I mentioned that I was more like my dad, to a close friend of the family, they said "good!" I am not positive mother had the most endearing personality, but socially she was prominent in her circle of friends. She never forgave her enemies, of which there were some, and carried a grudge forever. This was true when Walter Lilienfield (her father's cousin) sold the cigar business to the Consolidated Cigar Company.

There were compelling reasons to do so, including the financial pressures, involved by signing on a note for a personal loan of $2m for tobacco futures ($17m in 2012 dollars), a tremendous burden. My mother resented Walter for establishing positions for his sons as part of the agreement, and nothing for me. Well, his sons were already working in the business. I was just in my first year of college. It was the right thing to do for many reasons.

Apparently my great grandmother Beulah had a nice cache of jewelry, and my mother did not fall far from the tree. Since it was left to my children and their wives in her will, I never became familiar with it. The following article appeared in a number of Chicago newspapers. This is quoted from the *Chicago Tribune* edition of November 1, 1919.

Clever Porch Climber Takes $12,000 in Gems from Home as Owner Dresses *Search is being made for a clever porch climber who entered the bedroom window of Mrs. Eugene Lilienfeld's second floor apartment at 5247 University Avenue last Saturday night and escaped with $12,000 worth of jewelry. The theft was suppressed by the police until yesterday.*

The articles taken include a pearl necklace with platinum settings worth $4,550; a necklace of diamonds and emeralds worth $1,700; a diamond lavaliere valued at $4,000, and a coin purse containing $20. A purse containing $1,000 which Mrs. Lilienfeld had collected on Saturday for the Jewish Relief fund was overlooked....

.Other newspapers reported $10,000 stolen while family dines, $10.000 while woman bathes. *...later Mrs. Lilienfeld took a train for French Lic (a fancy resort located in Indiana) to meet her husband as she had planned.*

Obviously the sums mentioned were considerable for the times, (in today's dollars the heist would net $125,000). No doubt an insurance policy paid a portion of the value back. Let me mention that this was not "an apartment" but a house, and that such excitement did not prevent my grandmother from proceeding to the beautiful French Lic resort as planned, and leave it at that.

It might be noted that my grandfather purchased a 38 Smith and Wesson revolver in 1921 (possibly in response to the robbery)which he never fired and also acquired a Chicago Police Supervisors Staff badge which he carried on his gold key chain along with his car keys for the rest of his life. Badges were known to be given to prominent people, and even political contributors. Aunt Ellen once told me he was pulled over while driving with her in the car by a police officer, and he was so nervous about showing the star in an effort to get out of a ticket that his hand shook. I do not know the outcome of his gesture but the gun, police badge and the initialed gold key chain remain in the family. As it happens the gun was purchased in a hardware store in Arkansas, this information was courtesy of the Smith and Wesson historical department. Why the police star was received or why the revolver was bought I have no idea. The gun was in the original box when I inherited it, and it was never used.

I am positive that my family danced away the twenties and sloshed away the thirties. I remember hearing that my grandfather bought a large amount of whiskey from a restaurant when Prohibition was initiated and I remember the liquor closet in the basement filled to the brim.

In nearby Cicero, a town known for Al Capone and along the "Great White Way," near the University of Chicago there were many venues of entertainment for Chicagoans to imbibe in. Of course keep in mind that my mother and father did not marry until 1933, and my grandfather was widowed since 1923. During the late twenties father attended the University of Illinois, joined ZBT Fraternity, and eventually became President. Upon graduation he took over the family store and converted it from a general store to a prosperous furniture business.

Mother attended the University of Chicago Laboratory School and then National Seminary, a two year college in Washington D.C., one of the most prestigious women's school in the country. She toured Europe with her grandparents, and visited Hawaii for the grand opening of the famous Royal Hawaiian Hotel in 1927. She was attracted to the famous beach boys that were employed by the hotel and ran the water sports, the beach and cabanas, as described in one of her post cards.

It was discretely mentioned to me that when mother became eligible for marriage she was intent on making it happen, and dated some very wealthy men, who came to the conclusion that they could not afford her.

She panicked, for she was now 24 and still a maiden. How she met my dad, I have no idea, but on April 18, 1933 they tied the knot in the Rabbi's study (or home as stated in one newspaper), with no ceremony, no well-wishers in attendance, no wedding pictures, no reception or dinner. How strange. It was never mentioned that I can remember. One newspaper printed the following:

"Eugene W. Lilienfield of 5247 University Avenue, Chicago, Illinois announces the marriage of his daughter Mary Elizabeth.....yesterday morning..."

A second read stated:

"The marriage took place on Tuesday, April 18 at the home of the brides Parents sic. (only one parent)....*they will be at home in Kankakee upon their return from their wedding journey."*

The official printed announcement read:

Mr. Eugene W. Lilienfield
announces the marriage of his daughter
Mary Elizabeth
To
Sanford B Lassers
On Tuesday
the eighteenth of April nineteen hundred and thirty-three,
Chicago, Illinois

Who would ever get married on a Tuesday morning, with the venue either at her home or the rabbi's office with no wedding party, ceremony or banquet? The engagement was announced the previous October, and there is no one alive today that can answer these paradoxes.

I do not believe mother ever considered the idea of living in Kankakee, this would have been 'Hicksville.' She may have told my dad that she would, and not fulfilled the pledge. For the next 40 years father commuted 120 miles a day to his place of business. When we moved to the north side it became even longer.

While my parents sailed away on the Furness Line to Bermuda for their honeymoon in 1933, tramps, hoboes and the hungry knocked on our back door for food, and the cook would always come up with something for their effort. They would be very thankful for the handout and sit on the back steps and eat it. Whether or not we had regulars is speculation but I am sure Helen never turned anyone away. All these beggars would have jumped at a second chance in life if one was offered, but at the moment none was. In 1933 the unemployment rate was 25% of the work force, the watermark high for that calamity. Looking back I believe our family did their share for the poor.

It was strange that mother never associated with my father's side of the family. My dad drove me over to visit his folks twice a week in the winter and once during the summer because he played golf on Sundays at the country club in Highland Park, a respectful distance away. It seems that there was more silence than conversation on those visits and I sat like a mouse in the 'church corner' for 45 minutes of shear boredom. Until I became a teen, my dad could do no wrong and our relationship was very close. It, or I, would change.

During the thirties my father and grandfather tended to their businesses in economic tough times in order to keep our life style going and heads above water. They both rode the rails extensively, my Dad to work daily in Kankakee, Illinois a sixty mile distance into the farm belt of Illinois where he sold furniture out of the heart of downtown. His ability to cat nap allowed him to go out at night with my mother and friends and the energy to roll out of bed with the 6 am alarm bell the next morning. He never over-slept.

My grandfather traveled less frequently but when he did he was on the go, crisscrossing the country for extended periods of time, peddling Corina cigars which he manufactured in Tampa, Florida and New Orleans, Louisiana. It was a national brand that dated back to his father's time, and his travels on the high iron liveried trains of the New York Central, Illinois Central and the Union Pacific were long, arduous and done in deluxe accommodations. He would be gone for weeks at a time, working different parts of the country, I can remember when he telephoned home, once a week and always on Sunday when the rates were cheaper, and my mother would say, "...Papa is calling from California, say hello and talk fast." I was surprised to find imbedded in one of my grandfather's letters to my mother, "*Loved talking to Gene* (me) *yesterday, he was talking like a little old man.*" Finding this in a letter to my mother I was totally surprised I never thought he mentioned, or was concerned about me.

Telephone calls were expensive, and he had a silver timer which went up to six minutes with a reminder bell that would ring after three were gone, and again when six appeared. The first three minutes were a packaged rate, and after that the charge was by the minute.

Grandfather Lilienfield was originally an electrical engineer, and graduated from Armor Institute, later Known as IIT (Illinois Institute of Technology). He worked for the Pullman Rail Car Company after graduation. Electricity was still a new and challenging field, and his interest was on the cutting edge of a fantastic new industry. President Benjamin Harrison was in the White House in 1892 when electricity was first installed. He never used it for fear of being shocked and stuck to the old gas light fixtures during his term.

Big Gene had the heart of an engineer and when he was forced to go into the family business due to his father's failing health I am sure he did so reluctantly. He was not a natural salesman from what Aunt Ellen told me, but was shy and had to force himself to become outgoing and driven. By the time he hit the street he was the best. The cartoon included in this book showing him with a bull whip driving his sales force gives authority to this statement.

He garnered better service and received more favors by handing out five cent cigars, than most people could by passing out fifty cent pieces. He would always slip one to the train porter, taxi driver or waiter, anyone that could provide better service, and he would be anointed a saint on the spot. Big Gene was responsible for a number of patents for display boxes and the design of a cigar that made the Corina brand innovative and a best seller. It was a patented idea to have a hole in the center of the cigar so it was not necessary to clip or bite off the end to smoke it, and he was instrumental in introducing the idea in his line of cigars.

We were a family of educated people in America, at a time where few ever finished, grade, or high school, and attending college was a real achievement. A diploma much less a degree was a bridge too far for most young people.

Aside from my grandfather's education as an electrical engineer, my father attended the University of Illinois at Champaign and soldiered on to earn a liberal arts degree in History. He was a very good athlete and also receive a number of scholarship offers from colleges due to his swimming and basketball prowess. The best offer was a full athletic scholarship to the University of Alabama, but his mother did not approve of a nice Jewish kid venturing into the deep south for an education. His athletic abilities were so good that his moniker was "Greek" (the Greeks started the Olympics) and that is the name that he was called socially, while at work it was unknown, and he remained 'Sanford. On his Rotary membership badge they shortened it to "Sandy" a sobriquet I never heard used anywhere else.

On the distaff side only my mother went to an institution of higher learning, National Seminary in Washington D.C., receiving a two year degree after previously graduating from the prestigious University of Chicago Laboratory School. Her grades as her father's are still in the family archives, and ranged from B's to A's, no less was expected.

 Mother never worked a day in her life, which was the norm for many women at the time. Her passion was managing the household of four (the three of us and my grandfather when he was in town). She also directed the three full time service staff as well as the part time laundress. Rarely was there a necessity for her to do any manual labor, and she only dirtied her hands taking care of her fairly good size Victory Garden during the Second World War, (fertile patches of ground, planted anywhere space was found to grow edible fruits, and vegetables to eat locally). This helped the war effort by sending more food stuffs to our fighting men.

Mother's days were devoted to Victory Bond Work, (selling bonds to help the war effort, entertaining servicemen with dinner and activities, and working for the Community Chest (United Way) of Chicago. Lunch with the ladies, cards in the afternoon, restaurants or parties at night and on the summer weekends and holidays at the Northmoor Country Club, was the normal parade of activities for mother and dad as I grew up. She received an award for donating 2,000 hours to "entertaining" our boys. Enclosed was a ribbon bar and card issued by the Office of Civilian Defense as a citation due you for (2,000) hours of volunteer services rendered. The letter is dated March 31, 1945.

She was a good golfer and won a number of tournaments until bursitis made her give up the game. The love of sports was a huge factor in the marriage to my father. She would listen to the Chicago Cubs baseball team on the radio and attended a few games including the 1945 World Series against Detroit. As a stock holder in the Cubs, which at the time were owned by Phillip Wrigley, the chewing gum magnet, she was privileged to have the first chance at tickets. My dad had bought her one share as a birthday gift and she kept it until the Tribune Newspaper Corporation bought the Cubs and went private.

Mother was passionate about her Cubbies and at home read or sewed while listening to the radio broadcast of the games by Bert Wilson on station WIND. "..that ball is really hit, it's going, going, and caught by the right fielder his back against the wall of ivy in right field." Most of Bert's home run calls stayed in the park.

Avid sports fans, my folks had season tickets to the Chicago Bears football games for 50 years. I too would enjoy the great seats on the 45 yard line during the hot days of September and the last game of the year was in the frigid afternoon of a December cold. It was for the hardy, but that is what Chicagoans were in addition to *"hog butcher to the world,"* the name that the great poet and writer, Carl Sandberg, tagged the City with since it was the center of the meat packing industry.

We even went out in the summer evenings to tiny Bidwell Stadium during the war to watch the *Bloomer Girls* play fast pitch softball and the men play Chicago style 16 inch slow pitch 'mush' ball which looked like a melon floating crossing the plate.

While we were living on a different scale than most folks, incongruencies were still in play. The wash hung on pins attached to clothes lines in the back yard, since home dryers were unheard of. The stockings were darned by the upstairs maid if they had holes in them, and Helen, the cook might stride over to Fulloms Grocery store and wrangle with Dan the butcher over tough meat the night before. The clean plate rule was always in effect; it was necessary to clean your plate at dinner. After all there were starving children around the world, and waste was not tolerated.

I lived near the venerable University of Chicago in the upscale neighborhood of Hyde Park. It is hard to believe our old homestead today is but two blocks from President Barak Obama's home in Chicago. 5247 University was large, but in looking back not out of place for the neighborhood. It was comfortable, and traditional, but not posh as they say. My family was not ostentatious in any overt ways, and my folks always bought grey Buick sedans to prove the point.

There was no fence around the back yard, and the house was on a corner lot which ran even with a well traveled 53rd street. The porch was screened in during the summer, as many still are, and it was a favorite gathering place for the family to sit on hot days and tepid evenings even though the smell of the famous Chicago stock yards 12 miles to the west of us would many times drive porch dwellers inside for refuge. In the winter the screens disappeared into the basement, cleaned and readied for the next year.

The house contained a suite of three connected rooms for my grandfather, but one eventually became Hattie's, the upstairs maid from Stuttgart, Germany. She would have to troop the entire length of the second floor into the back and up the steep stairs to use the attic bath along with the cook.

It was the depression, and as I think back it was incongruous that Hattie would be darning the household socks to extend their wear. Helen the cook from Hamburg, lived on the same floor behind the hall door and at the top of the back steps to the kitchen. My parents and I shared a modest and relatively small bath and my grand- father had his own, bath tub sprouting legs. It was the only shower in a house of three and one half baths. When I was quite young, and he was away, I can remember Helen or Opel taking me in there to use the shower. His rooms would be dark and cold if he was gone because we did not waste utilities. I was always glad to get it done, and leave.

Carl, the chauffer/houseman and his wife lived over the separate facility at the back of the property. The three car garage was unique in that it housed its own gas pump which was serviced when we received fuel oil for the house furnace. Most homes still used coal. My grandfather had an interest in the Apex Oil Company which allowed for such an arrangement. Across the alley at the rear of the house was the local grocery store where Helen shopped for everything. She was waited on by Mr. Fullum the owner, Bill and Al the grocery clerks, Dan the butcher whom she would argue with if the meat had not been good the night before, and Jim the delivery man. Mrs. Fullom was the bookkeeper/cashier and no doubt was ringing up a bottle of milk at fifteen cents and a loaf of Wonder Bread for a dime at the time.

Helen was like a 'second mother to me, maybe a first. I spent more time with her in the kitchen and occasionally in her bedroom than with my mother, or so it seemed. I would have more quality time with her than anyone else in the household while I lived there. She carted me around to places by public transport or Carl might drive us. Her sister lived in the Ravenswood neighborhood on the northwest side, and often on weekends she visited, took me along, and I would play with Margaret, her sister's child.

Helen Lundalius was with the family for many years and had fallen in love with a debonair Berliner by the name of Charlie Dehn, and now was waiting for the War to end so she could get married. Charlie had been drafted into the German Army and served out his conscription at a supply depot. She had returned to her homeland in 1938 against everyone's premonitions that she would not be able to return to America, but some how she came back. Helen and Charlie were able to communicate by letter during the war, and they were married soon after it was over. He was a *bon vivant* Berliner.

He became a citizen of the United States, and worked as an electrical engineer for the Emerson Company in Chicago, and Helen went to work for the large advertising agency, J. Walter Thompson preparing food to be photographed for advertisements in print and on television. Sharon, my first wife and I saw them often, and the affection for me was always there until the end. Sharon had wanted some of her great recipes, but Helen never did divulge them, taking great food to the kitchens of St. Peter, where she now resides in great favor.

My great grandmother Minnie Price Lilienfield originally came from Cincinnati, and was still alive while I lived in my grandfather's house. After moving west from Ohio as an infant in the mid 1860's, she and her family moved to Chicago and were victims of the Great Fire of 1871, which burned most of the city to a cinder. She could remember running from the great fire, and crossing the Chicago River to save herself. She was just nine years old. Of course the family lived closer to downtown at that time as the city was smaller. Some 25 years after her husband's death she dwelled in a three story walk up apartment on the second floor just a few blocks from our house.

Minnie Lilienfield was convinced that her long-time maid Katy, who deserved a medal for putting up with her, was stealing. She did not trust her and always hid things, never to rediscover them. A good example was her purse that she slid behind the pendulum of the old grand father clock in the hallway. Whenever I visited, which was almost weekly she took her purse and found a rolled up ball of Kleenex in which was stuffed a few pennies which were given to me. Minnie was convinced that she was over-paying Katy too, and was never aware that my grandfather was slipping her another $25. per week under the table. Without the maid his mother was his to handle! She lived to be 93 years of age, and passed but a year or two before her son who had the responsibility for caring for a difficult, complaining and demanding mother.

I was not aware that my grandfather had a sister, it was never mentioned and came up only at my mother's internment in the family mausoleum in 1992. The Funeral Director pointed to a plot plan of the structure which was built at Rose Hill Cemetery for William Phillip Lilienfeld in 1911. There are two tiers with four crypts on either side of which two remain empty today. The Director referred to the mausoleum plan provided by the cemetery which recorded an unmarked grave in the floor.

To say that I found this extraordinary is an understatement. I made an enquiry to Rose Hill and found that William and Minnie had conceived a second child, a daughter who died two months after her birth. She had been buried inside another structure at the cemetery until the family's own mausoleum was built in 1911 after my great grandfather's death. When they moved the grave, no grave marker was put on the floor to commemorate her short life. Was the grief too great? We will never know nor was this ever discussed in my presence. He was always mentioned as an only child, but that obviously was not the case.

It was always said that Carl, the houseman and chauffer was there for Minnie. My grandfather was on the road for many weeks at a time and I don't think she ever drove herself. Also he performed considerable work around the house and drove numerous other trips so I am not convinced he was there just for Minnie, but that is how the legend was being cultivated. He would drive my great grandmother a couple of times each week, to one or two nearby markets, the Jewell Tea Company or the A&P. She had clippings from the previous evening newspaper advertisements with her, and was shopping the bargains except that my great grandmother sat in the Buick limousine while Carl ran in with the newspaper under his arm to buy the on sale items. It could almost be made into a movie but it is the honest to goodness truth and reminds me of the movie _Driving Miss Daisy._

I know for a fact that neither one liked the other, but were dependent on each other as life sometimes works out.

The last nanny I had, being a privileged young child, lasted until I was seven and her name was Opel Katz. She was studying at the well known Christian Moody Bible Institute of Chicago, and was working hard to graduate and become ordained as a missionary. Opel would be assigned to the West African country of Nigeria for service. I went everywhere with her, even to visit her home in the Western suburbs by train.

I attended Opel's Christian Church on Sundays, years before I began Jewish Religious School, and consequently I was tainted by the latter experience. I enjoyed the Christian bible stories for children and she told me once "never to believe anything they taught me at the Jewish temple," which I had yet to attend. A religious conversion? Hardly, but something I remembered. I did not walk around with a sign that said "Jews for Jesus," but it certainly led me to creating my own religion, my own standard of worship and well-being, and no doubt my personality. You could even say I developed a "Christian attitude" toward people and situations whereas my wife Linda likes to say, "I can play Solomon." I try to never carry a grudge, or get back at an adversary, even when someone has crossed me. Staying mad is a burden that you carry, a 'chip on the shoulder' until you discard it, and can move on.

We went to church picnics with the congregation, and other social activities over a three year period. I even attended bible school, how many times I do not remember. Opel spent the rest of her life in a Leper Camp in Nigeria and passed away at too early an age. She was special. I still have a letter from her to me in 1946 from the camp explaining her life as a missionary and the circumstances under which she lived. She was always most loving, kind, and giving to me as shown by her correspondence.

Sudan Interior Mission

Nigeria Br. W. Africa
October 16, 1946

Dear Gene:

How are you, big boy? I hope well and happy. I have just been counting up your age and I'm pretty sure you can hit a baseball over the fence, get the football across the field with a well aimed kick and swim like a duck. Am I right? It is probably a little cold for swimming in Chicago right now. When our good old African sun beats down on us with a vengeance, we forget that it is cold at home.

I would like to hear about your school work, Gene, and what you like to study best. Do you ever play the piano? I use my accordion for the song service in Sunday School. ...Timmy is getting better, and we hope will be symptom free from leprosy soon. Will you remember to pray for these little boys that they may all get better?

What a wonderful person. Opel was all about giving help to others, proselytizing and teaching the Christian bible among those who might accept it. She was on the front lines, bringing Christianity, modern care and sanitation to those in primitive camps devoted to leprosy victims in 1946 Nigeria. Her letter says it all as to what kind of person she was. I still pray for her daily, and have for over seventy years. If her soul is not in heaven, then there is no heaven.

I attended the University of Chicago Laboratory School, like my mother did, from Junior Kindergarten through the Fourth grade. Teachers named Miss Campbell, Adams, Oftadahl, Carter, Burris and others educated and led me toward adulthood. In the beginning either my mother or Carl drove and picked me up. When Carl did, I found it highly embarrassing because he normally took Minnie's limousine, and this caused undo attention. Eventually he would drop me a distance from the door that was safe but not obvious. The avoidance of undue attention is still a trait I embrace.

To help assimilate with other children I was sent to Zimmerman's Play Clubs in the afternoon for a number of years. The first five years of my existence I was sequestered and guarded over like the 'prince of the realm,' and did not play with that many other kids my age which I believe has affected me socially and carried over into adulthood. I remain shy today, but I try not to let it show.

I was picked up in a 1939 Ford 'Woody' station wagon and I enjoyed after school activities as well as summer programs. I recall they had boxing as one of the activities. We used over-size gloves and no helmets, and there was a bloody nose or two which apparently was acceptable for the times. Of course boxing was a much bigger sport during my childhood with the Golden Gloves annual national event, the Police Athletic leagues rings around the country, and every one listened to the Friday night fights from Madison Square Garden in New York. I must say, I was not happy being hit in the head by kids more aggressive, bigger or better than I was.

Although I knew many children from my parent's social set, my best friend Judge Puttkamer lived a few blocks away and closer to the University of Chicago campus. His father was the Dean of the Law School which was and still remains today a highly respected post graduate school. I assume his first name is associated with his father's profession. I would occasionally sleep at his house, but I don't remember him sleeping at mine. We did not have an extra bed set up in my room for anyone visiting.

Eventually mother, probably with prodding from others in the household, allowed me to walk to school by myself. I was seven years old and of course it was a less violent time in society than today. I say that knowing full well that Chicago was home for gangsters, mobsters, and serial killers, but little kids didn't drink, gamble, carouse or do drugs and they probably just left us alone. Yet the Crime of the Century, the Leopold Loeb case, took place just blocks away from my house 12 years earlier.

The trail to the classroom was approximately eight blocks through a nice neighborhood and past Stagg Field, the old football stadium and field house of the University. In 1939 the U of C had given up college football, once under the venerable leadership of Alonzo Stagg, the 'Grand Old Man' of football. There were some respectable teams before it was dropped as a sport by the school. The U of C was one of the original members of the Big 10 Football Conference.

The streets around the stadium always seemed so quiet, as if nothing was going on. Occasionally people would come and go in one's and two's but they were older than the athletes and were assumed to be faculty using the facility. It was not known until the end of World War II that the racquet ball courts under the stands were used to produce the world's first nuclear reaction. Under the tutelage of the famed scientist, Enrico Fermi, in collaboration with Leo Szilard, they created the first chain reaction of atomic energy. Ferme had convinced Arthur Compton, his boss, that the calculations were reliable enough to rule out a runaway reaction or an explosion. Yet the official historian of the Atomic Energy Commission called it a "...gamble." if he was wrong it could have created a catastrophic explosion in one of the most densely populated areas in the nation." No doubt, we all got a second chance when Ferme was correct.

The atomic bomb, the monster of destruction related to the experiment, would end the war with Japan and bring to a close the entire bloody conflict around the world. Eventually peaceful applications of atomic energy were discovered and put to use, but not without controversy.

Grandmother Buehla, whom I never met, died at the age of 38 unexpectedly on the dance floor. Below is the news item that appeared in the Chicago Tribune on June 2, 1923.

Woman, Dancing Falls Dead at Tavern Party

Dancing was in full swing at the Lincoln Tavern four miles west of Evanston on Thursday night when suddenly the orchestra stopped in the middle of a fox-trot. Every one gazed round for the reason. They found it in Mrs. Eugene W. Lilienfield 38 years old, 5247 University Avenue, who had dropped to the floor apparently in a feint.

Mrs. Lilienfield was taken to St. Francis hospital, Evanston. There it was learned that Mrs. Lilienfield was dead before she arrived at the hospital. Coroner's Physician Dr. John N. Goltra determined yesterday that death was due to heart disease.

Mrs. Lilienfield was hostess to a party of fourteen guests at the Tavern in honor of Mrs. Mark Hughes of New York who was visiting her .

According to C.E. Huff, proprietor of the tavern, no liquor had been served to the guests.

This happened during Prohibition (to serve alcohol was illegal) and I am positive that the restaurant owner was making sure that the authorities knew he was abiding the law at the time.

Big Gene remained a widower for 17 years but according to my understanding he was a very desirable bachelor around Chicago. A lady who was heir to the Kupenheimer Clothes Company estate (in 1880 they employed 1,000 people and sold over one million dollars worth of clothing) was after him for years but he never took the bait. He was well off in his own right, with a successful business to tend and a fine education to bank on. He matriculated to the esteemed St. Johns Military Academy in

Deerfield, Wisconsin, living away from home during his high school years, and from there entered the Armor Institute of Chicago (Now Illinois Institute of Technology), in 1894, graduating as an electrical engineer four years later.

Electricity was a new invention that was understood by the few so it was not unusual that he received an offer from the 'blue chip' Pullman Rail Road Car Company for employment. When his father William Philip passed on he left the rail car company and became a full partner with his Uncle Edward in the family business and was a very eligible man for the right woman.

That lady was Ellen Williams, a buyer for the California Hale Department store chain, who worked out of the garment capital of the world, New York City. They enjoyed a 12 year relationship before she laid down the gauntlet, and said they would get married or the relationship had to break up. After all she was 40 and he 62.

Ellen's grandfather came across country by wagon train from Philadelphia during the California Gold Rush and mined silver hydraulically in the "Mother Lode" country of the high Sierras near Angels Camp. Her Mother came to San Francisco later by sailing ship and crossed the Panamanian Isthmus by mule to board another ship on the Pacific side. The family was of Irish-Welsh heritage, independent people as was Ellen. Living in New York as a buyer she could hold her own and wound up on the East Coast after her first marriage failed in California.

Gene and Ellen were wed in Reno, Nevada, and they were perfect for each other. It was a second marriage for both, and solid as the rock of Gibraltar. His letter of May 10, 1943 from Sacramento, California broke the news to his daughter Mary:

Well dear here goes for some good news. Ellen, Burt, and I will drive to Reno early Wednesday morning, and we are to be married. I know you will be delighted to hear the good news. So now you won't have to worry about leaving me at home alone, and we should all be very happy as Ellen is a darling gal.

I am surprised that my mother was not more informed about Ellen after 12 years of the in and out courtship of her father, that tracked back and forth from California to New York. Thus the occupancy of the house increased to four persons plus servants and Ellen's acceptance was unanimous even by my mother who did not please easily. They became good friends.

She too was a marvelous person, and we got along splendidly. Aunt Ellen became part of the triple play that raised me along with Helen and Opal. Even after my grandfather passed, we kept in touch regularly, and when she moved back to California, Sharon and I drove up north to Stockton, and visited her often. It is too bad she never had any children of her own from her first marriage, just the problems of an alcoholic abusive man.

My Great Uncle David and his brother William (my great grand father) immigrated to America from Hanover, Germany in 1860. David took on a job as a clerk in the M. Israel Dry Goods Store (I believe he was somehow related to the family) in Kalamazoo, Michigan and in a few years along with his brother opened a retail cigar store, which prospered. The brothers expanded into selling wholesale wine and eventually added the Brunswick saloon on the main floor which was said to be one of the best stocked and one of Kalamazoo's finest drinking establishments with domestic and German beers being offered. Apparently there was a billiard parlor on the second floor and the building remains to this day, and is listed in the National Register of Historic Places.

The Lilienfeld establishment was also a respected local cigar manufacturer. In the late 1800's Kalamazoo, Michigan was one of the nations leading producers of cigars with an output of about "150,000 per day" from 38 different companies. Lilienfeld sold under the name of Lillies and Prides, employed 25 workers and sold two million cigars a year. A labor strike shut down and dispersed the entire industry in 1908 and the company moved to Detroit. For reasons unknown and never mentioned, William left Kalamazoo and moved to Chicago, Illinois to open a branch of the business, while David continued to expand the original successful enterprise.

The Lilienfeld's (the name was changed to Lilienfield during the First World War because of America's adverse feeling toward the Kaiser and Germany) had built a beautiful Victorian home in the city. Whether David remained after the city-wide strike against the numerous cigar makers is not known. The manufacturers moved the factories to other parts of the state and the country. Today the home is a bed and breakfast inn and is registered in the National Register of Historical Buildings. Linda and I made a special trip to spend one night here in 2011 and spoke with the owner at length about my heritage. I could feel the presence of my great grandfather during our stay.

My dad's folks were middle class Jewish American immigrants. His mother Bessie Bomash Lassers was born in Kalvari, Lithuania while his dad Jacob Aaron, known as J.A. was also born in Lithuania, and brought to America at an early age by his father and brother, who had preceded him. I believe my grandfather was an average businessman and certainly an ardent Zionist, Jews that were extremely vocal for a homeland for their People. This secular movement was founded in the late 19th century advocating the return to the homeland (Palestine) by all Jews, and has been controversial within the community and to others over the years.

His wife managed three small apartment buildings that they owned to help keep their head above water when J.A. retired from the dry goods business. Joe was a sick man for many years, and their income was slim. It was his business in Kankakee that my father would turn into a successful three store furniture chain.

The notion of my grandparents attending college was probably never a factor in their lives. College was for the rich or the brilliant, and they were neither. They had two boys separated by a number of years that turned out hating each other. My Uncle Alfred (the older brother) was considered odd, of genius mentality, and unstable. He attended the University of Chicago, and was the "black sheep" of the family. He never could hold a job and went off on creative business ventures that went bust. He married, had one daughter and they all moved from Chicago to Seattle in the early 1940's.

Alfred was supported by his mother for years and was a real trial to the family, and a despised person as far as his brother (my father) was concerned. He would not talk to him, and the hard feelings had trickled down to his daughter Noemi, who at one time I had a fragile and short friendship with. Upon his death he was returned to Chicago to be buried next to his mother and father. My father refused to attend the funeral. Dad also reminded me that he had papers in his safe box regarding Alfred that he wanted to be destroyed upon his death, but the opportunity never came for me in that I was not a factor in his estate.

What those papers concerned is anyone's guess.

Dad attended the University Of Illinois and joined Zeta Beta Tau national Jewish men's fraternity, and was the acknowledged 'star' of his family. He was elected President of the house at Champaign, and attended school during the years the renowned Red Grange played football for the University, the glory years of the institution. In the summers he counseled at Strong Heart boys camp and at one time may have considered becoming a camp director.

My father was always on the move. To work and back, out with my mother a few evenings a week and certainly visiting or having friends over on the weekends in the winter. Summertime brought the country club life and the folks spent weekends at Northmoor. They'd book a room, and play golf during the day and dance away the nights. The summer formal always featured a name band like Benny Goodman or Woody Herman.

Dad visited his parents on Thursday nights, and Sunday mornings in the winter. I always went with him because mother never did, something I never had explained to me. They never talked, mother, Bessie or J.A. The conversations my dad had with his folks, were certainly not interesting and I sat on the couch like a mouse in a church corner just listening and not participating much. I didn't really have much to say either. The biggest problem was the financial support for Alfred who always needed money. Once, my Dad was adamant about selling one of her buildings because it was in a slum neighborhood, a pain to manage and a risk to own.

As I mentioned nothing was ever said, about this being an abnormal situation, but little was said about many things that happened as I grew up and I still wonder about today. The only time I can remember mother and dad's side getting together was at his father's funeral. The ironic thing is she went to brother Alfred's funeral where as dad refused to attend.

After our move north in 1946, my relationship with my father became more distant, but I was growing up. He would occasionally take me and my friends to big sporting events, like the Daily News Relays, Golden Gloves boxing matches, hockey or basketball games and they still remember it to this day. It may be the same for other families as kids grow up, they distance themselves from their parents, reuniting down the line.

I believe it would be fair to say, that as the one and only child raised in a house of grownups, I was tolerated but not nurtured by my grandfather, loved by my Aunt Ellen, acknowledged with fondness by my father whose work and social schedule took up most of his waking hours and he may not have spent as much time with me as he desired. Just before he passed on he told me that "I was a better father than he was." I believe that if he counted quality time' that was true. Of course I was adored and spoiled by the help.

The relationship with my Mother was more complex and strained, but I believe I was always polite to her. Once in awhile I would pop off or throw a temper tantrum in my room and throw things. I'd be afraid to tell her things, was devious as to where I had been, and tried to sneak in at 2:00 am in the morning after a Saturday night out, to no avail. She was always up even though in bed. No doubt mom wished for a closer relationship than we had but I do not think she was raised to be a hands on mother, she didn't know how. Her mom had passed away when she was 13, and a plethora of aunts raised her to adulthood. While her father who was loved dearly (one of the few times I saw her cry was when he passed away) continued to travel extensively and exchanged affectionate letters home. A letter from 1923 from Beulah to her husband is a good Victorian example, as are others.

"My Darling boy, signed, *your gal Beulah"*

Beulah's mother Mary, date unknown: *"My darling girl....you are the only sweetheart I have to write to every day*

From Mary's father in a letter to French Lic on their honeymoon in 1933,

"Just a load of love to both of you."

A sign off on a letter from 'Bapa' (the name she called her father), to her on a letter sent as a bon Voyage message for a cruise on the SS Washington that my father and mother sailed on February 1, 1939

Mary Darling,,,,so good bye darling,
have loads of fun....lots of love Bapa

She turned out to be a fun loving person in an adolescent way and extremely prim and proper, and could carry a grudge the whole nine yards. Letters that she received and wrote to her boy friends are revealing for her desire to love and be loved in a storybook way.

Royal Hawaiian Hotel, 1927. Dear Mary: I hope the next time I'll get to know you sooner and then we'll both have a good time...My love is your love, but theirs (sic) one thing be sure of, and be sure of it...sealed with a kiss. Chick (beach boy at the Royal Hawaiian Hotel)

Letter sent from Mary in New York to Greek (my father),in Chicago, dated 1930.

Dearest of all......Came home and dressed to go to a cocktail party...by the time we left there I was going pretty strong. There must have been dynamite in them there drinks. I just received another letter from you so now I am the happiest girl in New York.

I have written, I am only interested in one fellow. Those fellows I pick up are just nice to pass the time with. I think I know a girl who is willing to have this man that is going to be hard to lose, and she to willing to stick with him for ever and a day, even longer. So get the glue and let it stick them together for ever and ever....I adore people who are fit and healthy, I hate people that are sickly. My darling I must close now.

This last is very revealing in that my family never had a sick day during my childhood. Dad went to work without fail, and mother never lounged around because of illness, and I never missed a day of school because of sickness. Maybe we were the *uber race?*

With all the love that abounded within my mother her marriage never came close to a fairy tale. Most marriages don't as the new paint wears thin and constant repairs are required to keep a relationship afloat.

Mother Mary was too spoiled in her upbringing, too influenced by the unique relationship to her father, who loved her and would give her anything she wanted. Living in the same house with him for 13 years of their marriage, having her own funds, and not having to acknowledge my father's place as head of the household stunted the relationship to where it is said my dad asked for a divorce and was talked out of it by his father-in law.

Father for all his *bonhomme* and his popularity did not extend that to his wife or his child. I kept my respect but found love elsewhere and his wife just grew cold and prickly. My father was not a romantic, any more than his own family was warm and fuzzy. Whatever my folks had going for them when they married, it burned out along the rough tracks of a union that was not made in heaven. Father gave up all his friends except one to become part of my mother's social circle of friends, who had the dough and the go.

Being the 'prince of the hill' in a lonely kingdom I was entitled to observe some of the daily rituals of my family's life. On a typical day the help rose early in order to be ready for service to the family. Dad was in the bathroom by 6:30, at the dining room table by seven, and then walked in the summer to the 53rd street station to catch his train. In later years, he was driven by Carl, the houseman, to the 63rd Street Station when that became the only option as the railroads reduced service. Of course this all changed when we moved after the War.

Grandfather stirred around seven, had his breakfast brought up to his sitting room, would drive himself or be driven to work and arrive by nine at 79 E Jackson Street in downtown Chicago to start his business day. In later years Carl drove him roundtrip to the office. He worked up to the day he died.

Mother had her breakfast in bed every day at eight-thirty. The upstairs girl served it, and the cook returned to pick up the tray, and at that time was given the menu for the evening. My mother then prepared for her day's activities.

After breakfast when the cleanup was finished, Helen the cook, went out to shop for dinner; the second story girl, Hattie made the beds and tidied up the rooms. By this time Carl the houseman was back from his morning chauffeuring duties, and worked on the grounds or in or around the house. Twice a week he had to take Gaga, Minnie, my grandfather's mother shopping or to visit the doctor, in addition to taking or picking up family members as required. He always wore his chauffeurs cap and suit when driving and in the winter a heavy coat. When doing house repairs or working on the lawn, work clothes were the dress of the day.

At ten he might sit down for a cup of coffee and at lunch the help including the part-time laundress would eat around the kitchen table. If I was home I might be sitting with them, under the care of Helen. Danes are independent and can be cranky. Carl Langdon was a Dane, and other members of the 'backstairs' found him ornery at times.

Helen, always busy, worked at canning fruits, making pickles, shopping for the evening dinner, with it's great desserts. On Sunday mornings fresh baked *streuselkuchen* or *Suzannebakenkuglof* would grace the table.

There was a rest period for everyone in the early afternoon before the evening chores began. Mother was in and out, for she drove herself from an early age in a variety of automobiles over the years. She was good at shifting, parking, and driving big heavy cars with no power steering, and an excellent driver. Play clubs delivered me home around five, my grandfather returned from work while dad would arrive by 6:30 pm.

Dinner was normally called for seven and was announced by Hattie in her blue dinner serving uniform (black was reserved for company) to the family gathered upstairs in the sitting room, having their nightly highball. We all waited for the invitation to go downstairs to the properly set table with its fresh flower centerpiece.

Big Gene frequently was already downstairs in the butler's pantry doing the important job of fixing martinis for Aunt Ellen and himself. Occasionally the help were poured one by my grandfather, and my folks, confirmed scotch drinkers, mixed their own. The meal was a formal affair by today's standards, and always consisted of three courses served on fine china, monogrammed linen and placemats, polished antique silverware with initials on every piece, folded cloth napkins, doilies, and of course, finger bowls between the main course and dessert were present.

Through this long ordeal I sat on one side of the large oval table listening to the adults converse, and left to entertain myself. I did well for the most part but eventually was making funny faces that were reflected in the large mirror over the buffet which were noticed with disapproval and became such an irritant that I was moved across the table where my back would now be to the mirror, and the problem was solved. After all I was supposed to be the perfect gentlemen, a tough regimen at a very young age.

After dinner, over coffee, the adults lit up Chesterfield cigarettes, my grandfather his cigar, and remained for another ten minutes in the smoke filled dining room. He delighted in putting the wet end of the cigar in my mouth occasionally, why I don't know, but it was something I did not like.

In fact, over the years until just before he passed, I was a bit afraid of Papa, a man that everyone loved and admired. My mother constantly encouraged me to visit him alone after we moved North and I could now drive. I finally got up my nerve to do this and we sat in the back yard and talked mano to mano. It was a good conversation and our last before he passed away. The only thing I can remember years later was I asked him how hot and cold water traveled through the same pipe to the spigot. Not exactly intimate for our one on one get together!

He was a man of many talents, self assured and imposing. He had a great sense of humor, as did my dad and I believe I have inherited a hybrid from both of them. There were family stories handed down about his practical jokes like physically nailing sample cases of calling salesmen to the floor without their knowledge, and other antics that kept the office going. He was well connected around town, and was said to have advised William Paley of the cigar manufacturing family on investing in something called a radio station. He advocated him to go ahead and do it. This purchase would eventually create the huge Columbia Broadcasting System, and make Paley a household name. After reading the 700 page biography on Paley, I have my doubts about this, but they knew the Sam Paley family well.

Grandfather loved golf and there are pictures of him playing at Lake Shore Country club in plus-fours with a vintage automobile driving by in the distance during the early 1920's. He loved automobiles, was mechanical and liked to work on them. He owned one of the first cars in Chicago and it was mentioned at times he advised the chauffer of Henry Armor of meat packing fame, on maintaining his automobiles.

I followed the action in World War II very closely as a child and in 1941 America was on its way to war. The Japanese bombed Pearl Harbor on December 7th, and Germany and the Axis threw their hats in the ring not long after. My father, although registered with a deferment for a child and business, was drafted, but by the time they did he was 38, over the age limit to serve. Instead of going off to war he and his male friends voluntarily performed hard labor once a week by cleaning down hospital walls and repainting them. World War II was the war that America really was involved in on both the home front and the battlefield. It was all for one and one for all in those years, and it brought the country together, maybe for the last time.

My young imagination was captured by these colossal world events. I followed the war closely at this very impressionable age and plotted the victories and defeats on simple maps. My bedroom wall was plastered with the Coca Cola cardboard picture series depicting America's fighting planes. I constantly listened to the big Emerson radio that was in my room for war updates and news from the front, and ran to my spread out battlefield maps, and updated them.

By the time I was six years old (1942), my parents were actively engaged in War Bond Drives, with mother working every week as a volunteer and receiving a commendation letter for her efforts at the end of the conflict. Almost every Sunday in the winter months we had three or four servicemen over for Sunday dinner and then took them to the movies, ice skating or bowling. They were always very polite, receptive and appreciative for the opportunity of being at a home away from home, and cared for and honored by the American public. Enjoying a wonderful meal and wholesome entertainment and company really cheered them up. My mother kept all the letters that she received from 'the boys,' and I have a stack put away that describes the special relationships with these young soldiers and sailors our family had, and a picture of this period in American life. Here is a short note on a post card which I will quote verbatim.

August 1, 1943
Pvt. Paul Behling
Camp Walters, Texas

Hello Gene:

I didn't forget you I just have been awful busy. I am in Texas and from what you can see I am taking basic training in (sic) Infantry. I am in a heavy weapons company-that means machine guns and mortars. The weather is awfully hot and the work is hard. Getting used to this heat and enjoy the training. How's Play Clubs? I'd like to be in the pool now.

So long,
Your old friend-Paul

We received letters from all over the world from servicemen who graced our table. My mother kept up the relationship after they'd left for foreign or stateside duty with letters, food and gifts. Of course there were many families expressing their support for these young men who would be putting their lives on the line for America.

Mary, I don't really need a thing for Christmas
Jack Petty, Pearl Harbor, Hawaii.

I would always join the table and the guys would play with me which made it loads of fun and interesting. I believe it was this learning experience that encouraged my interest to follow a path toward a military commission. The guys would always remember to include me in their thoughtful correspondence.

How is Gene, say hello for me
ACCM Robert Hudson, Beleville, Texas

Tell Gene I'll keep my promise about that Jap helmet
Pvt. Jay Jackson, West Du Pere, Wisconsin

How is Gene getting along? I remember how Bob and him use to wrestle around.
Bill Welsh, AMM 2/c Pearl Harbor, Hawaii

Thanks for the picture of Gene. I would say he looks more like a Lilienfield than a Lassers, but he looks like he is pretty big for his age.
S/Sgt J. Howard, Cairo, Egypt

I am glad to hear that Gene is coming nicely on the swimming. Yes it sound like Gene is growing up.
Pvt. B.H. Boehling,
New Guinea

My folks circulated in a large group of close friends, most of them reformed Jews, but gentiles also, and they were all smart, successful and wealthy. Most were German Jews and they marched to a different drummer. They lived on the fringe, the rim, the thinnest lip of Reform Judaism in Chicago. One could call them a member of another Tribe since they were so far removed from the religious tenants of the faith. They could even be called 'extreme reform'.

They were Americans and proud of it, and totally assimilated in their minds. During the Loeb/Leopold "Crime of the Century" murder case and trial of 1924 which included members of this powerful enclave of prominent people, they suffered extreme shame and embarrassment about Jews killing Jews, and homosexuality. In fact the Leopold family would change their name to Lebold, to disassociate themselves from this horrid black mark on their forehead, and for their own protection. Mother knew 'Dickie' Loeb as she grew up and was 15 at the trial of her close neighbor (four blocks).

My dad's parents were more traditional in the practice of Reform Judaism, in fact my father was Bar Mitzvah at the KLM Temple, although I cannot recall him ever talking about it. My Grandson Samuel Brandon Lassers, just had his Bar Mitzvah, the first to accomplish this in the last two generations of the family, and his sister Erin shall do so also. The only thing I remember him commenting on in regards to his religious education was how they had to keep a sharp eye out for a band of Irish kids that would try and beat them up for being Jewish. J.A. and Bessie probably were not pleased that he married into an irreverent group of American Jews, that wanted to leave the old traditions behind. This was America, the "New World" and this generation was born here, was part of it and were all cut from the same rich cloth.

The Reform fringe in Chicago demanded that the religious services be in English, and be scheduled at a more convenient time. The Christians had it right, going to church on Sundays. Friday night was time to party, and this sliver of the Reform congregation would rather gather socially than attend services, if they attended at all. Above all the services would be shortened, and the children Confirmed rather than Bar Mitzvah, which was much easier for all concerned. They would not be shortchanged; the gifts were the same as if they went through the trials of becoming a Bar Mitzvah.

I adored the comfort zone and the love of Opel, my nanny until I reached seven. It was wonderful yet embarrassing to still have a nanny, and relieved my parents of any responsibility for my care. I still remember the sound of our 1941 Buick starting up near my bedroom window during the evenings, when the folks were on their way to play cards, or a dinner party, and I would be going to sleep. I thought that this was normal, still most families stayed home during the week. It was the age where the children of the wealthy were raised at arms length, like the upper class English did.

At Christmas time, we celebrated with a tree, and no embarrassment, but no mention of the manger. On my birthday and Christmas I received over 30 gifts. Much to my dismay, when I was old enough to write, my mother made me record who they were from and send a written thank you note in return. What a drag. Is there any reason to wonder why I do not enjoy receiving gifts today? When the rest of the family was done unwrapping their Christmas gifts I still was going strong, recording names for another 20 minutes so I could thank them.

All my life I was fascinated with different modes of transportation, especially airplanes. Of course I could not tell an airplane from a safety pin at that age but the fast moving world of aviation left some benchmarks in 1936. Amelia Earhart raced her stock Lockheed Vega in the Bendix Trophy Air Race which by now had moved to Cleveland. Howard Hughes, famous as an aviator and film mogul started planning for his historic around the world flight of 1938. Jimmy Doolittle an aviator and best known for his daring raid on Tokyo during the Second World War, was just transferring back into the Army reserves from civilian aviation and employment with the Shell Oil Company. The world soon would be in flames, and the future story of fire, brimstone, and abundant black crepe was yet to be written. The dreamers and isolationists still held sway, as the Axis nations put their chess pieces in place, and the future story of fire and death was recorded in the book of world history.

No doubt about it, if a man-made object moved, I had an interest in it. Trains, planes, automobiles and ships fascinated me from my earliest memories. Both my dad and grandfather took the rails, and I went to see them off or meet them on their return which only reinforced my interest. As to flying, I am doubtful that Big Gene ever went up in a plane. My folks flew from Miami to Havana in 1933 so they indeed achieved pioneer status. The 90 mile flight was in a Pan American amphibian and my mother encountered an ear problem due to the altitude pressure differential, and did not fly in an airplane again for 17 years.

Dad was not fond of flying but did so, many times in small planes to go fishing. He always said he wasn't comfortable in the air during rough weather. Airplanes were not pressurized during this period and thus flew at lower altitudes where the air was rougher and the storm clouds if present were more intense during the trip.

Would I be like my dad? Could I overcome this fear? The answer was in the clouds which lay ahead, and not visible yet. As I started to read more stories about the military, my bookshelf soon expelled the *Hardy Boys*, and the *Last of The Mohicans*, and replaced them with modern books of conflict.

In my room I had numerous toys which replicated the moving phenomenon of the world of transportation, and my reading eventually centered, and still does around stories of ships, trains and airplanes. Transportation or the military certainly wasn't a vocation that was of interest to our family, although Big Gene loved trains.

My future path still remained uncharted. Jewish children seldom grow up to be pilots, train engineers or cowboys for that matter. All that hard earned tuition money spent on an excellent college education is meant to produce careers in accounting, jurisprudence, medicine or taking over the family business, and not for learning the skills of aviation. Of course there are exceptions, the Israeli Air Force is considered the best in the world. But even at this early age I had wanted to pilot a fighter plane, command a ship or drive a tank. Could I, would I? There certainly was no precedence in my family to predict that I would.

Secretly, I hoarded my war books. I preferred reading about daring submarine missions and man to man fighter duels to the end. The enemy could throw anything at me but I was invincible to their thrusts. I admired our front line soldiers and adopted their persona as revealed in books, knowing that I could be a fighter jock, handle the mortar bombardments on my ground position, or take the retaliatory depth charge attack by the Nips (Japanese) after I had sunk one of their big Maru tankers.

How was it that these men could survive mentally and physically under such intense conditions? Could I do it, I wondered. Lying on my stomach on a soft designer bed I took it all in, and rationalized the horrors away like a Walter Mitty dream. I could "look the elephant in the eye" and walk away proud, or so I thought.

Dad enrolled me at Camp Nebagamon from birth, (it was that hard to get into), and now I was 10 years old, and soon off for eight weeks to northern Wisconsin, and a new experience. That Memorial Day the family was in the 'country', and dad was playing golf while my mother took me to visit a friend nearby. Their sons Tom and Dick Keim were older and rode bigger bicycles than I was used to, but I didn't let that stop me from tagging along even though I could hardly reach the peddles. On Sheridan Road in the suburb of Highland Park the street becomes a series of sharp curves as it negotiates *Snake Hill*. I had never encountered hills before on a bike, and I could not reach the brakes to slow my decent. Add to that a steady stream of weekenders driving their cars on a one lane road in each direction. Before I knew it I was out of control and the next thing I remember I woke up in the hospital. Apparently, I fell off the bike, hit my head on the pavement and was unconscious for twenty hours. I was fortunate the cars swerved around me and I was not run over. My first memory was dad sleeping in a chair next to the bed where I spent a number of days recovering.

It was my first experience of being given a second chance, but I did not realize it at the time. I was alive without any known consequences from the incident, and I still would be able to leave for camp at the end of the month. How my dad got my mother to buy in on that I will never know. "All aboard," the camp train is now leaving.

Chapter 2

Laggard at the Elite
Francis Parker School

I was set to enjoy my first summer at Camp Nebagamon while my parents moved across town to the trendy Near North Side. Mother, at age 37 left the house she had lived in all her life, as I would until I was 10. During World War II "Big Gene" had remarried and now that the conflict was over, it was time for everyone to get a little more breathing room, and move on to equal but separate homes. My folks moved to the upscale near north, better known as the "Gold Coast," which lined Lake Shore Drive where all their friends had moved.

It was expected that city children from families of means would attend summer camp for a portion of the long vacation months. The under-privileged camps for the poor lasted a week or two at most, while top camps like Nebagamon ran for eight weeks. A major concern for parents was that the dreaded Polio season peaked during the hot summer months that were associated in people's mind as the cause of the crippling disease. To be able to leave the stifling July and August heat of the city was a God-send. The Salk vaccine which eliminated polio had yet to be discovered so the scare remained very real. Both my dad's mother and a good friend were polio victims and afflicted with the crippling physical debilitation from it for the rest of their lives.

Since birth, I had been signed up at the extremely popular Camp Nebagamon. Boys from all over the Midwest and the South traveled to Chicago the third week of June for the over-night camp train which slowly chugged its way north to Heyward, Wisconsin. Nebagamon was located on a large lake of the same name approximately 30 miles south of Superior, Wisconsin. The

Director and founder was a man by the name of Max Lorber, a former All American football player from the University of Indiana, and was also a leader in the field of recreational camping.

During the summers of their youth, dad and Lorber worked together as counselors at Camp Strong Heart, and here they became life long friends. I believe my father had considered camping as a career at one time as they grew up. Lorber, who was better known by his sobriquet "Muggs" and my father, had double dated together, and Dad was going with a gal named Janet who would turn out to be Muggs future wife down the road. It would have been interesting if Janet and dad had hitched up together because she was totally different than my Mom. I was registered at the camp shortly after I was born. It was plain and simple that if you did not sign up years in advance, you were never accepted. My father wanted me to attend, and I was primed for years by attending the annual winter camp meeting in Chicago long before I became eligible to become a Swamper, (youngest participant) at 10 years of age.

Through the war years the camp continued to operate under the hardship of the times, as rail equipment like everything else was prioritized for the American military effort. 1946 was my first year at camp, and It would be the first time that actual sleeping cars were back for the over-night trip, the first time since the war started. The tired train would take nine hours to waddle up to Hayworth, Wisconsin where we disembarked into an abandoned field of waiting vehicles for the short trip to Lake Nebagamon, breakfast and the beginning of camp.

On 'train' day children and their parents would converge on the large station in Chicago to board the chartered coaches which would take us to camp. Many of the excited boys connecting to the camp train had traveled from distant cities like Birmingham, Little Rock, Memphis, Cincinnati and St. Louis to join us for this segment.

The special train carried four hundred kids and counselors wild with anticipation for the camp season to begin. The car sleeping sections would already be turned down and small kids slept two to a lower birth while only one was assigned to an upper. Being that I was tall for my age and asthmatic I drew an upper. Pillow fights and similar activities would breakout, but soon would simmer down as the counselors herded the boys to bed and lights out. Jewish children are controllable even when faced with the wonderful anticipation of summer camp ahead of them, a great breakfast awaiting our arrival and the smoke and cinders of a bumpy train ride.

I attended this fantastic camp for five summers, from age 10 to 15. The first two years my dad came up to see me on visitors weekend, after that it wasn't necessary in his mind or my mother's, who had been prohibited from joining him and bringing illegal treats from the 'manor house' carpet bag of entitlements to me. It may be one of the few things my Dad really held her to comply with, and she did. Camp allowed me to have the opportunity to learn new and different skills, as well as practice old ones, with friends from all over the central part of the country. I especially enjoyed the three to seven day canoe trips into the wilderness, with their deep foliage, rushing rivers and placid lakes stocked with Pike, Walleye and Bass. The older and more skilled a camper was, the greater the variety of arduous voyages they could choose from.

The longest trip each year was the ten day excursion to and along the Gun Flint Trail that separated Minnesota from Canada. The drive to reach many of the launching areas ranged from three to five hours and was made in an old Dodge army truck towing a specially built trailer with racks for eight canoes. In the early years they were mainly of wood and canvas construction; aluminum boats would soon make the traditional canvas canoes obsolete. The metal boats were stronger and lighter, a big factor when you had to portage them yourself from one lake or rippling stream to the next over varying distances and terrain. It was interesting to note that these portage paths were part of the Conservation Corps work of the depression and were measured in chains, the equivalent of approximately 16 feet in length.

As dawn became a reality and the sun peeked over the horizon the old Dodge army truck would be already loaded with canoes, paddles and provisions. Campers and counselors had pre-packed there miserly allotment of allowable items, i.e., socks, a few sets of underwear, T shirts, an extra pair of long pants and another set of shorts, and your toilet kit a misnomer since there were no toilets, were all placed in small bags that were then combined into large packs that rode in the back of the truck. Your knife and ax would ride with you on your belt. The campers were fed a hardy meal and then boarded the open truck with its canvas top in place and the matching canvas sides packed away to be available for use in case the weather changed. We all sat on upholstered but hard bench seats that in comparison today would make an equivalent American Airlines coach seat comfortable. The driver, Harley, kicked over the engine and black diesel smoke blew out the tail pipe and with a mighty roar and a possible wave and hardy best wishes from a few staff we were off on our adventure.

If you were headed the short distance to the Brule River or the Eau Claire Lakes it would only be a couple of hours, still trips up to the *Land of a Thousand Lakes,* in Minnesota required a lunch stop and additional travel time thereafter to the destination. In those years the boys utilized pit stops, which were known as "pine tree plumbing" along the way if a rest stop was unavailable. The normal complement of campers was 15 boys and three counselors. If luck was with you and the sun shined bright on the truck, trippers would warm up by 10:00am. After awhile you would doze off, bouncing along the rural road through the tall trees and by the silent fields. There were no transistor radios, electronic games or cell phones to take our minds off the beautiful scenery or the gorgeous lakes. There was no GPS (Global Positioning System) for Harley to use, just old worn and creased dirty maps. We knew nothing else, and therefore never missed it.

I always looked forward to tripping, getting away, enjoying the wilderness at this time in my life. Bugs and the bears we heard about but never saw were something else. This said, Nebagamon and the Army would be the last of camping for me and I can live on the memories, thank you.

In addition to our personal items we carried standard camping equipment for the group. There were tents, stakes and poles to set them up with, canned goods, SOS pads, sand was always a good substitute, a fold-over shovel, a few fishing poles and reels, a handy first aid kit and t.p. We were expected to catch our meals whenever possible, otherwise the eating would be thinned out to accommodate our failure. It was not possible to pack any more canned goods, and by the second dinner all the fresh items were gone. The fish were there skimming over the lake for bugs to eat early in the morning, and evening at sundown. There were swarms of skitters flying around our boats as we trolled for our breakfast, it was worse at night.

On arrival, everyone pitched in, unloading the packs and canoes from the truck, and carrying them to the waters edge, where they would be beached stern first. Next we brought the rest of the items from the vehicle as quickly as possible, so that the driver could be on his way back to Nebagamon. He had a hard day's night as it was!

Depending upon our arrival time the group pitched camp at that location over night, or pushed off for a short paddle to our first camp site and set up. If moving on we loaded the canoes, careful to balance them because they could tip over at a moment's notice, with our belongings and supplies lost forever. A camper took his shoes off, waded out and pulled the canoe so it was just beached in the bow and the stern was afloat, and hold it against the current. If you did not do that it was very hard to get the canoe in the water and in a floating mood. The packs were then placed into the dead weight area. Usually two canoes held three persons. Soon the campers paddled off creating lasting memories of the vast quiet lake or tumbling stream that could become turbulent, or choppy in a minute's notice. We were prepared for anything.

I still can hear the boats being pushed off from shore by the bowman, and starting out with a dip of the paddles into unsoiled lakes, and lifting out of the pristine water, only to have it drip off the paddle again, ready for another stroke. We would slide across the lake in a ragged convoy of happy campers and our "big brother" counselors. The world was ours for there was no other world as far as we could determine as we never saw another human being.

Keep in mind, camping is work. Through self sufficiency, nothing happens unless you make it happen, so the group would pitch in to make our trip pleasant and survivable. You were only as good as your weakest link. Trippers were expected to paddle hard, be good companions, and do more than your share while watching out for your buddy who just might save your life. I do not remember wearing life jackets so either way if the boat tipped over you would be in the water and had to swim back to its half-submerged hulk. It would keep floating, but in all likelihood your cargo of packs, carrying a portion of the camp's general items and your personal possession were now on the bottom of the lake. You would just have to wing it during the rest of the trip. UPS did not serve the area. Civilization was not close and 911 had not been yet invented.

Ah wilderness!

The word portage is defined as 'carrying boats and supplies over-land between two lakes.' Let me add that to portage a canoe is hard work. You must lift it out of the water, pick it up and flip it over your head while placing the yoke that is attached to the gunnels on your shoulders. The strongest of us would carry a pack also. Carrying this awkward load over your head with very little room to look out, while stepping into mud ruts and under hanging branches was dicey. Insects never failed to buzz around your sweat-laced brow. Relief can be only a few rods or a 100 rods (a unit of measurement used in surveying. 1 rod equals 16 ½ feet) away and only occurs when you reach the next lake.

The best time to catch your breakfast or dinner was to fish the early light of morning or the receding shadows of the day.. I was amazed how many insects swarmed on and over the water at this time of day and how the fish in the coolness of the new or setting sun would jump out of the lake or river to feed on them. The catch was good that night and from the four canoes we probably landed 14 keepers. Nine were eaten at dinner. There was no sense in preparing the remaining ones until breakfast when the live fish could swim on a stringer in the water, strung through the gills and tied to a near by tree. They would wiggle all night and be fresh and ready for frying in the early morning sunlight, or so we thought. We were aware that there were snapping turtles in all the northern lakes, but never thought about them attacking our breakfast only leaving the heads and the bones. Dried cereal anyone? No time for gripes though, we had a long day of paddling and portaging ahead of us.

Cold water swimming and bathing was the norm. I am not sure what the temperature of the water was but only the hardy stayed in for more than a few minutes. Besides, there are some large snapping turtles that can nip you, yet I don't ever recall this happening. They would eat your fish up to the head if you left them on a stringer in the water over-night, but not your toes.

Accidents were rare, but occasionally a camper got sick and somehow he had to be brought back to camp. Thus, only those with the skills and the sufficient physical stamina were allowed to make voyages of extended duration. One trip the group ended camping near a nest of hornets which really got mad and stung most of the boys. It was fortunate there was a telephone in the vicinity and the voyage was terminated early with the welcome roar of the old Dodge truck entering the camp site.

As mentioned, the Camp Director, was close friends with my dad and thus he took a special interest in my welfare. Muggs, unbeknown to me, was keeping my father updated on my experiences and progress. After my folks passed on I found the following letter in my mother's personal correspondence. It was written during my fifth and last year at camp.

Camp Nebagamon For Boys
Lake Nebagamon, Wis.

July 24, 1950

Dear Greek:

You certainly never forget. Thanks for your birthday greeting. In view of the cabin being broken up I didn't think that this would be a good year for Gene. One never knows because in my opinion this is his best year. He is out-going, friendly and has displayed much more warmth than hereto-fore. He is extremely popular with his group and his tripping reports are something!

I am enclosing his Trip Rating sheets. Read them and return them to me. Most of the boys' reports are pretty critical – these speak for themselves.

You and I know how a boy's personality and character is stripped naked on a trip so it makes these reports all the more pertinent. I know you will be happy to receive such good news concerning your calling card I'd be interested in receiving reactions he has revealed in his letters to you. Your guy is pretty

closed mouthed about complaints and he may have fooled me,
but I think he is happier this year than ever before.

With fond regards, I am,

Sincerely, Muggs

Muggs was right, it was a super year!

One thing not mentioned previously was that I suffered from
acute asthma attacks in the summers, and it seemed to be
exacerbated by the 'North Woods' environment with its molds
and fungus. Some nights I had to sleep at the camp infirmary
under medical care to recuperate from the worst attacks. I would
wait at night until I just couldn't breathe any more and then I
would drag myself up the hill past the dining hall and the
younger cabins to the cure center of last resort, the infirmary. I
can remember sitting up in bed and panting for breath until the
adrenalin shot I was given kicked in, easing my gasping, toning
down my blood pressure and allowing me to drop off to sleep. It
is scary not being able to breathe and when relief comes it's a
blessing. A letter dated July 29, 1949, confirms my general
condition and it's outcome during my camping years.

"...it will not be necessary to send Gene home because of his
asthma, but to give you an idea how bad it was on his trip he
took 3 pills a night and three days ago we had to give him two
shots of adrenalin. Muggs"

I did my best to not let it interfere with my summers but it did
have its consequences. The symptoms eliminated me from the
"big trip" along the Gun Flint Trail where rescue was
problematic. It also eliminated my chance of being a CIT
(counselor in training) the next year because of the possible risk

and incapacitation liability that I would saddle the camp with. It was a hard pill to swallow, but it was an important learning experience to realize that I was not dealt the same physical fitness cards that most other young people held at my age.

At the close of this adventurous and fulfilling summer I returned to Chicago from camp. My parents had moved from the Southside to the "Gold Coast" area of Chicago, to the 'near north side. My mother, who always had excellent and expensive taste, had leased an apartment in the 20 E. Cedar building at the top of restaurant row, where Rush meets State Street. In 1946 the monthly rent ran about $500.00, a princely sum for those times, and I believe even her father cautioned her about paying such an exorbitant amount. This did not prove to be a deterrent and I lived there for 13 years. My parents continued to do so for an additional five before they were forced (the building was being subdivided into condominiums and they did not want to buy, but only rent) to move to another elegant building located at 1550 Lake Shore Drive over-looking beautiful Lincoln Park. The unit had a wonderful three corner view of the Chicago skyline. The irony of the situation was that this building they moved into from Cedar Street eventually went condo and they had to buy in anyway.

I still have professional pictures of the interior of our apartment (please see picture supplement) which was a two story affair with the elevator opening right into it on both the 16th and 17th floors, the top tier of the building. All the units were similar and except for a few apartments that were four to a floor, the rest were two. We had the entire two floors which made ours unique. The Cedar building at the time had relatively unobstructed views of the downtown skyline with the Palmolive Building and its rotating Lindbergh Beacon being the nearest and tallest in our panoramic view. The piercing light could be seen for miles and in earlier years it was a path for primitive airplanes to find Midway, Chicago's only airport at that time. The famous Wrigley Building (William Wrigley of chewing gum note) was lit up every night, its granite white walled exterior shimmering in the distance. On a clear day the Gary, Indiana steel mills could be seen 50 miles away, their smoke stacks pouring out black soot.

Visitors would be admitted through the entrance by the doorman who announced their presence to our residence. If visitors came by car, most visitors used taxis, the doorman could double park it on the street, because he had made his monthly payoff to the police so they would not ticket cars for infractions. The building had no garage. No surprise there, remember this is Chicago, the land of the bribe. My father later in life was the manager of a large building on famous Michigan Avenue. Every year he had to pay-off the elevator inspectors to be issued a renewed operating permit.

From the doorway the guest would be shown the way to the front elevator which still had an operator. The back service lift was for deliveries, the servants and walking the dog. The elevator would proceed at a leisurely pace to the 16th floor where a door bell would become visible once the sliding elevator door was opened to expose our front door. An identical set up would be on the 17th floor except there was no door bell, and if any one was so rude to come to this door they would have to actually rap their knuckles the old fashioned way on the wood, to gain attention. The best use for this entrance was for the morning paper to be slipped under it at 6:00AM every day.

The doorbell was rung and if it wasn't the servant's day off they would open it and let the caller into our stunning black and white diamond floored foyer with its small lit display cabinets on each wall. This entry way was approximately 10 feet by 12 feet with an entrance to the coat closet and powder room off at either side. Right in front of the visitor was the spiral staircase to the second floor with the huge vertical windows all the way around to take in the spectacular view.

To the left was the lovely dining room with its corner views of the lake and skyline. The recessed overhead lighting featured a spotlight in the ceiling directly over the table for 14, which was covered with a black reflective glass, and the light was beamed to just cover its surface. The entrance to the room had two white banquet doors which were closed for special occasions, and opened with a *voila*, at just the right moment, revealing the room and the beautiful table settings whenever dinner was called for the guests. Of course under the carpet at the hostess chair was an electric call bell to bring the serving person for whatever reason. It was good to be king!

To the right was the most spectacular room of the entire apartment. The two story living room with huge windows over looking the Chicago skyline with a majestic 24 foot ceiling. Off a small alcove was a wood burning fire place and this area was where the Christmas tree, something we had every year, a tradition on my mother's side of the family was set up. It was a Hanukkah bush as far as the extreme Reform Jews were concerned.

Next to the opulent living room was the bar cove which also served as an alternate small eating area for breakfast and lunch. It had a miniature liquor bottle collection which easily totaled 400 different brands. Twice a year they were taken down, dusted and returned. We did not do this ourselves in case you were wondering. Inside the bar counter was a custom built large glass fish tank that my mother put a cactus garden in since fish were for eating, and it was a good call.

The entire living space included four and a half bathrooms and three bedrooms upstairs. My room was in the back yet was unique in that to enter a person would have to step out on a small balcony over the living room between the hallway and the entry into 'Gene's lair,' a distinct disadvantage to me when there were adults over for dinner or cards sitting in the living room below me. If they looked up they could see if I ventured forth.

As a 'true little prince', and representative of a wealthy family, I always was asked to come down to meet the company, something I dreaded and was slow to do, but do it I did. Hello Uncle Hubert, Aunt Wilma, Uncle Shorty, Mr. Phaelzer, etc. After escaping back to my room from this dreaded chore that was odious and no doubt a factor in my developing shyness, I could not leave again to go elsewhere unless I slowly opened my door and silently crawled on my stomach, so as not to be seen, to the safety of the main upstairs hall where once again I could assume the stature of a human being and not a reptile.

The place was spectacular. My friends at school were amazed when they came over, as I was, even though I always told people we were middle class. I actually almost talked myself into it, but I became suspicious that I might be gullible. We were probably more of the middle of our class, a sly distinction. I never wore our wealth on my sleeve, because my dad didn't. My father worked hard for his paycheck and he expected me to do so also. He always warned me about not becoming like so and so, who lived off the wealth of the family, and never amounted to anything. I would not forget this. I became defensive about our apartment because I never wanted to be considered rich, and today I still wonder about those times. It is not a factor in my life at this stage. Although I received piecemeal help from my folks, the bulk of their estates were left to my children, and so it should be. We have been able to make it on our own, since my divorce, but it has not been easy.

That fall I entered Francis W. Parker private school at the fifth level and I acclimated myself to all new friends, many that had been enrolled together since kindergarten, a tight knit group to say the least. The class was diverse financially for scholarship children were taken, and minorities admitted, though from my recent understanding with a classmate, it was on a quota basis, two students to a class.

From the start I would take the bus on Lake Shore Drive or the trolley on State Street (where the cars were still vintage 1920's with open platforms and no heat for winter days and only adjustable windows on warm ones), for the 20 minute ride to school. The trolley stop was more convenient and in winter I did not have to battle the cold wind blowing off the lake by riding the bus. My mother never took me, my dad couldn't and there was no chauffer as on the South side, so public transportation for a dime with a student card each way was the only means of getting there. I, along with the other children, was very independent from the beginning.

I would only have one incident with a predator during all my years in Chicago. It took place on the west side of State, Street, downtown, near Marshal Field and Company, and I was alone and maybe 12 years old, cruising a Woolworths five and dime store looking at some items on one of the huge counters that these variety stores were known for. I was standing next to a man in an overcoat and hat so his dress was not unusual. Suddenly I felt an unwanted hand in my crotch and immediately moved around to the other side of the counter watching him all the time. When he moved one way I moved the other and this kept on for about five minutes. Now either I ran out when he turned his attention elsewhere or he gave up - no matter, no harm no foul, this was the big city, you were on your own. I can still see his face today.

My school, Francis Parker, looked like a huge house, but I believe it was originally built as a school years before my attendance. In fact it was founded in 1901, and it occupied a city block while the kindergarten through third grade classes were taught in a modern building across a blocked off adjoining street. The 330 Webster address bordered Lincoln Park on the East and busy Clark Street on the west, with its noisy metal wheels on metal rails, street car traffic streaming past. There was a separate building that contained the cafeteria, library and art class room.

A few bungalows were used as the print shop and for other activities.

On Clark Street just two buildings away, was a riding stable for the nearby Lincoln Park bridal paths, and the horses would walk up the street to get to the park. Today it is an apartment complex and before a riding stable, it was a garage which became infamous as the scene of the Saint Valentine's Day Massacre. Seven men were lined up against the wall in a gangland assassination during prohibition by the Italian led mob of Al Capone from the South Side. The killings were in retaliation for Buggs Malone North Side Irish mobster's machine gunning Capone's headquarters. To say the least it was an interesting neighborhood.

Over the stage of the school auditorium was the venerable motto of Francis Parker. *Everything to help and nothing to hinder.* This imbedded the philosophy of the noted educator, founder and guiding light of this progressive education institution which used the methods of the renowned philosopher, psychologist and educator John Dewey. "A School Should Be a Model Home, a Complete Community and an Embryonic Democracy," Parker believed that education should include the complete development of the individual; mental, physical and moral. John Dewey called him the "Father of Modern Education."

My adjustment to the new school environment was tentative. I was the new kid on the block, apprehensive and not up to the level of advancement that my fellow classmates were, or so I thought. I did not make friends easily so I remained aloof, outside the regular cliques that were already in place. I felt self conscious and it took me a long time to become 'one of the gang.'

George, a fellow classmate whose father was a prominent clergyman in Chicago wrote this in my yearbook

"...You've been a good friend and a fellow loser at hearts (keeping girl friends) through out high school, and, don't wonder when they look at you in college like we did in fifth (grade).....Curly"

Apparently, my shyness, lack of assimilation and awkwardness did not go unnoticed at my new school. May it be said that George had a sarcastic and flip side to him and he was very streetwise in other ways for his age. His life included unexpected twists and turns that others in the class would not come close to experiencing. We were all raised on the streets of Chicago and this made us more savvy, more self assured and to think outside the box. We learned that we were able to survive on our own in an urban environment. We would get ourselves in trouble and yet skim by with luck, speed, or God's blessing! The thoughts of my first days in Parker were still with George seven years later, scary!

The fifth level where I entered numbered 43 students that would be introduced to not only advanced studies and individual help but a true relationship with each of the faculty. Social events and friendships blossomed as our group moved as a self contained module through the next eight years of school until we were out the door. In my case, except for summer camp, I had no other friends, for we spent all of our time together. Yet, saying this, on the weekends the Jewish kids hung out together. They were the dominant portion of the student body.

Through Parkers rules and dress codes for the girls no one could trump another classmate on jewelry or clothes, it just wasn't allowed. White blouse, blue skirt and white sox and shoes kept differences when it came to dress at a minimum and created a level playing field environment.

I went home after school alone for many months and involved myself in adventure books, spinning records and building models, most of them of a military nature which had grasped my entire interest. I still studied World War II closely and the daring of soldiers on all sides appealed to my psyche. I enjoyed building military ships, vehicles and airplane models and no doubt pictured myself operating them in battle. I never was any good at the balsa wood kits, but the easier plastic were the ones I could glue together and enjoy.

The military was something I could picture myself involved in as I continued to read books about World War II. Five of my cousins had served as Officers; I would also like to do so. With my interest in combat at that early age I did not understand the consequences or the results in a conflict. In my mind I knew I could be a sniper in a tree, blast targets from inside a tank, torpedo a convoy of ships, and escape or out maneuver an enemy fighter for the kill. I could hold my position in a box set up of bombers over Berlin while German anti-aircraft shells burst around me throwing out deadly shrapnel and downing my comrades. Now at 77 years of age I am wiser and deem there are no "good wars," and other means of solution of political or economic problems are preferable.

Back at school the arts and the manual arts were articulated, and student government, assemblies, drama and music were part of the curriculum. The art, shop and printing departments were examples of this, and special chorus with a gifted leader and music teacher, Chauncey Griffith was a favorite if you could carry a tune. If not, you were free to sit out.

Reviewing some of the plays which were given by the upper school during my senior year I found names like *Lost In the Stars, Antigone, The Patriots, Suppressed Desires, The Monkey's Paw and Riders to the Sea, the Pinafore and Peer Gynt* by Ibsen which was our Senior Play in 1954. Very impressive indeed for high school thespians.

Athletics were enjoyed by many students as Parker belonged to a Private School League and played similar institutions around the Chicago area including Harvard, Wheaton, Latin and North Park, to name a few that I remember. We fielded a strong basketball and bowling team, played football with old style equipment and baseball, which remains obscure in my memory, plus inter-mural sports. The school had a new part time football coach who was a practicing attorney and until we had a game injury an anonymous Christian Science practitioner. When he encouraged the student to continue playing on what turned out to be a fractured ankle without removing him from the game for medical treatment he was replaced with a believer in medicine.

My former classmate and good friend John Shapira, was a smart guy, and a good athlete, especially in basketball. He probably would have won the league scoring title if the guy who did win it, John Loeb, another classmate "…..would have passed it (the ball) to me," He cordially states.

Every year John and his wife Jane travel in the winter to the San Diego area and we get together and laugh about the "Arrai Affair," appropriate or not. Allow me to explain. It was in our Junior year, John, as mentioned, was a fine basketball player and one of the regulars and Harold Arrai was a rider of the pine (a reserve player), like some others of us and the first half was winding down. Our center, a Nordic looking chap, was playing his heart out on the floor for the glory of Parker. With a minute or so left on the clock his jock strap broke and a remnant was hanging down from under his basket ball shorts for all to see. It may have caused a twitter or two but the horn for the end of the half sounded and we all trooped back into the locker room for the 15 minute time break.

The coach told the center to check his bag to see if he had another supporter replacement. Nope! Then he asked if anyone on the team had an extra one for the center to use. No luck here either. It was now desperation time. The coach turned to Harold and said how about giving him yours and not coming out for the second half? No sweat and that is actually what happened and it was always remembered as the Arrai Sacrifice!

Eventually I formed a close cadre of friends, some of whom I still visit today. We played together after school, engaged in antics that bordered on vandalism, and played poker. My skills and discipline were marginal and most of the time I came out a loser. I would double date with the guys as we socialized with girls in our class and some from lower grades. All this started at an early age and I remember my first date with classmate Karen Meyer. We went to O'Connels Restaurant for a hamburger, shake and conversation. She remembered it "fondly" when signing my year book in our senior year.

"To a real swell fellow. We've had a lot of fun together for four years. Do you remember that first date in 7th grade-oh Lord! Good luck, Love Karen."

I cemented my relationships as the class years passed by. Those years still are retained in my mind as to what the class studied. The Persian Empire would come and go as sixth grade ended. South America was interesting with Ms. Marshall in seventh, while Ms. Greenebaum, a fixture at the school for years was brave enough to teach during the McCarthy era about the Soviet Union and China. I recall there were whispers about her being a Commie, but that did not phase her. She made Golda Meir look like a wimp, and I am sure if offered the opportunity, could take Senator Joseph McCarthy to the mat just by looking at him with her glass eye.

Once we reached ninth grade students circulated around to individual classrooms for language, science, mathematics and social studies where we tackled ancient history and studies of the "Back of the Yards," referring to the stock yards of Chicago and the working class people that lived there. The class broke up in teams and actually, hit the bricks to film and interview the residents, for the years assignment.

In 10th grade I took my second year of impossible French from Madame Richards. It was torture and all I wanted to do was *ferme la bouche*, for I could not form the words, acquire the accent or do the bookwork. I dreaded Madame calling on me in class, her demeanor and tongue took no prisoners. I believe I was the poorest student in the room, although others were struggling too, while some excelled. Looking back it makes me sympathetic to students today. I believe we need to aim education more to their abilities and interests rather than a shot gun approach curriculum in high school that covers a wide spectrum of subjects. This way more of them will stay engaged.

One day near the end of my second year, Madame asked me to stay after the class was over, and made me an offer I could not refuse. Madame would pass me with a C this term as long as I would not take a third year. Deal or no deal? I will let you decide. I am sure that at the time it was like the "second coming."

Maybe it was surrender on her part, not only from the frustration of working with me, but also because the biology lab was next to her room and it was emitting an odious new odor. The usual smells had all been classified by sophisticated noses, and was now exacerbated by a new addition, a wild choice by yours truly for what pet that I would have as a laboratory animal. The class was assigned to buy, keep, study, and care for an animal of their choice during the second semester.

While the others were buying mice, rats, hamsters and a garden snake or two, somewhere I found a raccoon for sale. I named it Bebe' and it sort of belonged to the class. Mr. Meyer our Biology teacher allowed me to keep it in a large cage adjoining the wall next to the French class room. It was my job of course to take care of it and although I would let it out in the classroom to chase frogs for dinner it was relatively tame and eventually smelly. Meyer was also our homeroom teacher, and remembered by me as a "piece of work," went along with it. Although Madame wasn't sure where the smell was emanating from because the lab always smelled, she one day stuck her head in the door and spotted the raccoon, and that was all "she wrote."

She let Meyer have it with both barrels and he instructed me to get rid of Bebe ASAP! Well, easier said then done. I had no idea where to take it. I finally found a zoo in Wheaton, Illinois just outside of Chicago that said if you bring it, we will take it.

The "love of my life" at that time and the heartthrob of every other living male student was Paula and I convinced her to come with me and we drove the animal to the zoo in my folks Buick. What made the trip memorable, and attracted the stares of startled motorists and their passengers was that Bebe rode on Paula's shoulder the entire way without a mishap. The mishap was that I eventually would lose Paula.

By eleventh grade, our studies became more serious and after Biology the sophomore year, students were faced with mandatory Physics or Chemistry courses, both would be dreadfully hard to pass much less endure. I was doomed to take Chemistry, a course of little interest to me. In reality I did not have a scientific mind to grasp its essentials. I just knew it would be a trial and on that I was correct. Looking back I fear I did not face the challenge maturely. Ironically, Doctor Richards, was the husband of Madame the French teacher, and was the butt of many jokes and class pranks over the years. He was extremely knowledgeable but should have been working in a University environment, rather than a high school.

Both of his sons attended the school and could have given him some insight into student behavior, which on the whole was very good, but he remained a very bright and naive teacher lost in his work. He spoke with a heavy Austrian accent which hindered the material he was teaching from penetrating and there were incidents of boredom and rebellion in his class over the years.

Students would hook Bunsen burner hoses up to the sink faucet and let the water fly on command which put Doc Richards into a tizzy. One student ahead of me orchestrated a great prank that the gullible Richards bought hook line and sinker. A boy by the name of Art set up a scene where a fellow student snuck down the outside fire escape which passed by one of the wide open huge windows, and upon reaching the ground lay prone under the window on the sidewalk. Once he was in place Art yelled at Doc that so and so fell out the window, come and look! Doc raced to the window and was flabbergasted and after yelling at the prostate student who did not move raced down the inside steps while the student, cued by Art, zipped back up the fire escape steps. Doctor Richards was not amused and no doubt assigned extra work for the suspected culprits, while the class was in peels of laughter and disorder, but this was de rigueur in his class.

I was indeed a card carrying member of that year's Chemistry class, but I found myself lost in the woods and more absorbed in childish disruptions than in the good doctor's lectures. No other instructor would have put up with it, nor would they have had to. We were basically a respectful bunch of kids, but I was so bored that I came up with the idea of tying the old fashion shade string to the belt loop of the student next to me. This I did and with the class bell ringing he got up and quickly pulled the whole shade down creating laughter and confusion. That was my ticket out of Chemistry. Doc kicked me out of the class and I am not sure what I did to make up the credit. It may have been for the best. Classmate Rowan Schmidt wrote in my yearbook, *"....we missed you in chem....you lucky dog."*

I may have been off Doc Richards radar, but he was still on mine. For as long as I attended Parker I was the first one to arrive at school in the morning. That was because I left the house with my dad every morning after breakfast and I would be there by 7:30 along with the janitors. Twice I took the bolts out of the three hinges on the chemistry lab door and twice when Doc opened the classroom for the day the door fell on him, but not hard enough to injure him, but he just did not understand this tenet of gravity, and kept contacting the maintenance department to rectify this phenomenon.

I do not recall how I came to be co-editor of the yearbook. There were only three ways to becoming an editor; appointment, election or volunteering. Rereading the comments written next to Bill Freehling's picture who was my co-editor it says he was elected so I guess I must have been too. The yearbook is always the highlight of the end of the school year. It was an assignment that I really enjoyed, working with the new printer we found and the new layouts and art ideas from our creative staff.

Bill took after his mother and was a true genius who overcame his physical disability to participate fully with the class and his friends. He was the only one of 43 students to be accepted at Harvard. Everyone did go to college, with most of them ranked in the top tier of educational institutions. I note here that my co-editor became an American Historian and Singletary Professor of the Humanities Emeritus at the University of Kentucky. He has written eight books and received the Allan Nevins Prize of the Society of American Historians, 1967 Bancroft Prize, elected Senior Fellow at the Virginia Foundation for the Humanities, and was a Louis R. Gottschalk Lecturer in 2007. Quite a resume.

With Bill and me at the helm of the 1954 yearbook, the undertaking was accomplished with a staff of 36 students and two advisors and received kudos from everyone.

Congratulations on the most terrific Parker Record....Thanks for a marvelous 1954 Record...a real great job with the book...one of the finest Records in years...congratulations on your great Record....it is certainly terrific....thanks for a swell record.

The yearbook has been a treasure, pleasure and resource for me all these years and it may have been the first hint of any literary abilities that I might have possessed.

The Senior Play was always one of the highlights of the year and it was selected by the class as a whole. As mentioned previously, Parker was into dramatics, and we had a drama teacher on staff full time. Helen Gharrity held the position for years but when she was chosen to produce the renowned Chicago Rail Fare Pageant (which ran for two years (1948-49) on the lakefront with a cast of thousands and real railroad engines and rolling stock), John Holabird took her place, He remained working full time for the famous Chicago architectural firm bearing his family name of Holabird and Holabird, but in his heart he was a real thespian.

The class made the ambitious choice to give the classic play "Peer Gynt" by Henrik Ibsen which was first produced in 1867, and is the most widely produced play in Norway, and frequently staged throughout the world. The original play was written in five acts, but our merry company had it reduced to three. It was a large and demanding production featuring dancing, music, and singing. All of the costumes, scenery and masks were produced in house with the help of an adult support group of mothers, including mine. The play had two performances on a Friday and Saturday night in May. Peer Gynt, the lead was played by my good friend George Walker who now lives in the Washington D.C. area, recently retired, and has close ties to the Obama White House. Other students would be assigned parts based upon their abilities and I was designated to play King Brose, a character with one important line. We rehearsed for weeks after school and on weekends and I had my one line cold! "The time for your death has arrived."

Now, during the real production in a storage area under the stage there was a running poker game raging with stage hands and minor actors of various unsavory backgrounds involved, and I was part of it. My appearance occurred in scene 6 of Act 1, so what else was I going to do while waiting? Throwing in a good hand as scene 5 ended I went upstairs to be in position to enter stage left and as I was waiting for my cue I kept repeating my line to myself. "The time for your death has arrived" or was it "approached," must have been arrived, and then I heard my cue and out I marched and promptly said in my most arrogant manner "The time for your death has *arroached.*" After a split second of silence the audience broke into peals of laughter and it was then and there in this career guiding moment, that I knew the stage was not in the future for me.

"Idle minds are the devils work shop" goes the old saying. I am not sure my mind was ever idle, it seems I was always thinking up diversions or designing the world's next great egg beater or some other lame thing. Something as wild as stealing Doc Richards desk from his classroom and driving it over to his house and putting it on his lawn would be the next challenge. I believe that my year book co-editor was also in on the initial planning. There would eventually be six or more "Band of Brothers" involved, and we would have to pay a heavy price, the penalty for such a rude indiscretion at a very well respected private school.

The idea germinated because of my knowledge that the keys to all rooms were left in the lab coat pocket of Mr. Meyer each night. The last thing he did was take it off, hang it on a hook in the teachers cloak room and put on his jacket before leaving the building. The stunt all tied into the senior play and our being in the vacant school after dark for the production.

Now the plan went down like this: stuff a wedge in one of the emergency exit doors after the play was over and no one would notice. Leave the school to return to a vacated building an hour later in the top down convertible of one of "the brothers," and park it near the exit door. Meanwhile the "Parker Plumbers" stealthily made their way in and grabbed the keys from Meyer's coat, went up the stairs to the lab where the prize lay behind a locked door, that soon would be sprung open. The drawers with papers in them, including tests, were laid on the floor undisturbed and the desk was carried down the stairs to the waiting car to be transported 5 miles to the Richard's house at the charming hour of one o'clock in the chill of the Chicago morning. We unloaded the desk gingerly placing it on the lawn unseen, departed and returned to the school and retrieved our own automobiles to head home to warm beds and white sheets, the color of untainted driven snow.

By the time school started on Monday the second 'Spanish Inquisition' had begun with classmates being singled out and questioned in the principal's office. The administration was steamed up and gossip about the heist had now gone viral around the school. The faculty needed to know how the desk robbers got into the school. The perpetrators had signed a blood pact not to tell, which was only as good as its weakest link. Brother Kenny broke and the jig was up. The criminals, aka the "Band of Brothers" ran for the sewers. Ken ended up in New York City in a large accounting firm I believe, but still tainted as a fallen felon.

The penalty inflicted was to stay after class each day and paint the ten foot high wire fence that surrounded 3 sides of the one block property until it was finished or they stopped making green paint, which ever came first. Our parents were now on notice that they had raised juvenile delinquents and that aside from the fence painting assignment we would not receive the diplomas at the graduation ceremony but one day late. No longer were we the "bros" but now the "One Day Late Society." How embarrassing to our families, and humiliating to ourselves.

Graduation came and we all marched to our seats to the music of *Pomp and Circumstance* for the ceremony. Placed under our chair was the hardcover folder with the diploma inside for the law abiding. Maybe I thought "I would rather laugh with the sinners than cry with the saints, because the sinners have more fun," words which had not yet been written by composer and musician Billy Joel.

At the end of the proceedings, all the graduates were asked to reach under their chairs and retrieve the diploma which was inside a special hard cover folder. We were greatly surprised and relieved that ours were in there too, and I gave my steely stink eyed parents a thumbs-up to let them know they would not have to leave town after all.

The memories of the heist remain etched in my yearbook.

George W. wrote in my yearbook: *"To my partner in crime from our 6th grade job to the latest one. Best wishes...no crime in college."*

John S. wrote: *To....partner in crimes, social as well as desks*

Michael H. noted: *"...glad you made it"* (graduated)

Paul F. signed: *"Congratulations....Hope you do as well next year when you graduate with us."* Paul was one year younger than I was, and maybe more sarcastic.

The Faculty of The
Francis W. Parker School
Certifies that
Eugene William Lassers

Has been a member of this School for eight years, has completed the full High School Course of Study, has satisfied the faculty in respect to conduct and is now graduated from the school.

Given at Chicago, Illinois, this sixteenth day of June, nineteen hundred fifty-four.

Herbert W. Smith
Principal

It was good to get a second chance and to graduate on time.

Summer time
and the living is easy,
fish are jumping
and the cotton is high
(*Summertime from Porgy and Bess by George Gershwin*)

Well, my folks never heard this song or if they did they never lived it. I never saw goldfish jump at my house, nor did we have tall cotton. My summers were always busy, no loafing at the Lassers house. It was 1951, camp days were behind me especially since my bid to be a CIT (Counselor In Training) was turned down due to my asthma, and I don't blame them. I would be more of a liability than a help, but without the infirmity I would have been chosen, according to the Director.

The next summer would be devoted to learning to type, at least five weeks of it. I was now typing with two fingers but my father wanted more skin in the game. He never made many demands on my activities, but here he was adamant. His hand writing was passable but mine was not and remains today the work of a skilled physician, and he was going to correct my means of communication. Thank goodness he did, because the way it was I would definitely have ended up in the blue collar workforce, not exactly what I was raised for.

At the time I hated attending secretarial school, I was the only male student, and certainly the youngest amidst the ladies clacking the keys on the old standard office typewriters that were provided. All this would take place in downtown Chicago in the heat of summer with no air conditioning, just large windows that when opened brought the noise of the street below into the classroom on the second floor of the old building. My fellow students had one objective in mind, a job. My royal standard typewriter if used to its fullest would earn me a ticket to college.

I was not pleased to be there, but I was diligent in my work and enjoyed the challenge of the timed test against the clock that was given throughout the four hour daily class which validated one's speed and precision. I could type 100 words a minute, but to do it perfectly was a tough go. Remember, no white out or computers back then, and rubber erasers usually left a smudge, and this was deducted from your over-all score. Eventually the five weeks passed and the rest of the summer was mine. Thank you dad for making me do this!

Harry Stoll was a powerhouse businessman and a friend of my dad's from his days as President of Fish Furniture Company, Chicago's largest furniture outlet. He was now General Manager of Mandel Brothers Department Store, and because he was, I hired on for the summer of 1952. I would work in sales, and stock shelves while rotating from department to department each day. I was 16, and was paid a dollar an hour (minimum wage) plus 1% of my sales. Dressed in a suit and tie I rode the street car downtown five days each week to report in at 9:00 am for work. Quitting time was 5:30 pm with a half hour off for lunch, which I took across the street at a cafeteria.

Mandel Brothers, was established in 1865 in a huge building that housed floors of merchandise. Its entrance was on famous State Street at the corner of Madison. The Mandels were very prominent in Chicago society and also quite wealthy.

I always enjoyed selling and had previous experience working for my dad at his furniture store in Kankakee, so I wasn't afraid to ask customers if "I could help them." I was tall for my age so at least the customers thought that child labor was not being resurrected. I worked the men's shirts, socks and undergarments, the notions and sporting goods department and others, rotating to a different one each day. There was very little introduction and training from any of the managers of the different departments, I do not even think they remembered my name after I reported in to them. As for Harry Stoll, I never did see him during the two months, but it was a great opportunity, and the experience was priceless

I finally ended up full time in the sporting goods section and I really enjoyed the placement. Here was a department where I knew the games and the merchandise needed to play them. One day they yanked me out for duty in the basement and the inexpensive men's suit department which was having a two day sale that would be advertised heavily in the four Chicago daily newspapers. I was not overjoyed by this assignment but of course I accepted it.

The first day in Mandel's bargain basement was spent putting the sale items in order and tying new mark down tags on them. The best suits were "shark skin" and they were shiny but about as numerous as sharks in Lake Michigan. I spent most of the day retagging suits with discount sale tags for the big event. The thing that caught my eye was that the price was the same, only the tag was a different color sales tag. That meant that there was no discount, and only a few miscellaneous suits were left on the bargain rack.

The second day was a real learning lesson for a sixteen year old kid. I reported in at the regular time but two things were noticeably different. There were additional salesmen on the floor, collecting customers at warp speed, customers who were already pawing through the "bargains." Today it would be my job to sell suits. The only experience I ever had in regards to this was being fitted myself at Sak's Fifth Avenue men's department, a world removed from Mandel's bargain basement.

Not only did I have to sell the suits but I had to fit them and make the soap hash marks for the tailor's guidance through the process of finishing the suits for the buyer. I found a piece of soap in the backroom and proceeded on to the sales floor, tape measure hung around my neck. What greeted me were short foreign sales men grabbing each customer as they entered while having a stash of pants and coats on their arm from people they already corralled. If I was going to make any sales I would have to take the initiative. I became very aggressive and as customers came in I ran as fast as my colleagues who were old dudes to coral their business. Soon I was walking around with clothes hanging off my arm and this day would turn out to be my best sales results while I worked there. I sold over $1000.00 worth of merchandise, something I never would do again that summer.

Ah, the memories of trying to fit one particular customer. The coat fit well and only took a mark or two on the sleeves for the length. The pants were a bit more dicey since they were too large and as I crimped the waist in the back and asked the customer if this was better he said yes, and I made a soap mark at that location and again on the cuffs and sold another suit. God wonders if the tailors who cleaned up after me would know what to do. Thank goodness they transferred me back to sporting goods the next day, and any complaints were beyond my ears.

The summer of my Junior year was also a working one. My Folks would keep me in the squirrel cage once again. My cousin Bob Silberman, was an executive at Bell and Howell Camera Company located in suburban Chicago, and through him I secured a job in the shipping Department. At 17, I already had two years of driving experience and because the plant was on the outskirts of the northwest side of the city I needed a car for transportation. If you can drive in Chicago downtown traffic you can drive anywhere, trust me.

My dad made arrangements with the Plymouth dealership in Kankakee to rent a new 1952 four door for my use. It was a manual shift and my last. Because our apartment building at 20 E. Cedar did not have a garage my parents parked in a public one with valet service. When they wanted to use the car it would be dropped off at the building and on return picked up by an attendant who dropped us off and returned the car to the garage. This arrangement was not an option for me and I was required to keep the car on Cedar Street which never had any parking places. Looking for a space could be a half hour proposition.

The work in the shipping room was basically packing and loading merchandise for the mega camera company. Most of it was sent by truck but we did have a rail siding and it was the only time I ever unloaded a box car in the stifling summer heat of Chicago.

The people I worked with were older, many with European accents, and I was ignored except when conversation was required regarding the job. The way some of the packages of projectors or other sensitive items were thrown into trucks I wondered why they would not be returned as defective or broken for replacements or refunds.

I always anticipated the morning and afternoon ten minute breaks, and the 30 minute brown bag lunch whistle. Quitting time was a mirage far into each day's twilight zone. On the drive to work I would try and memorize a popular song playing on the radio to keep my mind off the boring repetitiveness of shipping room labor. One week they put me in the place of a man on vacation whose job was to run the Pitney-Bowes postage stamp printing machine at the end of the line. On the second day I forgot to change the date on the imprinter and half way through the shift I realized my mistake and reported it. All I heard were things like "you're in for it now," and "bye-bye kid, it's been good to know ya." As it happens the Post Office did not notice the mistake and they did not send the feds out to dock the company for such a dastardly deed.

During my last week at work I was driving home hoping to make it to the train station to pick up dad, looking forward to having a few minutes to be alone together. It was seldom that we could do that and I do not remember our relationship as being close, but always respectful. Meeting his train was always ambitious since the station was an additional 20 minutes past our apartment with no traffic.

The end of the day bell rang at four, and I was out the door and jumped into the Plymouth in no time. Peterson Avenue became jammed as expected and I took the short cut through a residential apartment area around the mess over to Foster heading for Lake Shore Drive. Each corner of three story apartments I passed was uncontrolled by stop signs or lights and I paid no heed, exceeding the speed limit by ten miles per hour minimum. Out of the corner of my eye I saw a car to the left of me at the next intersection and it was not going to stop even though I thought the right of way was mine. I sped up and it plowed into the rear door behind me and pushed me into park cars on the other side, or "T" boned as they say today. I was alive, unhurt, and totally scared to tell my Mother, who was always the bump in the road, the bad news bear for her controlled anger, and disapproving look.

The Plymouth now looked like a 'green camel' because of the hump in the roof and the trunk of the car. Of course a cop eventually showed up and took a report. Giving me his card he said my father should call him, the report and any tickets would wait while the investigation was under way. In other words he was looking for a bribe, it's Chicago.

The outcome of the entire mess was my Mother came and picked me up, and she was quite upset/angry, the two words are interchangeable, and still gave me the third degree which was worse than the grinding metal experience still dancing in my head. So the bottom line was: the car was totaled, my father did not take the cop's bait, both drivers were cited, and the Plymouth dealer said he would never rent to dad again.

The last six months at Parker I was introduced to a young lady four years my junior and still in 9th grade. I had enjoyed dating Senior girls from my own grade during the year so I knew that this was not going to last, a short time relationship. At best she was a footnote, a chance happening, a bit player who soon would be gone once I moved on to the University where the adults were, but whatever similar strings that kept us together was good enough for now. Her name was Sharon Joyce Banovitz, and we would marry five years later and have three children together, and many memorable times.

College called, not a moment to soon, and I would answer!

Chapter 3

Saguaro Sojourn,
The University of Arizona Years

Children were enrolled at Francis Parker school because it was an accredited and esteemed institution, and opened doors to the best colleges in the country to well prepared students. Parker delivered on a well earned reputation.

Bill went to Harvard, John and George to Brown, Christine to Berkeley while Judy attended Mills. Dorothy stayed close to Chicago and attended Northwestern, and Gene departed for the barren Southwest and the University of Arizona. Obviously the table setting was not level for all of the students because some could not afford the cost of attending renown Universities while others, like me did not have the grades to do so.

I had always wanted to go west to school and naïvely applied to Stanford, receiving no reply. Pomona College turned me down and the University of Arizona, a State University where out of state students paid higher fees, and were welcomed with open arms, accepted me.

My parents occasionally wintered in Arizona, and mother's wealthy family stayed every spring for two months, at the Arizona Biltmore. They played golf, rode horseback and congregated around the pool in their own cabana. They enjoyed the desert warmth, the rustic location of the hotel, and left the harsh Chicago winter behind.

My first visit to Arizona was in 1948, when my parents journeyed to the Biltmore Hotel. We arrived on the train from Chicago, and at the moment our attention was fixated on George Halas, owner of the Chicago Bears, and his wife who were also detraining from our car of deluxe Pullman accommodations. My folks had attended the professional Bears football games for years.

The Halas' stayed for at least two months, and had brought clothing and other essentials, including a case of Scotch for the long vacation. The station porter was helping them remove the items, took the case of 25 year old Scotch from their train compartment on to the platform, stumbled, and dropped the treasure, which then collapsed with broken shards of glass and wood sitting in a pool of Scotch. Halas, known as volatile on the field, went ballistic, and the porter feared for his life, as the platform fell silent except for the hiss of the escaping steam from the standing train.

My father was standing near the catastrophic scene, and a Scotch drinker himself, offered his sympathy and condolences to Mr. Halas, who accepted them This introduction resulted in dad playing golf with 'Papa Bear,' on a regular basis during our stay. The downside was the relationship had no effect on upgrading our seats for the coming season. For me it was a wonderful experience and created a real desire to live out west, away from Chicago's weather and its lifestyle. As icing on the cake I was able to visit the New York Giants baseball team spring training camp, and a fellow guest with connections took my autograph book, and filled it with signatures of the team including Manager Frankie Fritsch, the National League great all-star from the thirties. Even better, Hank Greenberg, the Detroit Hall of Famer was vacationing at the hotel, and had a cabana near ours by the pool. He added his signature to the treasure which somehow has disappeared from my grasp over the years.

The west was etched in my heart and affected my choice of where I desired to attend school. My grades at Parker were average, and even with the school's reputation, my acceptance by a state or small institution was about the best I could expect.

I did not apply further, and I gave it no more consideration, nor expressed any disappointment, for there was none.

My parents drove me to the Chicago La Salle Street Station clutching bags of school clothes and linens to board the Rock Island Railroad's *Golden State Limited* for Tucson, to start my freshman year.

> *The Rock Island Line is a mighty fine Line*
> *The Rock Island Line is the road to ride*

…so the well-known folk song goes which was popularized by a man known as Lead Belly. I found upon arrival the days were hot and the nights were warm, and most campus buildings were cooled by swamp coolers which were not nearly as efficient as air conditioning. No wonder the school year started at the end of August and concluded in early May. The heat in summer was always over one hundred degrees, and a good reason to leave town if you could.

Upon arrival I was placed in Yavapai, a Freshman dormitory, and given the choice to join the fraternity 'rush'. Although this was a normal routine, in reality the 'rush' for Jews and minorities of color was a segregated affair. The front door was open to visit all the houses, but only the Jewish frats would 'pledge' you to join, and the blacks and Latinos were marked down to dorm material. The Civil Rights era had not yet happened, so those who were not wanted did not participate in this charade. I should note that our house pledged the first African-American to join a fraternity a few years later.

I was 'grandfathered into Zeta Beta Tau, one of two Jewish houses on Campus because my dad was a 'Zeebe' at the University of Illinois. It wasn't my charm alone that allowed me to join the smartest house on fraternity row. ZBT won the scholarship trophy year after year, while sports, and drinking trophies decorated the fire place mantels and display cases of other houses.

Bob Farber, an active member who lived in Chicago had actually pre-screened me, and dropped by my home to chat during the summer. After some general 'get to know you talk', he asked what I was most interested in studying at the University. When I told him Reserve Officer Training (R.O.T.C.) he was speechless. He may at that point have wanted to check to see if I was Jewish, for this was not the normal response from a "Mogan David" lad entering the 'halls of ivy,' or in this case cactus.

In the 1950's and for many years after, every able bodied American young man was subject to the Selective Service Act and had the obligation of military duty. Thus at 18 years of age I was required to register at my local Post Office. The University of Arizona was a "Land Grant" University, the term dates back to the Lincoln Administration, and the Morrill Act of 1862. Therefore mandatory R.O.T.C. was required for men during the first two years of college, unless medically excused.

The Jewish boys were not Imperialists, but rather realists, and many were in the Corps because they'd rather serve as an officer than an enlisted man. Today there is no requirement for public service from our young people, only entitlements, and the country is worse off for it in my opinion. Many countries around the world demand such sacrifice. America is poorer because it has been eliminated. By serving the country young people have a different perspective, a chance to pay back, return a piece of their good fortune, and be proud of their service, and homeland.

Once ZBT accepted me I moved into the old and decrepit frat house they called home, a convenient location three blocks from the main gate of the University. The Pledges lived in the attic while the Actives (regular members) resided downstairs, rank had its privileges. It certainly was different than my home in Chicago. Our class had 20 Pledges trying to make grades (C average) and get through the rituals and hazing that would make us 'brothers.' Fortunately Jewish kids are not infatuated with hazing.

Our group was a mix of middle-America, with a few wealthy young men thrown in for contrast. Two pledges had exotic automobiles while the majority of us had our shoes. Lyle drove a beautiful white Jaguar 140 drop head convertible while Jack had the first model Corvette, hot off the line. Lyle lasted two years before leaving us and had the nerve to take his beautiful automobile with him, while Jack killed himself by hitting a stray cow while speeding in Mexico. Maybe shoe leather was not so bad after all.

I came unprepared for how studies were conducted at a large public University. Students were pretty much on their own, and they handled the responsibility of college or they didn't. The actives in the house kept their eye on your grades, for the future of the house depended upon it. Still it wasn't Francis Parker where I had 43 classmates in my senior year, and concerned teachers. There were many distractions including the fraternity, and it was easy to let your work slip, especially the courses you detested. One subject, Humanities, required the entire Freshman body in attendance while others were held in smaller study groups. Many of my academic requirements were boring and the afternoon laboratories in Accounting and Botany were dreadful. I always was cursed with identifying weird things through the microscope which I couldn't see, and cross footing a spread sheet that wouldn't balance.

No doubt my parents had grave misgivings about my success at college when I failed both courses and had to retake them again. I remained a Pledge during the second semester, by not making grades along with five other dunderheads. I'd be lying if I did not admit that I constantly wondered, if college was for me? If not, what else was?

However the next semester employing extra effort, and enjoying fewer diversions I did make grades (C average), and I was initiated into the fraternity that fall. To accumulate additional units I attended summer school at Northwestern University in suburban Chicago. I was able to complete two courses which were required by my mandatory curriculum at Arizona. It did not mean that my problems were at an end only that the end was in sight.

After my first year I remained eight units short of where I should have been. Still, Biology and Accounting remained my nemesis. Finding an image through a microscope or scribbling on a balance sheet still confounded me. I always begged the laboratory proctor for more time, and it was already four-thirty in the afternoon. No doubt he was thinking about something more interesting like a beer.

In my Sophomore year I carried 23 units, a heavy load to say the least, (normal was 16), to catch up. I truly think that the ambition to achieve the impossible, becoming a Commissioned Officer drove me on. I still was enjoying the good life of an under graduate, like participating in the all fraternity pledge five mile race, and coming in first for our house. I never ran five miles in my life and I was wheezing, huffing and puffing like an old steam engine with asthma at the finish line, but if you want something bad enough, you might just get it.

That summer I drove home to Chicago with a frat brother, and returned to Tucson with another. Vaughn Binzer's family lived in Palm Springs during the winter and Vincennes, Indiana the rest of the year. He was driving home once school let out via way of Palm Springs, where he closed up the family home and prepared it for the long hot summer. I joined him and we drove west to go eventually east. Palm Springs at this time of year was hot, even hotter without air conditioning, and everybody that could left town until the fall when cooler weather prevailed.

Before dawn broke, our cross country path turned due east on old Route 66. There were no Interstate Highways at that time and this was the quickest and most direct highway to travel. Along the way we occasionally sang the popular song written by Bobby Troup about *"Route 66."*

> *If you ever travel west,*
> *Take the highway that's the best*
> *Get your kicks on route 66*

When it was time to return in late August I drove back to school with another frat brother and good friend, Jim Block, from Milwaukee, Wisconsin. We cruised along in his brand new 1955 Chevy convertible. The top was down for most of the trip and both of us turned as red as lobsters.

I still was considered a Freshman, because of my unit deficiency. It was make or break time if I wanted to finish my advanced education in four years. The fraternity had now purchased another house more suited to our needs and we all moved into the new facility. I still was studying Biology and Accounting and it was necessary to retake the first semester over again. I continued to carry additional units just to stay even.

I noticed during my first year a few students engaged in passing out free sample packages of cigarettes to others on campus. The job paid $300.00 a year which was easy money for the effort that was required. The entire operation was handled as a marketing educational experience through the office of the Dean of the Business School. I had the good fortune to find that the American Tobacco position would be open soon and since I was a business major, and applied first, it was mine for the asking.

For two years I passed out 'Cancer Sticks' to unsuspecting students, and I am ashamed to admit that I did it. The program was terminated just after my second year of addiction creation.

As a note, I have never smoked cigarettes, and never was tempted to even though my folks puffed away without concern

As to my social life it was relatively bland even though there was a young lady from our sister sorority Alpha Epsilon Phi that was fun and pretty. My heart apparently was still back in Chicago with Sharon who was now a Sophomore in high school. It was remarkable that we still cared about each other.

During my first year I became quite close with a plebe in the fraternity from Tucson, by the name of Benji Gross. He was very smart and after only two years of undergraduate work was admitted to the University of Southern California Dental School, at age 20. Benji spoke fluent Spanish, played a brassy trumpet, was short, and the only Gringo in a six man mariachi band, that played in a dive on the Mexican side of town.

With the blessing of their families both he and another local, Howie Goldwyn were planning a two month trip to Europe, and asked if I had any interest in joining them? Indeed I did if I could sell my parents on it, and to do that, the trip could not be over the top expensive. My mother had journeyed to Europe in 1927 when she was just 18, albeit chaperoned by maiden aunts. Maybe she would buy in, for she loved to travel and had always encouraged me to do so. Mother always said "...they can't ever take your memories away from you." She made my summer, and gave her blessing and money to join them.

We had planned to do it for $2,000.00 dollars, and it looked like a once in a life time opportunity. The idea came full circle in the Spring of 1956. Prepayments were made for the most expensive items, airline and steamship tickets, and the car lease, but everything else was doled out on the go. Keep in mind that every country had its own currency, and we would travel to twelve different ones. Our wallets looked like a cornucopia of colorful pop art of unknown pictures except for the Queen of England on the pound note.

The great journey started with a flight home to Chicago, and preparation and packing before flying up to Montreal on a brand new Trans Canadian Airlines Viscount turbo prop airplane. It was over the same route where a sister aircraft a few weeks earlier lost a propeller, and it sliced through the cabin and killed a lady in the rest room. We would all gather over-night and catch the tramp steamer for England the next day.

The three of us boarded the bare-bones *Castel Feliche*, a name that makes you want to scratch yourself just saying it, along with a fistful of other eager students. Normally it plied the waters with European immigrants, still escaping the devastation of the war to America, Canada, and Australia. The price of the 10 day ocean voyage was $150.00 and we were birthed eight to a cabin. Two tiers each of four bunks for the hardy and the young. The 12,000 ton 'beauty of the seas' sailed full of wildly enthusiastic students for Southampton, England. Dormitory style bathrooms accommodated our needs, and we ate from long family style tables, serving hardy, if not tasty food. There wasn't caviar, or fine pastries, no live music to dance to, but a booming bar business alleviated those depredations. As long as you could see over the countertop you were served, no questions asked.

The weather remained fine allowing mingling, and for some, co-mingling, and even sleeping on deck if you had a snuggle to do it with. Walking around the ship at night could be awkward, especially in dark places as it had a tendency to roll even in light seas. We all stocked up on cigarettes and Canadian Club, not that we needed them for our own consumption, but they were goods that could be bartered for inflated favors on a Continent of recovering economies.

Upon docking in Southampton the entire ship transferred to a chartered train up to London, still pulled by a steam locomotive. Upon arrival we explored for seven days and found the rate of exchange was staggering since the pound was worth $4.60 to the dollar making everything extremely expensive. It was the only country that we'd travel to where the exchange rate was higher/negative to the dollar.

Our visit coordinated with the monarch's official birthday in June, (different than her real one), and we gathered in front of Buckingham Palace with a huge crowd to watch through cheap cardboard periscopes, Elizabeth II, ride side saddle on her mount to review the parade of "Red Coats" marching in the Queen's honor. She had only been on the throne for four years and was still a young woman.

Leaving London once again by train and journeying to Dover we boarded one of the numerous ferry boats that plied the turbulent channel to La Havre, France, and arrived in Paris, expeditiously, courtesy of the French Railways. Staying in a moderate but centrally located hotel was a good choice. It was near the Opera, the Louvre, the Seine, and the Metro. Moving around in this, the first foreign language country we had ever visited, the location was perfect. It was necessary to call a housekeeper to bathe. She drew your tub in a public bathroom and brought a towel in case one was needed. Toilets were in a different accommodation and the room was provided its own sink next to the bed. Of course we all shared a single room.

It was still a custom to tip the housekeepers in Paris, and no one escaped from their Velcro grasp. When guests checked out and called for the porter to help with the luggage, he came up, immediately pushed a bell, *ring, ring,* and out of nowhere maids appeared as if by magic awaiting your departure, their hands out! It was best to have your gratuity ready, or be prepared for some Parisian rudeness, sprinkled with words probably not covered by any high school French language class.

We picked up the brand new prearranged Renault 4cv sedan with the temporary red license plates and hit the road *"Jacques, and don't come back no more no more,"* as the Ray Charles song goes. The world was at our finger tips. Those were really the days when the dollar was good as gold, cigarettes were ours for trade and Americans were loved, for saving Europe. We were king of the road. Hail Caesar.

Dinner each night erupted into a sound bite as to whether we would drive, walk or taxi to the restaurant. The parking was brutal in the major cities, no different than today, and many times the three of us would need to lift the light automobile into its parking place as a last resort, indeed a Trojan effort.

I had the task to call my parents twice while I was away. The place and time were up to me, which was indeed a fair arrangement. Of course making an International call in 1956 compared to today's wireless world was truly a Herculean effort. The best place to call was from a post office in a metropolitan area, They were set up for it, where a hotel had to verbally receive the charges from the operator once the call was completed and bill the room for any amount they chose, and there was no way to verify that was correct, something I don't think Vegas would give odds on.

On the day to telephone home I spoke with the person in charge, and requested to place a call from Lucerne, Switzerland to Chicago. While waiting they called the International Operator who in turn relayed the call to the New York International Operator who rang up the Chicago exchange.

I continued to wait as Chicago rang up Delaware 7-3260, to verify that the person to person party called would be home at the specified time to receive the call. This was confirmed back verbally to the Lucerne Post Office. Once booked, I needed to return at the appointed time to place the call, and to leave a deposit.

When the time came the procedure was once again repeated and lodged in a phone booth I eventually heard "go ahead Lucerne, your Party is on the line." Then the shouting along with the static on the line increased, thus allowing very little communication over the crackling connection from an international call via a 100 year old cable stretched beneath the Atlantic Ocean. At least my parents knew I was all right. Indeed, two thumbs up to them, living with so little contact from me. Aside from this they wrote to different American Express Offices, and I collected my mail upon arriving in major towns, and returned the favor, sending letters back home along the way.

Leaving Paris, the 'City of Lights' we started our Continental driving adventure and headed southwest toward the Basque Country over the Pyrenees Mountains which separate France from Spain. It was in San Sebastian that I witnessed my one and only bull fight. In this case the bulls took the day by goring three Matadors of a lowly rank, sending them to the hospital to mend. Next was the capital city of Madrid where Dictator General Francisco Franco still ruled the Spanish people. Spending five days exploring we now turned east toward the Costa Bravo, and up to the French Riviera, and then dropped down to give Italy a thorough once over.

All roads lead to Rome and ours did too. Arriving on the Fourth of July the town was sold out and sweltering in the summer heat. We found a room on the second floor in a third rate neighborhood where our windows were wide open to catch a breath of air. Below us the 'ladies of the night' made their rounds, but we were not buyers of their services for their negotiated affection.

Of course we had to visit St. Peters Cathedral and its huge complex. What a surprise, there were throngs of visitors, flocks of Nuns phalanx's of Priests and hordes of vendors in the mammoth square hawking every imaginable item. There were scarves, Parker Pens, rosary beads, leather goods and Zippo Lighters, to name just a few. When we stopped to look at the lighters, all lying on a blanket across the ground, the vendor after his appeal to buy in broken English asked, "...are you *Lanntzman?*" Shocked, we acknowledge that we were Jewish, not knowing it showed. He came closer and said. *"..don't buy any of this stuff, its all fake."* Wow, it's good to be Jewish, and exposed to some insider trading.

Venice was hot and sticky but enthralling as the three of us walked the cobblestone ways, and crossed tiny bridges over the canals. Much to our surprise we ran into a couple of our old cabin mates on the street, what a coincidence. Over an espresso we learned that they had just driven here after visiting nearby Yugoslavia which put us in shock. Nobody we knew ventured close to this Communist tainted country, unless you happened to be kidnapped. According to them all it required was a Visa for entry into this forbidden land. They purchased theirs from the Consulate located just a few hours north in Trieste, a city without a country, an International city-state in 1956. It was a temptation that the three of us could not pass by.

Goodbye Venice, hello Trieste and that was where we headed the next day to find out if this was true. The city belonged at one time to the Hapsburg Empire, and then Italy over the years and today it is once again back in the possession of Italy. My parents had warned me about dealing in 'black market monies' which were so prevalent everywhere on the continent after the war. So far none of us had touched any illicit currency, but our cabin mates said we must buy the Yugoslav Dinars off the street in Trieste, because they were considerably cheaper than the over-valued official rate of exchange once inside the country by about three to one.

Motoring into Trieste we saw that money was being exchanged on every street corner, openly and illegally. Naturally before long we were sucked in, parked and soon were sitting in the rear of a small restaurant, trading the Yankee Dollar into Yugoslav Dinars at a great savings, never thinking this was a crime. It was only a crime to all the others doing exactly the same thing, but apparently not to us.

At the border it was necessary to fill out forms of entry, show our passports and proceed to have the most meticulous search I have ever undergone. If it had a serial number they wanted it recorded, how much money were we carrying, how long were we staying and where were we going, was asked as the Border Guards pawed over our Renault. Our answers were guestimates but apparently good enough for they let us pass. We were literally walking on our illegal money, and the customs and immigration never made us take off our shoes. If they had, we still would have been locked up in prison. Youth is for the brazen, the stupid and is wasted by most of us.

We were young, brash, thoughtless blockheads, and extremely fortunate to still have a life. Piling back into the car and driving south for about two hours over poor roads and passing more horse drawn wagons and carts than automobiles, we ended up on the northern tip of the beautiful Adriatic Sea in the small resort town of Opatija. Pulling into a large dowager grand hotel that had seen better days, and was listed in Frommer's Guide book at $5.00 a day with breakfast, we parked, and seeing so many German tourists milling around the lobby, we knew we had a good deal. They had a habit of traveling on the cheap, finding the best hotels to stay in, and often vacationed off the beaten track.

Our decision to stay on for five days turned out to be brilliant and an unexpected adventure. The beach was pristine, the breeze pleasant and the water mild. Spending time swimming in the Adriatic Sea, and on the sand with our former enemies in their Speedos and revealing bikinis went well. Every day a row boat selling fresh fruits worked the area and it had a scale on the front to weigh your purchase. I was carrying one of the first all metal Polaroid cameras in which the photos had to be retouched with a developing and finishing solution, but still was quite phenomenal. We drew a crowd, to marvel at the instant pictures that I could not give away fast enough to the bathers surrounding us.

It was the first and last time that I ever swam in open waters surrounded by shark nets to protect the beach and bathers from marauding schools known to frequent the Adriatic Sea. After seeing what looked like a black laundry line, barely visible in the distance I asked my traveling buddy Howie to swim over and check it out, after all he was on the University swimming team while I would have been classified as a 'sinker' in anything aquatic.

He soon returned and said the nets only extended about two feet below the surface and he was not positive that this was adequate to fend off these fearsome creatures. From then on we all stayed near the beach, checking frequently for anything near us that could make 'fin soup'.

Our room location required riding the lone elevator, operated by a teenager a few years younger than ourselves. His English was faultless, his mind sharp and over the stay we befriended him as he did us.

Gino Zamlic invited us to his home for dinner which was a real treat, and extremely generous. His shoemaker father had lost a leg fighting the Germans with vigor during the War. Now he harbored tremendous resentment as he was surrounded by the returning German Army in tourist clothes. The Zamlics served a hardy dinner with steak for the main course which must have been quite an extravagance. The entire conversation had to be translated into Croatian for his parents to understand, and our communication was stilted, though it was a great evening.

The next night he guided us to the larger nearby town of Rijeka, where we dined on Octopus, and drank local beer while listening to my first and last Zither player. Each morning he was back on the job running the elevator. He even took us out to the local Tuberculosis sanatorium where his brother was a long time patient seeking a cure. It was a large, light and airy building with huge windows that swung open to catch the sea breeze of hope.

Over the years we corresponded back and forth to each other in a timely manner. I even subscribed to the National Yugoslavian travel magazine, much against my father's warnings. Anything that was Communist was toxic, and with the McCarthy era of witch hunts just over he felt I was exposing myself to be labeled by the government as subversive. I received the publication for five years and emerged unscathed.

The next time I visited Opatija, in 1961, was with my wife Sharon. We came unannounced and Gino was not there. He was studying Medicine in Russia, with plans to continue his Residency in East Germany. Even after he became a physician I would hear from him occasionally. He called me one year from the Mayo Clinic in Rochester Minnesota where he was traveling as a personal physician to a major political figure in disguise.

In our conversation he mentioned "... things were unraveling fast in Yugoslavia, and I soon will be moving to Munich, Germany and fade into the countryside," and indeed he did. I lost all contact with my good friend who had become a regular 'pen pal.'

Back to the oxcart roads of this communist country, and driving east to Zagreb, now the capital of the country called Croatia, we spent overnight in this gray and dismal city. The next day the Renault and passengers crossed into the French zone of Austria (the country remained divided into zones after Word War II), with its beautiful fields, and majestic mountains. Spending time in Vienna, we then moved on to the historic city of Salzberg, and motored on for a brief stay, or so we thought in Innsbruck, Austria.

In a few days the Renault was headed up again toward the famous Brenner Pass, which runs over the Alps into Italy. We had planned to stay in a remote Austrian mountain village. 30 minutes off the main highway. The little car was huffing, and puffing, up the pass and in a few spots two of us would get out, and walk behind to lighten the weight with hopes that Saint Nicholas, elves, and raindeer would soon be here and help get the car up the pass.

Once off the main road, Howie continued to drive aggressively at a good clip down this narrow country road to the village with abandon. There was very little traffic in either direction. It was my turn in the back seat where I always rode sidesaddle, because of my height, legs across the seat in order to fit. Benji was the only one who could ride comfortably in each of the seats. Our Mexican Gringo was in the front. He could gain secondary employment by being shot from a cannon for he stood a bit over five feet and change. We were a clown car of Americans, traveling down a narrowing road with one and a half lanes and a Mercedes bus at below average speed coming the other way.

As the road narrowed we both brought this to Howie's attention who acknowledged it and said "...I have plenty of room, no sweat." The vehicles hit with a light touch and the result was that we had a bent over fender, and the bus had 40 concerned citizens all yammering in German, and wanting to know how we were. We gave them the two thumbs up sign, we were fine, especially after retrieving and opening the Canadian Club whiskey in the trunk and swaggering a gulp or two of liquid fortitude.

The fire department responded to our predicament with flashing lights and a tow truck, and down the mountain we went back to Innsbruck, The German passengers much relieved, boarded their scratched bus again to resume their journey on to the unknown.

We were now back in town for 10 days, awaiting the repair of our Renault, which required a new fender from Paris. In fact we returned to the small inn from where we started which was just around the corner from the body shop. Leaving most of our belongings, including overdue washing for servicing, and being fit and adventurous, we rented bikes to charge back up the Brenner Pass. It was about an eight hour trial of peddling and walking the steep parts, panting and sweating through this insanity. We finally reached the little village that we intended to stay when we had the car, and spent four nights of mountain bliss in a boarding chalet.

Soon we returned to our lodgings in town making the trip in less than three hours, sailing downhill like the wind of a tornado. It was an exhilarating experience in what seemed to pass as a nanosecond. Driving the short hop over to Switzerland with its breath-taking beauty, mountain lakes and inviting landscape, not that Austria has to take a back seat to anywhere, we allotted seven days to take in the northern Cantons which included Zurich, Lucerne, and Basal.

Departing for Germany, and a brief stay along the Rhine River in Heidelberg, we spoke with numerous post war young adults our age. They acknowledged their homelands roll in World War II, and blamed their parent's generation for perpetrating it, and were ready to move on, and they did. Germany showed few signs of the War, the most notable was the church tower in Cologne which still remained under restoration. Of course in East Germany things were considerably different, but I did not see that since it was off limits to travel there as a Westerner.

Leaving northern Germany we proceeded on to Belgium and the Lowlands by driving through the Ardennes Forrest where the *"Battle of the Bulge,"* played out, and we drove across the famous and strategic Nimejan Bridge, featured in the movie '*A Bridge To Far."* We visited Brussels and Amsterdam in the Netherlands, but when we arrived in the city of Rotterdam, it still remained reduced to rubble, courtesy of the German Luftwaffe. The following week our car was returned to the agency in Paris where *voila,* they gave us back more than we paid for it, and we immediately taxied to Orly Airport for the short flight to London.

It was time to make the long trip back to New York on Trans World Airlines, in an era where air travel had very strict limitations on baggage weight. Everything was weighed, a definite problem for us because of our extensive purchases. Piston engine aircraft did not have the power of the jet engine and their operations were severely restricted by weight. Our flight had a scheduled refueling stop in Gander Newfoundland, thus making the trip to New York's Idyllwild Airport (now JFK) a 16 hour affair.

On check-in the TWA Agents meticulously weighed all of our luggage including the little carry on flight bag which contained the heavy items we had purchased during our trip. Being aware of this procedure the three Caballeros figured out a way to beat the system and bought identical carry on flight bags before going through the weigh-in process.

Checking in individually, the other two waited until the first was finished before joining the line. At that point the airline tag was removed from the first flight bag and transferred to the remaining heavy untagged bags, and the same one would be used again by the next companion. In the bag used for check in were items that weighed only a pound or two at best. Thus when we were done each of the carry-ons had the proper tag, as well as excessive weight. I do not think Howard Hughes, the owner of the company, missed the money.

On the long flight home we reminisced and evaluated our wonderful trip. England and Germany still displayed some damage ten years after World War II had ended. Goods were extremely inexpensive, leather items in Italy for only a dollar or two, camera equipment on the cheap in Switzerland, and American cigarettes and Canadian whiskey to use for trade was like gold! Of course these are ancient memories as things have changed dramatically in 55 years.

To do what I did as a 20 year old was exciting and full of adventure. In the future I completed another four crossings of the Atlantic in propeller aircraft before the jets took over. Nostalgia and good memories are what all of us dwell on. In 1956 flight attendants still took an interest in each individual passenger, engaging them in lengthy conversation. They were young, pretty, courteous, and the food was excellent, as each airline touted and competed over their meal service.

The long flight times, questionable safety records, constant noise and vibration from the piston engines, no entertainment except reading or sleeping in a comfortable seat, and enduring the turbulence at the lower altitudes was what passengers were subjected to at the time. Putting it all together I would vote nostalgia out and the modern era in.

During my junior year I moved into an apartment with three other brothers from the fraternity house. It brought some sanity to my life and better grades. For whatever reason, rebellion, interest in adventure or actual need, I bought a Harley Davidson motorcycle, the big model EL, not that I was looking for this type. I had never ridden anything with two wheels except a pedal bike, and why would a knuckleheaded kid want one to begin with? A vague justification was that I could ride to campus for my classes and find a parking place nearby for bikes and cycles.

I looked through the newspaper want ads for days until I spotted a HD for sale. It was a nine year old 1947 'Hog' and the owner was asking $500.00 for it. The sale was made on the basis that the seller would teach me how to ride it. I must say that the cycle had seen better days. It had a worn sheep skin seat, faded paint, pitted chrome, and sun baked Plexiglas wind screen, but it's hard to stop a runaway train once it gains momentum.

I do not remember the lessons, but they must have been rudimentary at best, and probably most of the learning curve came from riding it to class, my job and eventually to the airfield. I still retain memories of soft desert winds at twilight, blowing through my hair as helmets were not required, and the cool clean smell of the morning air when I rode to attend 7:40am classes. Such joyful reminiscences can be extinguished by the fact that there was no automatic starter on cycles like today, and an engine turn-over was accomplished by jumping up and down on a pedal for start-up. It was a mean device that if the spring loaded pedal was in an ugly mood it could snap back and break a leg before any blue exhaust emerged from your tail pipe.

The big red Hog could kill you if it was mismanaged. I often had trouble shifting from first to second as I went through the four gear cycle with the shift handle that was mounted on the fuel tank and the accompanying swivel clutch just above the left foot plate. It required coordination and it seemed to have a mind of its own. Give it too much gas, and the HD would do a buck and wing or rear on its hind wheel like a black knight's charger in battle. This could be disconcerting. Too little gas and it would die like a wounded serpent. It was 50 years later that I learned that the EL models had the dreaded "suicide clutch," which created instant terror, I remember it well.

On military drill day, after a night of rain still awash in the street gully's, I would lift both legs as I swept through them to keep my uniform military bright and spotless. Sharon, many times rode on the back, with her arms around my waist holding on tight. The cycle left its permanent burn mark on her exposed leg one day when it touched a hot cylinder and it was initiated to the perils of 'motor mania'.

I was living quite an exciting life for a college guy in the 1950's, the only thing missing might have been the coonskin cap and the college pennant, but this was Tucson, where the old west still ruled. I soon upped the anti by taking flying lessons; maybe I was really out of control. Pushing the envelope further I would take on my third paying position in addition to the gig for American Tobacco, and the stipend for attending advanced R.O.T.C.

My speech instructor announced in class one day that he would conduct interviews of students interested in representing the University on the CBS statewide news program at noon. My hand was up quicker than a surrounded bank robber. What a thrill it would be to read the daily University news for five minutes on a statewide radio network

The wind was behind me as I was chosen as one of the rookie news readers, and it was five minutes of terror I had volunteered for. The U of A had its own broadcast department so the "patch-in" to the network originated right on campus. I never realized how long five minutes of non-stop reading was until I started to broadcast. With sweat on my brow and nervous twitching at the corners of my mouth I made my best effort with only a few stumbles. I was speaking to thousands of people statewide, and I could not see any of them. Maybe that was for the best.

Little did I know that this was an entrée for a two year job on the brand new FM affiliate of the prominent Tucson radio station KTKT. My Professor was also working a second job as program director for the station and he offered me a chance to become a disk jockey for the frequency modulation side of the dial. In 1957 FM had a limited listenership, because it was necessary to buy a special receiver to tune in the station. There was no such thing as both modulations in one set. To enjoy wonderful classical music in the dry desert sun listeners had to put more skin in the game, for access to names like Beethoven, Hayden, Bach or Vivaldi. KTKT-FM was in the mix of new stations entering the frequency modulation era, and my Prof would be at the heart of it. He did everything but go on the air in this low cost operation. There was no other staff except the disc jockeys in the old Quonset hut located on the western fringes of the Tucson grid.

The station transmitted 24/7 using a reel to reel tape machine for the Musak elevator music, being piped into buildings, restaurants and offices. This format was interrupted during the period from five to eleven in the evening when we were live. The buck ($1.00) an hour jock arrived at the station about 4;30pm and retrieved the stack of records that the Program Director had set aside for the night, and then moved into the broadcast booth to set up. At five minutes to the hour it was time to start flipping switches and turning dials to put the station on the air, checking gauges and meters to make sure you were ready to start broadcasting. Three turn tables were cued up with long play vinyl records, and the clock read five, and it was time to cut the Muzak off and go live.

"Good evening ladies and gentlemen, this is your announcer Gene Lassers, and welcome to another evening of classical listening pleasure from your pioneer FM radio station, KTKT-FM. First, let's turn to the news…"

The news came off the teletype and the announcer could cut and paste as desired on what to report to the listeners. Next came light selections until 6:00 and then into serious classical music for the rest of the evening. Although I was familiar with the basic tenets of long hair presentations I certainly was not a professor at the conservatory. I mean, what do you expect for a 'buck' an hour? My best attribute was a voice which was pleasant, and melodious, and this probably is why I was chosen for the job in the first place.

The Program Director daily drove out to "Indian Territory" or what seemed to be since the building was so far from town and lined up the evening selections in the order of play and listed them on the scheduling sheet. All the announcer had to do was be able to read, talk, cue up the selection and chew gum when the mike was off.

I convinced my boss that Saturday nights were a good time to roll back the rug, break out the beer and play some dance music or even 'hot jazz.' He bought in and kept it in rotation on the schedule for as long as I worked there. The great thing about the job was that I was spinning long play records, some of them two sided, and I could get some studying done while the Philadelphia Orchestra with Eugene Ormandy conducting covered for me.

Unfortunately one of my steady listeners was Mrs. Fisher who was raised in 'Main Line Society' in Philadelphia, and was now living out her days in the scrub brush of the Sonora Desert. As some pilots had "God as their copilot," I had Mrs. Fisher as my persistent critic. When KTKT FM was on the air she would be listening, and if I killed the pronunciation of Tchaikovsky or Rimsky-Korsakov, the phone by my knee rang as sure as the sun rose in the morning. I never could shake her, and she kept my pronunciation in line, and I even learned a thing or two as she shadowed my every decibel.

The station shuttered each night at 11:00pm, and at that point I could play my favorite song, *The Star Spangled Banner*, and head for the barn. The opening procedure was reversed and the dials were turned the other way, the switches went into the down position, and the lights were dimmed. I would step out into the vast, quiet desert night, lock the door and pray that my Harley would start and break the silence.

One evening I was on the air and I heard a knock on the entrance door. This had never happened before at our remote and isolated location. Since a long play was spinning I was free to get up and answer the knock. It could be the Program Director, but instead it was an unknown character speaking to me from the other side. I could not hear what he said and opened the door which was a no, no since he was drunk as a skunk. I tried to show him the way out, but he just wandered into the waiting room, and I scurried back to the broadcast booth and locked the door. The current record was just about over so I waited for it to finish. Meanwhile I opened the door and yelled, "... if you don't leave, I will call for help," and hoped that I had a listener base out there in FM land that would lend a hand. This done I continued to watch the intruder through the glass that surrounded the booth, my fortress in the desert.

Then the outside door slammed as he left, but I will say when I closed down that night he was on my mind as I poked my head out the door, eye balled the area, and raced for the car, which I happened to drive that night rather than my cycle.

The summer between my Junior and Senior years I was obligated to attend the Army Cadet summer camp in order to advance in the Reserve Officer Training Program. It was an eight week 'vacation,' all at government expense and comparable to what an enlisted man was required to endure in basic training. I left from Chicago on Northwest Airlines for Seattle where the Army was waiting to transport Cadets to Fort Lewis Washington. Two thousand were arriving from all over the western states to participate in the demanding eight weeks of tactics, weapon familiarization, firing, rugged exercise, and boots on the ground exercises.

It was not the Camp Nebagamon of my youth, and of course it had been my choice to attend, since my asthma would have been a disqualification for military service. The fact that I was so focused on receiving a Commission in the Army, I cast all caution to the wind to try and achieve my goal. In reality I wanted the bars on my shoulders, like my seven cousins who served as Officers in both the Army and Navy. They were all such an inspiration to me as I grew up.

Consequently I hid my disability card to "get out of jail free," if you will, facing the possibility of becoming an enlisted man, and having the fights in the bars rather than the bars on my uniform shoulder. This would prove to be a bigger challenge than I had imagined, yet I was never sorry for my decision to continue with the program.

We were broken down and bunked alphabetically. My two story barracks consisted of the last of the K's and the beginning of the L's. In reality I was only friendly with two of the guys on my side of the aisle, which in today's world beats the relationship in Washington between the Democrats and the Republicans.

At the end of the hall on each floor was the latrine, and at the other end the room in which our regular Army Sergeant in charge slept. After two nights I quickly learned that the barracks washroom was not the same as I had been use to in civilian life. What a mess to get your toilet taken care of with the entire platoon rising up at 6:00, with inspection at 6:45 and chow at 7:00. Oh, don't forget to make your bunk with square corners and the blanket tight enough that a quarter bounced on it.

So I found an answer to this total bedlam. The Sergeant came by my bunk at 5:30 for the latrine, beating the rest of us, and guess what? The next day I was right behind him, problem solved.

The second day of inspection by my Airborne Company Commander brought him face to face with me in the roll call line up. "Did you shave this morning Cadet?" He barked.

"Yes sir."

"What kind of razor did you use?"

"Electric razor Sir."

"From now on you will use a safety razor. Do you understand that?"

"Yes sir."

And until this day I still use a safety razor. Of course the current models don't take a pound of flesh mixed with blood off your cheeks which was reminiscent of Attila the Hun slicing the enemy in battle with his sword. I don't miss those old Gillette 'blue blades,' no siree Bob!

Before entering the mess hall all of us lined up and did three mandatory pull ups on a bar placed near the entrance. I never had upper body strength and occasionally I held the line up as did others who were lacking. The guy behind me would once in awhile give me a boost up as needed. This was more constructive than the few cat calls I or others received.

Each day "campers" participated in field maneuvers, tactical instruction, weapons orientation and demonstration. Occasionally there would be live fire exercises which ranged from the minute to the massive. Cadets were made to crawl under thirty caliber machine gun fire that was set up about four feet above the ground. The good thing was the machine gun had a block of wood under the barrel so it would not move, the bad thing as they told us very seriously was that if you panicked and got up and ran, "..you were dead."

The heavy weapons end I found fascinating. As we sat in bleachers they demonstrated the large 155mm Artillery guns that had a range of over five miles. The amazing thing was that you could see the shells fly through the air and demolish targets of opportunity in the field.

Twice we had night maneuvers, which demonstrated how tough it is to move around in the dark, and how inept we were in the first place. Getting lost, trying to use the compass, looking at the map under a pencil of light, and then tripping over cows in the field and stepping in who knows what, were some of the fond memories I have retained.

I remember an exercise where we combined into a Company of four platoons to assault a military objective. At the whistle we stormed the hill, and the enlisted regular Army cadre circulated among us, and threw fire crackers at various cadets charging the enemy and yelled, "you're dead."

In the line of battle certain weapons are more valuable than others; like machine guns, Browning Automatic Rifles (BAR), and mortars. The doctrine was that if a soldier carrying one of these went down, another was to pick up the weapon and use it. I was carrying the heavy BAR, and when I was pronounced dead I thought I went to heaven and some other poor bastard would have to lug it. As I lay on the ground I noticed that the entire line of fighting men passed me by without notice, and I ended up in the back with the walking wounded, and dead, carrying the heavy weapon.

The modern Army of today no longer must perform Kitchen Police (KP). They have civilians to do this for them in areas where it is safe. I was instructed to be at the mess hall at 0500 in the morning, ready to work until the evening meal was through. It would be a 16 hour day, and I did not know the telephone number to the Child Welfare Department of the state of Washington to complain.

I reported in at the required hour, and was the last one of the detail to arrive. My reward: the pots and pans, the hardest job, and the privilege to do it all day. The only time not on our feet was when we ate, and after seeing what I saw, I wasn't very hungry, besides this wasn't fine dining. My boots were not broken in yet and the pain in my feet was excruciating, plus my hands needed a spa treatment when the day was over.

It was a learning experience and the next two times I pulled the duty I arrived at 0430, and got one of the "cushy jobs," cleaning the mess trays, tables and benches. It was the only time in my life I wanted to sweep the floor.

During the first four weeks of boot camp we were confined to base. After the Saturday morning parade, with both battalions marching 'eyes right,' the rest of the weekend was ours to squander. Many used the recreational facilities, the movie theaters or bowling alley on Post. Dinner at the Officers Club was on the privileged list too, while others just hung around the Company Day Room, writing letters, playing ping pong, cards or board games. Of course sleeping was always a high priority, and shining your dress shoes, combat boots, brass, and doing the laundry was a constant. The Platoon Sergeant made sure his charges changed their bed linens each week and washed their towel. We could count on him to appear again bright and early on Monday for the barracks bed and foot locker inspection.

After the fifth week we were permitted to go off post, and into Tacoma or Seattle. The first time three of us decided to "rip" into town together. We booked the best hotel in Tacoma, and took the roof top executive suite. From there on it was room service and hot baths. Saturday night we decided to take in a movie close by since we didn't have a car. The two choices were the *Drill Instructor* with Jack Webb, and *Tammie and the Bachelor* starring Debbie Reynolds, and Walter Brennen. I will let you guess as to which one we attended, after being put through the grinder for the past five weeks. It was a one horse race.

Throughout the entire time at Fort Lewis, sleeping across the barracks aisle was a cadet whose name came at the last of the K's. His father was an Air Force General, he was extremely athletic, and his proficiency scores put him at the top of the list of 2,000 attendees. He had brought his guitar to camp and many times would sit at the end of his bed singing softly, and playing lightly. He was attending Claremont College in the Los Angeles area, and went on to become a Rhodes Scholar and much, much more. My association with him never amounted to much and it wasn't until years later when I saw him in the movie *The Lieutenant's Wife* in Albuquerque, New Mexico that I realized it was "the guy across the aisle." Kris Kristofferson was a huge Country & Western singer and movie star, and his life was a road map of twists and turns that would make the average person dizzy.

Before I knew it my senior year at Arizona was here. I moved into a new apartment with Jim, the fraternity brother I had driven to Tucson with a few hears back. He would only stay for a half year and graduated in February. Inducted into the Air Force as a Lieutenant, he was ordered to serve at a distant base in Libya where he spent most of his time playing tennis on behalf of the Command. Stan took his place.

One of the first requirements on my return to campus was to check with the R.O.T.C. Department regarding the results from summer camp. I did not have great expectations; I proved that I wasn't the Sergeant York (World War I American hero) from the University of Arizona. I thought I passed, but not with flying colors, partly because of my asthmatic flare-ups. I was in the bottom 'percentile no doubt and it was the Army's call if I could go forward with the program. My acceptance into advance Military Science was partially based upon the summer camp results.

Captain Foxx, the military advisor was in his office, so I stopped to chat. After a brief exchange of polite conversation, he said "Sit down, I want to go over your summer camp results with you." Fair enough, he had zeroed in his sights on me, but I did not expect him to start lobbing hand grenades too. I must say I do not remember the particulars, but the summation of my performance was similar to the smell of three day old fish left in an alley. The Army's expectations were not met by my efforts at camp, and I was encouraged to drop the course and the quest for a commission.

To say the least I was shocked. All my dreams of becoming an Officer were now dashed. I was stunned, devastated but not defeated. Extremely concerned but undaunted, I knew I could bring reason to the table. I returned his fire with facts; I had three years of straight A's in the course, plus my extensive reading of military books, was a real plus. The enthusiasm I exhibited for the curriculum was another good reason to let me continue. Of course I could not play the asthma card for that would have been all 'she wrote.' He shot and I defended.

Again he said "…it would be best to resign from the course." I countered with a proposal to continue for another semester and see how my grades penciled out. I was wearing him down. He picked up my file and thumbed through it, readjusted his glasses on his nose, a good sign, and accepted my proposal. Either I was persuasive or he had a soft spot in his heart, but he agreed to monitor my progress for another semester. It was a second chance for a determined young man.

Life never seemed to stand still for me, not even in my senior year. I was now able to carry a normal load of 16 units having made up my deficiencies while still performing a part-time job, plus R.O.T.C. with its monthly check.

Much to the dismay of mother, my girlfriend Sharon from Francis Parker would be joining me at the University this year. I am sure she thought that the puppy love flame would have been extinguished by now, but it had not. Her grades were good enough to have attended an eastern college like her sister Ruth did at Wellesley, but she chose to follow me with her parents' consent. My folks were never happy with the whole infatuation to begin with.

Her presence was a major factor in the improvement of my grades, and I actually discovered the Library. Graduation on time became a reality. Sharon studied hard, received good grades, and was the 'warden' at her dormitory where she served on the "knuckle rapping council for wayward girls," those who violated the rules and would be punished. It did not make her the most popular resident of the hall, and we always had to make sure she was back in the dorm by curfew to set an example..

It was time to "Look the Elephant in the Eye," as was acknowledged by soldiers of the American Civil War, and test my courage further. I'd check out the joys and fears of flying. It is said, when you fly there are hours of boredom interspersed by seconds of sheer terror. I would find out. My years of aviation activity are covered in the chapter *Wilber, Orville and Gene.*

If I had only elected to study business courses for my degree I'd have died of boredom, Thank God the curriculum allowed for one elective course each semester. Two of the courses which were most tantalizing were Criminology and Penology. Both were over-booked, because the Professor was dynamic and the subject intriguing. Sharon joined me in taking both classes.

There were field trips that included the State Prison at Florence, a facility for 'exceptional children' in Coolidge, Arizona and the state mental institution at Phoenix, enticing bait to say the least. No wonder the class was over-subscribed.

The town of Florence remains one of the oldest in Arizona, and was established after the Civil War in 1866 by Colonel Levi Ruggles who was commissioned an Indian Agent for the U.S. Government. Once the prison opened in 1908, after its construction by convicts from the Yuma Territorial Prison, the rest of the prisoners were shipped north by train from Yuma. The town was right next to the prison and mirrored the dust and decay which the old walls reflected. Today the facility has been relocated west of Phoenix.

Back then it was a scattering of windblown, sand blasted homes snuggled near the penitentiary walls and when there was a prison break the inhabitants were subject to auto theft, and fleeing cons running across their property on foot. People seemed to accept this inconvenience since the prison was the town's main source of income, and many of the citizens were on the payroll.

The class was excited to be on the way to visit the "Slammer" and upon arrival we were unloaded from the chartered bus, and briefed about the facility, safety and what to expect. After that on a fine cloudless Arizona day with a nice breeze blowing from the west, the group was led up a staircase and outside to walk around the top of the prison wall surrounding the main yard. We all pressed forward to look at the caged men below who seemed just as interested in us. They soon began waving, cheering, and whistling. The class waved back, with the girls receiving the most attention.

In a moment of horror the coeds realized that the cons were looking up their skirts with glee, and they immediately moved back from the railing to the disappointment of all below. The guard who was leading us soon got the drift of what was happening, and told us it was time to move on. Somehow Sharon and I became separated from the others and wandered into the prison gift shop, which was still safe territory, and managed by one of the inmate Trustees of the facility.

Trustees were 'model' inmates that lived outside the walls and were housed in one story barrack like facilities which were located behind barbed wire. They had greater freedom, possible opportunities of employment with pay on site or in town, and were being rehabilitated to once again reenter society.

The gift shop merchandise consisted of handicraft items made by the prisoners in the hope that visitors might purchase them. If so, the money was credited to their prison sundry account and used for toiletries, snacks and stationary items. We ended up talking with the Trustee for awhile, a nice young man about 20 years old with a good attitude, gold tooth, and a pleasant smile. His name was Chuck. He loved to play baseball on the prison team, and hailed from Waco, Texas. What was a nice kid like this doing in a hell hole like Florence? The tour caught up with us in the gift shop, I doubt if they even knew we were gone. We went on to view other aspects of prison life, all an incentive to keep our lives on the straight and narrow path of honesty. The staff packed us back on the bus for the two hour return ride to campus, and that was that, but it wasn't.

Sharon and I had developed an interest in Chuck, and he said we could come and visit him whenever we cared to. His family never did, which was said without malice. For the next two years we trundled up to Florence on old state route 79 to visit our new friend. One Sunday each month was visiting day. Groups of relatives, many quite poor milled around outside the prison gates in the hot sun waiting for them to open and give access to husbands, sons, and relatives who were incarcerated behind the giant doors.

The prison band entertained the visitors, and sounded like an old accordion winding down, playing in the hot sun under the watchful eye of the tower guards. Visiting Sunday was the best chance the gift shop had of selling any of the home crafted stage coachs, covered wagons, leather purses, lamps, belts and ash trays among other items, and Chuck was always there. I actually purchased a stage coach and covered wagon which were finely crafted with limited tools.

Why we came, I don't know. Maybe it was the mystique of associating with a person living in "The Big House," and visiting the prison as outsiders. It is possible that we thought that Sharon and I could make a difference? There but for the grace of God go I? Sometimes his best friend helped in the shop, for he was also a Trustee. His Job? Run the blood hounds that tracked any escapees that headed across the barren desert, with the guards and deputies on horseback in hot pursuit. You never got far when you were on the run.

It took a few visits to find out the facts behind Chucks incarceration. He and his friend had sacrificed their youth on the altar of violence at the age of 18. Leaving Waco, Texas they headed toward "Sin City," aka. Las Vegas, where they gambled downtown on Fremont Street, the avenue of broken dreams. It was here that everybody was welcomed and no questions asked. Broke they hitched a ride out of town with a guy in a pickup truck. It was the era of thumbing along the highway and eventually a good hearted soul might stop and pick you up.

Chuck was sitting in the middle, next to the driver, his chum by the door. Near Phoenix, and maybe with the thought of stealing the truck the Waco "Kid" by the door pulled out a gun and killed the driver. Where the gun came from, what was their thinking, and why did they do this, I will never know. They emptied the dead man's pockets, dumped his body in the brush and took off, only to be arrested by Arizona's "finest" down the road.

Tried as adults, the boys were committed to the State Prison. Why they were paroled earlier than what would be expected for a capital crime has always remained a mystery to me. Now they were Trustees living outside the dreaded walls, with real jobs.

We visited Chuck on a regular basis for two years and hopefully brought a little sunshine into his life as well as his buddy. When there we would catch up on the "skinny" of what was going on inside the prison. Once he told us about a con in for embezzlement, his former job on the outside was an accountant. With good behavior he became a Trustee, and his new job was taking care of the prisoners' sundry accounts. Once a con, always a con, he embezzled money from his fellow inmates, and was sent back inside the walls with an extended sentence behind bars, and facing the wrath and anger of his former clients. "The "boys did a good job on his face," Chuck told us.

Another time there was a prison break and the blood hounds were dispatched for the chase. Sharon's mother picked up the news in Chicago, and telephoned her that the escaped killers were heading for Tucson and we should be careful. I am still waiting for them to ring the doorbell.

Our friend was up for parole and it was granted. His family could not pick him up, so we offered to drive Chuck to the Phoenix airport which he declined. We learned later that felons never return to where they 'fell' (were caught). He would leave from Tucson. He did ask for a suit-case, which we were happy to buy for him, and that was the last time we saw him, his buddy, or ever returned to Florence.

We did receive a few letters. His family took him in, he fell in love, married, had a child, and started a bakery with the help of his kin. A success story? We certainly hope so. At no time did Sharon or I feel at risk, or uncomfortable, and it was an interesting sub chapter in our lives.

> *"but I shot a man in Reno, just to watch him die.*
> *When I hear that whistle blowing,*
> *I want to hang my head and cry."*
> *(Folsom Prison by Johnny Cash)"*

Graduation was in May and I received my Bachelor of Science degree from the school of Business Administration. At a separate ceremony on the stage of the University auditorium our Army R.O.T.C class was commissioned as Second Lieutenants, and I was assigned to the Adjutant General Corps, which guaranteed a staff position wherever my orders sent me. So much for the gallant and nimble tank commander that I always wanted to be. It probably was for the best. With my eyesight I may have blown up the wrong town.

It was a disappointment that my parents did not attend my graduation and commissioning into the Army. I soon would join them and my Aunt Ellen for a return visit to Europe. Sharon pinned my bars on my uniform instead. The upcoming trip was designed by my Mother to convince me to leave Sharon in the dust! Edward VIII was not dissuaded either, He gave up the throne of Great Britain and was exiled the rest of his life, not my fate yet.

My commission was indeed a second chance, one of many I have been fortunate to receive during my life. In turn I have always tried to give others, the same leeway, not always with success. Captain Foxx would have been reassured by his decision to let me continue if he had read my fitness report while on duty from my superiors.

"...Lieutenant Lassers is an extremely conscientious Officer...He has performed all assigned duties in an outstanding manner under difficult conditions...,"

and the Certificate of Achievement Award presented to me upon the end of my tour of duty by the Chief of Staff at Camp Irwin..

"...for outstanding performance of duty...his readiness to seek and accept responsibility mark him as an unusually adept commissioned Officer."

My orders called for me to enter the service in February, nine months down the line. It was inconvenient timing, but the outcome was all for the best. I had never considered obtaining a Master of Business Administration degree, but a tip from a fellow Officer led me to the program. My friend in Sigma Alpha Epsilon, Joe Lumpkin, said he was deferring entering active duty by enrolling in a Master's program. The Army Regulations specified that if you could graduate with an additional degree in one year, your date of induction would be extended.

I'd have had a better chance of being hit by lightning than returning to the University and cracking the books again, yet this is what I did. My original approach to all of this was hesitant, after all only accountants, doctors, attorneys, academics, and in

Arizona Indian Chiefs required another "sheep skin." The upside was the degree itself, and for military pay and allowance purposes I would have another year in rank.

Off I went to the Deans office to inquire if I could enter the program. After a lot of chin scratching the Dean checking my records said, "...over the four years of undergraduate work your grades have improved significantly." He would give me the first semester to prove myself. If I did, I could "...go for the gold." It was unusual that Arizona awarded an advance degree for only enduring one additional year of studies. Checking their website recently they now require 22 months to complete the program.

It would be my fifth year at the University, and the first semester grades turned out to be straight A's. Of course this was a green light to complete the program, which required an oral examination at the end. The second semester was a mirror of the first, thus I was set up for the Oral's, which I faced with trepidation. I never tested well under intense interrogation, and this was to be conducted by three Professors and would be received by one scared student. The day came and I was extremely nervous. There wasn't a clue as to which subjects would be covered, and they could shoot from the hip. My only life saver was my Professor and advisor, Joe Gill who also sat on the Prosecution side during the grilling.

The day came, the inquisitors showed up, and after three hours of cross examination I felt like a mechanical duck in an arcade shooting gallery. They asked me to step outside and have a seat in the hall and await their decision. I am glad there wasn't a parking meter by the bench, I would have run out of change feeding it, for I waited an hour.

The door finally opened and I was asked to step back inside for the verdict. It was simple, I had failed. As I dragged out of the classroom my advisor sidled up to me and said, "...let me work on them, I will talk to you tomorrow." Joe was the only ball in play, and I needed a Hail Mary pass, and an immaculate reception. If this was granted I definitely would have turned Catholic. The next day I met Joe in his office and he told me they had changed their minds and I was awarded the Masters of Business Administration degree after all. Since I missed graduation it came in the mail, and I remained Jewish!

The Army had my number, and I had my orders. It was time to move out!

Home of David and William Lilienfeld, Kalamazoo, MI.
On National Register of Historic Places.

Photo by Andrew Jameson

Cigars: David Lilienfeld

David Lilienfeld came to Kalamazoo in 1860 and took a job as a clerk in the M. Israel Dry Goods store. Within a few years, he and his brother, William, opened a retail cigar store. The business did well and they expanded their product line to include tobacco and wholesale wines. They built a store on East Main Street in the main commercial district.

William left the firm and moved to Chicago, but David, who like the Desenbergs became a Mason, went into manufacturing. The Lilies Cigar Company was one of many cigar makers in Kalamazoo in the late 19th and early 20th centuries. In response to a 1908 cigar workers strike, most local manufacturers closed their shops and moved to more anti-union environments. The Lilies Cigar Company moved to Detroit.

LILIENFELD'S
With its charming storefront, Lilienfeld's was a popular cigar and wine shop on East Main Street.

William was my great grandfather.
Courtesy of the Kalamazoo, Mi. Historical Society.

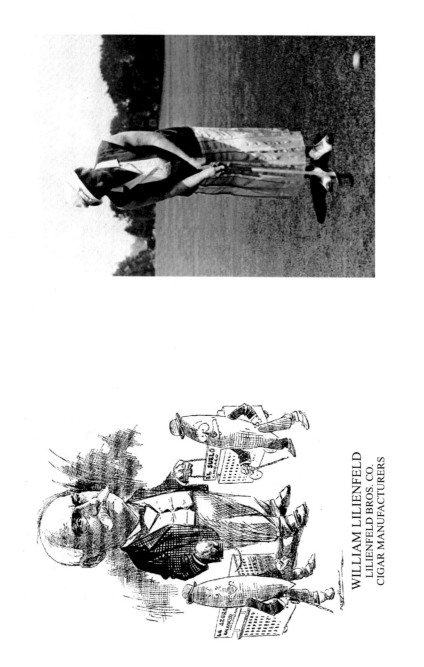

Mary Silberman, my great grandmother

WILLIAM LILIENFELD
LILIENFELD BROS. CO.
CIGAR MANUFACTURERS

William P. Lilienfeld, my great grandfather
(Chicago Historical Museum)

Beulah Silberman Lilienfield, my grandmother, in WW I Red Cross uniform. She died on the dance floor in 1923.

Grandfather Lilienfeld, aka Lilienfield, St. Johns Military Academy (circa 1895)

Silberman family (my mother's side of the family) driving with their chauffer. Circa 1915

Joseph and Bessie Lassers, my grandparents on my father's side.

Cartoon of grandfather Lilienfield, making sales calls.

Aunt Ellen. My grandfather Lilienfield's second wife.

Gene. Circa 1938

Sanford (Greek) and Mary Lassers, my parents on their honeymoon (French Lic, Indiana 1933).

Family Christmas Card at Age 5

Formal picture of Gene, 1939 (3 years old).

Chapter 4

Don't Shoot Until You See the White Out

I was born to fight, pillage, to lead the charge, torpedo a ship, and shoot down an enemy aircraft from my fighter plane in a blaze of glory. None of that came to pass as I was assigned to the Army Adjutant General Corps (AGC). If I were to meet my death in the service, it would have to be inconspicuously, like being hit by a falling file case.

The AGC was established in the American Army during the Revolutionary War and its first commander was Horatio Gates, a former British General Officer. The Corps is assigned to Combat Service Support and requires "...astute and innovative Officers to plan develop and operate personnel management," as it is described officially.

My military orders directed me to report to Fort Benjamin Harrison, located in Indianapolis, Indiana since 1903. The Fort was named in honor of General and then elected President Harrison, and today it is no longer active.

I was married to Sharon Joyce Banovitz, my high school sweetheart in June of 1959 and the wedding took place in Chicago. The honeymoon was a cruise in the Caribbean, a wedding present from my folks, and elegant for the times.

We became engaged over the previous Christmas Holiday and out of a scene from a movie of the 1920's a jeweler to the "upper crust" of Chicago, brought uncut diamonds in tissue sleeves to my folks apartment for her perusal. Sharon looked the selection over along with the help of my mother, who was picking up the tab. No price was displayed on the hand picked samples. Remembering back I believe we were both over-whelmed and did not appreciate the gesture at the time. As I write this now it seems more like a period scene out of Masterpiece Theater. I am not sure Sharon had any idea of what she was looking at or for, and I certainly did not. I never was into jewelry.

The wedding was the first event held at the Ambassador West Hotel's Guild Hall since the reception and dinner for Queen Elizabeth II of England, during her state visit to America. It cost my-in-laws $10,000 (2010 with inflation computes to just under $75,000) if it cost a dollar and was quite the affair. 'Putting on the dog,' (show boating) as they say, wasn't the bride and groom's idea, and we would have been happy to have some of the money in our bank account. Sharon's mother wanted to showcase to family, friends, and society her youngest daughter, the first to marry at barely 19 years of age.

The room was set in a garland of white motif, adorned with silver service, fine china, and formally dressed white gloved wait staff. Flowers were in abundance, and music filled the air from the 10 piece orchestra on the dance floor. Each of us had five bridesmaids and groomsmen in attendance with two of her nieces as flower girls. Our temples Rabbi, Louis Mann officiated and I still have the wedding picture book to prove it all really did happen like this.

No yarmulkes were in evidence, even on the rabbi, and the service is a blur of fractured memories as my friend John stood up for me at the ceremony. Sharon's sister Ruth was her Maid of Honor. My dad was almost late to the ceremony. He worked that day and when he came home his pants did not fit, so he frantically hailed a cab, and raced down to the tuxedo rental shop for a new pair to replace his own trousers.

In the end we were pronounced man and wife, and happy. Soon we'd be on the *Twentieth Century Limited* luxury rail to New York for a two week Caribbean cruise on board the Grace Lines SS *Santa Paula*. In another 12 hours the "all aboard,' would sound and we were out of there except for one thing. Mother had set up an appointment with her high powered attorney for us to draw up our wills the morning after the wedding. You have to love being of German heritage!

My folks could not understand the grandiosity, and lavishness of the event, and I believe mother looked down her nose at the lineage of the Banovitz family, and carried an air of superiority in her demeanor. She blamed Sharon's mother for promoting the chase, and the catching of her son. Of course my mother was married in a very small ceremony in her home, with but a handful, if that present. My parents marriage was an extreme in the opposite direction, and today, begs the question why there was no public ceremony or reception.

Looking back it might be said that my mother-in-law, Faye, was out to prove that the working-class Russian Jews were equal to the haughty Germans who came to America first, and of course that included my family. Sharon's mother's side were Zees, and included a doctor and a very successful juvenile store started by Faye's mother, where the other children worked, for most of their lives.

Her father, Morris had been adopted as a infant by a related family and his upbringing is murky, but the siblings were very successful. One, Sam Banowit (changed his name) was one of the big financiers in the country, owning the Chrysler Building, and a portfolio of numerous other high profile national properties and was active in the development of the huge Huntington Harbor home project in Southern California.

He had his picture in Time magazine wearing a full Indian headdress at a ceremony opening the famous Spa in Palm Springs. The local Indian tribe had finally leased their sacred land for the Spa and Casino to bring in needed cash flow to the tribe. This was one of the first development ventures on Indian property.

His house in Beverly Hills was sold to Harry Karl, the shoe magnet, then married to movie star Debbie Reynolds. Sam was eventually investigated for selling 150% of his partnerships to clients when there was only 100 % available. He died suddenly two weeks after Sharon and I ate dinner at his house. His new 'trophy' wife was the center of the gossip mill, with the wild thought that maybe she had poisoned him for his money, but that never moved past the point of speculation, and there was no autopsy.

At our wedding no expense was spared, no item over-looked by the wedding coordinator or the family except a wedding night room for the bride and groom. For the money spent we should have had the penthouse, but we didn't, we weren't even in the same hotel. No arrangements were made for us, and the Ambassador Hotel was full up when this was realized a few days before the wedding.

At the last moment I reserved a room at the old and historic Stevens Hotel (Hilton), twenty minutes away in downtown Chicago. At the time it was the largest hotel in the world. We received a very poor room next to the noisy elevators for the short 'Motel 6' night stay. With no limo waiting, and under a hail of rice thrown by the wedding party, we took a cruddy cab from the taxi queue for paradise. I believe the entire event was an ordeal for both of us.

Our honeymoon cruise aboard the Grace Line was all that it should be, and aside from the gifts that Sharon had bought for everyone and their uncle being stolen by a shady dockworker who said " I'll load this in the cab for you," and didn't, it was super.

Once again home I had a lead on a nicely furnished apartment in Indianapolis, our temporary duty station, and I flew over and rented it on the spot for the ten weeks that I would spend at my military school. The unit had two bedrooms, a kitchen and living room. The building was a newer two story walk up, perfect for newlyweds. The train trip to Chicago was only 3 hours and ideal for Sharon to visit her parents often. It was lonely to live in a town where you knew no one with nothing to do.

The first night's candle light dinner in our new home started with the aroma of smoke and burnt chicken wafting through the apartment, and ended with many open windows and alternate plans at a nearby restaurant. It would change as Sharon became more familiar with a stove. We could still laugh about it years later.

My training comprised of classroom hour after classroom hour on subjects that interested me little, and it was boring to sit for eight hours each day to learn the material necessary to pass the course. I slipped by but certainly was not on my way to immortality like General Gates the founder and hero of the Corps. I could not wait for the ring of the four o'clock bell to let us out for the day. Maybe I had ADS, (Attention Deficit Syndrome), or it was just boring.

During the last weeks of our indoctrination of "how not to catch your finger in a file drawer" rather than what I had fantasized years before as how not to catch your thumb in a M1 rifle when loading the clip, we were asked to choose three domestic locations for our permanent assignment. My first choice was the *Presidio*, the beautiful post in the heart of San Francisco by the *Golden Gate Bridge*, Fort Lewis in Washington State where I had previously trained was second, and last, Fort MacArthur in San Pedro just south of Los Angeles. The assignment that was ultimately authorized was duty for 21 months at Camp Irwin, which was located equal distance between Death Valley and Barstow on a one-way road. Was this retribution for my marginal work at the school? If it was, so be it, I would do my best. A fellow Officer from my R.O.T.C. class was stationed there and had spread the word that he was housed in the mental ward for lack of space until months later when housing was found. Not a good rumor to start with.

When I called home with the news of my assignment, mother said she would call me back after looking it up in the atlas. About twenty minutes later the phone rang and she said "tell them you can't go," and she was serious. I assured her that the military did not care if I liked it or not, that was where I was headed, and that was that.

She had no doubt located the facility on the map, a one time outpost for the Army during the Plains and Indian Wars. It was reactivated and closed a number of times until World War II when it was used as an anti aircraft training facility. Again it shuttered in 1945 and by the time I arrived it had become a permanent infantry and tank training facility. Its' claim to fame was the ability to fire heavy artillery and tank weapons in a 360 degree arc and not wipe out a town. Irwin was so remote that it was possible to run a five day tank exercise in a circle, and not retrace your tracks. No other base in the country offered this advantage. The Fort is today the main training facility for fighting in Afghanistan because of the terrain similarities.

It is possible that my mother may have thought she had connections to get me out of the assignment, but I doubt it. She had not voted for a Republican or a Democrat in the last three elections and instead cast a throw-away vote for Norman Thomas of the Socialist Party of the United States. If she did, and they offered, I would have turned it down. It would have been cowardly and un-American to do so.

I was driving an older car at the time and I was surprised when my folks bought me a new 1959 Chevrolet station wagon for the trip west. We loaded it down with some superfluous items, a slew of boxes and bags and headed out to join famous Route 66, and followed it west for most of the trip. On our first night we bedded down in St Louis. It was the spring of 1960, yet the next day it hailed the size of snow balls and I thought for sure that my new car would be dinged and scratched. After the storm cleared we checked it over but found nothing, and continued on westbound, eventually to turn south to visit Tucson and old friends, in that we had a little time to kill before reporting in for duty.

Once back in "the Old Pueblo" as Tucson is called, I dialed up my former roommate Stan, and Sharon went to visit some old dorm-mates. She was no longer a student at the U of A, but the wife of an Army Officer, and following the trail of U.S. Grant who was once stationed at a desolate post in California a hundred or more years earlier. Looking back I am sure she is sorry she did not graduate, yet it was normal for the times where women married and left the degree behind.

Stan, my former roommate was a mega character and eventually became an NBC television news commentator in Los Angeles. I could write books about him but I will condense it to something manageable. He was a good looking creative guy who's father was a Vice President with Union Bank in L.A., and his mother was a neat freak. Stan, a typical college student only worse, left his dirty clothes on the floor, had smelly feet, and used my toothpaste until I substituted a decoy tube of shaving cream in its place, and he smartened up, and quit the petty thievery.

He was in the habit of parking his car anywhere he felt like on campus, and the "Key Stone Cops," as we called the University Police, gave him ticket after ticket which he never paid. If he had one he had 50. No doubt to graduate he would have to pony up. There were no wheel boots in those days.

Indifferent about his studies, I remember sharing an English class with him and the professor assigned a term paper due in a month. It could have been a year, the results would have been the same in his case. For a reason I never understood he chose the World War II battle of Guadalcanal as his subject. He wrote the entire paper in two days with little reference to books or facts, making most of it up as the pen hit the page. Unfortunately he chose the wrong subject to scam on since the professor was very knowledgeable about the battle, he was there! I don't know how he passed the class or if he ever graduated, but he was still in Tucson when we came through.

"Mr. Suave," had a side job at the CBS radio outlet in town where he frequently broadcast sports interviews and other stories. During spring training the New York Giants baseball team was tuning up in Phoenix while the Cleveland Indians practiced in Tucson. He told me about interviewing the Giants veteran utility infielder Dusty Rhodes, a baseball character in the mold of Casey Stengel, and Yogi Berra. Recently Rhodes had been thrown off the team airplane due to overindulging and inappropriate behavior, a story that made the national wire services. When Stan asked him about it he said "..they were making a mountain out of a mole hole." Of course the correct last word was hill, but James Lamar Rhodes was a country boy from Mathews, Alabama.

Leo Durocher the iconic manager of the giants once said of him "a buffoon is a drunk on a hitting spree." Rhodes a good old southern bubba spent seven years in the majors and another 25 years after on a tug boat working for a friend. He claimed that when Durocher left the Giants, "baseball wasn't fun any more."

Stan said he could not meet with me because he was on assignment to travel to Fort Huachuca located near the town of Sierra Vista the next day. A story about an amazing hunt by the government for gold was breaking, and tomorrow was the big day for the climax. He asked if I wanted to go with him, and of course I was on board to join up.

The base currently was designated as a Signal Corps development Center. When Private Robert Jones, an illiterate black man from Dallas, Texas was inducted into the service in

1941, it was just a remote installation, and a sequestered post for black troops and white Infantry cadre only. Out of sight, out of mind might have applied. The service was still segregated until 1948 when President Harry Truman signed Executive order 9991 and desegregated the military. The isolated fort at that time was ideal to train soldiers who were black.

The haunted Huachuca Mountains are full of legends about the Spaniards and their buried gold, which has been sought by many treasure hunters over the years without luck. The value is rumored to be in excess of $100 million. Legend says some of the gold was melted down into bars by a bandito named Juan Estrada and buried in the canyon on the military reservation. The old trails crossing the area dipped into Mexico close by, and were known for carrying shipments of precious metals.

When Jones was there he became close friends with another soldier, Private Sam Mays. One Sunday just before Mays shipped out to North Africa they took the day off, packed a lunch and walked out to a remote area, two miles from the barracks for a quiet afternoon. During the hike Jones, ten steps ahead of Mays fell into a depression at least thirty feet deep and into a dark hole. He could not see anything but the hole was more than just a shallow chasm. Mays saw the calamity and yelled, "Jesus, where did you go to?" In reply Jones yelled "help."

Unhurt he called up to his buddy for his cigarette lighter and when he lit it a shimmer of gold bars revealed themselves in an underground cavern. He was staggered, but did nothing more and asked to be pulled out, using long vines that lay nearby on the ground. They trudged back to the barracks acquired a flash light and rope and returned once again. Jones now confirmed what he thought he saw, a room stacked full of gold bars.

Excited, they left the area after marking a nearby rock with Jones reversed initials to identify the spot. They kept it under their hats and returned in a week, found the hole and Jones once more entered it with a hatchet, and cut off a chip of one of the bars. He was pulled back out by Mays. In the barracks he tried to get his mates to acknowledge the find as gold including his Platoon Sergeant Matt Verbles, also black. Verbles told him he was "*Mucho Loco,* and to concentrate on his training," his fellow soldiers ignored him.

On his next free day he asked for and received a pass to go into the nearby town of Douglas where he proceeded to an Assayers office and had his find analyzed. A man, later thought to be a Mr. Fox took a look at it and said "…do you have any more to sell?" Jones was afraid to say yes and Fox paid him $890.00 which he rolled up in a sock and gave to him. Jones scampered back to the barracks with his stash.

It was soon time for the 93rd Division to ship out so Jones decided to throw a Company party with the money, a man who had nothing and was earning little, spent his entire wad on his buddies. He would use the money in the sock and leave the rest of the wealth in the ground. It was his and Sam's secret. He was scared of the military, afraid of some of his fellow bunkmates and spooked by the incident. Neither Jones nor Mays returned again until years later, and Mays not at all. He was killed in North Africa.

Fast-forward now to January, 1960. A huge black man in bib overalls strolls up to Fort Huachuca's guard at the front gate and says, "I want to see an officer." He has just come 1,000 miles from his clapboard house in the black section of Dallas to seek permission to "find his gold". After his discharge he had constantly petitioned the Army to return to see if it was still there, and the Army over a period of time had evaluated him as being truthful in his story and psychologically sound, but it was a don't call us we'll call you situation. Now he was back, 19 years later with two friends in tow for support.

There was not much traffic crossing the entrance at the time, and the guard pondered the request, scratched his chin, called the headquarters building, why not? It was fortunate that the Sergeant answering relayed the call on to Colonel Elbridge Bacon, the Inspector General on Post. It was a 'bingo' for Jones, the right man at the right time. Bacon was an intellectual, creative and sympathetic to the request, and a student of Arizona lore. A little "digging for treasure," might make his job on this lonesome base more interesting.

Permission granted. The next day the three black men were back on site with picks and shovels, and a MP (Military Policeman) in tow checking out where they expected the treasure to be. They found the rock with Jones initials inverted. They had one day to find their Eldorado.

In January the days are short, and the wind can be curt even sharp; the 22nd was no different. The sun rose, the cold wind blew the sand and sage brush, and the sun departed behind the mountains in the early afternoon. The results, a few scratches on the desert floor, a couple of dozen rocks removed from their time honored place, and no gold was found. Jones pleaded "for more time, the gold was there." Bacon remembered that there was a post bulldozer that could prove this once and for all, and told the men to return tomorrow.

The sun blasts its way skyward the next day, and is big and bright for the dig to continue. It's the weekend and the post is quiet, all is at rest except for a pickup barreling down the Huachuca Creek road and the rough motor of a bulldozer on the way to the site of the elusive earthen vault, and its treasure. The work begins, once again under the watchful eye of the M.P.; if gold is found the government will get its share. At noon the dozer operator stops and yells out "Better call the Colonel" and stopped work at an estimated depth of twelve feet. "We've water gushing in from the sides of the excavation," he stammered.

Bacon came immediately, and a minute later yelled "fill her up," and sent the three men back to Dallas, while the dozer waddled back to the motor pool.

Jones found a Texas attorney with gold fever that would roll the dice for his fee, and he wrote Colonel Bacon with additional evidence. The word gold does something to all men whether they have a silver eagle on their collar or worn suspenders on their shoulders. Bacon investigated further, met with Jones old First Sergeant and found Fox the Assayer, still in Douglas. "It ain't over 'til it's over," Yankee catcher Yogi Berra often said, and neither was the reality show taking place in the Arizona desert. The Army with permission from higher up, contracted with a civilian company to bring in heavy equipment and put the story to rest once and for all, and in June they did just that.

At a $1,000 a day a 'clam digger' started once again at the site and again water rushed in. This time pumps had also been brought along to handle the 50 gallon a minute deluge which was now creating a pond that crumbled the walls and the digger was taking tons of muck out in return. And then they hit rock. Jones said the room he entered down there had a rock ceiling. The contractor said his machine could go no further, but Bacon was as determined to close the book on this dream as Jones was to find it. Tomorrow they would blast the rock; it would be all or nothing.

The next day Stan and I headed for Huachuca and arrived 2 hours later. He showed his media credentials and told the Military Policeman that I was his assistant and they waved us through with directions on how to find the "big dig." Upon arrival he parked among a few other cars and near a small group of people milling around a huge heavyset black man in bib overhauls and straw hat perched on a bench alone. The site had been worked on for two weeks now at a "grand" a day with a huge steam rig and ancillary equipment that in the near distance could be heard puffing and chugging while wisps of smoke lifted from its cigarette like stack into the clear air.

Jones told Stan that "… so far the excavation had run into the water table which required large pumps to continue digging. There was no water when he found the gold," He speculated that the table had risen over the intervening time. Either that or they were in the wrong spot, but, "there were his worn initials." Jones pointed out. No matter, today would be the final effort and the Army was going to dynamite the rock to see if there was any lost treasure to be found. If not they would cut and run! He was resigned to it and said even though if nothing was found, "… he had outside investors who would back him in the future."

At the end of the day a whistle sounded, a sharp yell cried "all clear,' and the blast echoed and rebounded off the surrounding hills and mountains as 36 sticks of dynamite blew dirt and rocks skyward dropping them back to the harsh desert floor in different patterns. Nothing was found, and the hole was said to be closed forever as far as the Army was concerned.

Stan reported his story on the air. The government never allowed Jones back to look again, and the incident made Life Magazine with a follow up letter and picture in a later edition by yours truly. Case closed, it was time to move on to Irwin and report in.

On a quiet Sunday, Sharon and I took off across the Sonora Desert tracing the highways that once were trails and home to the Butterfield Stage and the Pony Express. After lunch in Barstow we followed the signs that said Camp Irwin 35 miles ahead on a shimmering oven baked two lane desolate road basking in 100 degree heat with sand, rocks and a crackling radio station to keep us company. Over the last rise on the highway and now past *Dead Man's Curve* the base soon revealed itsself in the distance spread out below us like pixels in a picture. There was no doubt now that this was the hot, desolate, barren, non-forgiving country that we would be living in for the next 23 months. We expected nothing, and it was delivered.

Tuckered out in my best kaki uniform with jacket and pants colloquially called 'pinks,' I parked, put my coat and hat on and went inside the rudimentary headquarters building and reported to Captain Price, who had the weekend duty assignment. He was dressed in the standard Army desert uniform of shirt and shorts which looked and felt like canvas and long woolen stockings and black shoes. Since it was Sunday he gave us a key to a room in the Bachelors Officers Quarters (BOQ) for the time being, and asked me to come back on Monday to finish up the formalities, and to meet my superiors.

The next few weeks revealed the following: the Camp was a forgotten base used mainly for National Guard and Reserve training during the year. The permanent compliment was some 120 Officers, 1,800 enlisted personnel and about 50 civilians who were involved in civil service work for the Army. The housing consisted of old migrant worker homes with a waiting list of over a year plus a trailer park that was available, but full. Most of the married personnel had to drive or bus the 70 mile round trip from Barstow each day, on their own time and their own dime, and be on duty by 8:00am. By the way the BOQ compared with a grade 'D' motel used by hustlers, and pushers. It was pretty grim.

The weather varied from frying pan hot to bone chilling cold accented by sand pitting car damaging winds in the winter. The recreational facilities were mediocre and for a really good time people drove to San Bernardino, a two hour trek each way, to blow their paychecks shopping or having a good meal out. You could get drunk cheaper on base!

The officers billeted here were for the most part at the end of their careers. There were many mixed marriages because the remote post was safe territory from the prejudice of the bigoted outside world. Irwin was also a good place to put soldiers who had screwed up somewhere down the line or were just unlucky. This was the end of the line. Being assigned to Irwin was a career change or a retirement for most. One lieutenant who graduated from West Point, the Military Academy resigned his commission after spending two of his three year stretch at our resort.

We had a diverse cast of officers. The Chief of Staff on base had been a 'boy wonder' during World War II rising to Lieutenant Colonel at a very young age. Now 15 years later he was still in the same grade praying to hang in there until he had 30 years of service, and receive three quarters retirement pay. His biggest project at Irwin was the creation of a golf course that blew away with the winter winds, dried up in summer, and had the additional ambiance of an occasional rattle snake in assorted pin hole cups. It became obvious that your best club was your wedge or sand blaster, and by the way - always look in the cup before you retrieve your ball, there might be more than the ball in it!

Or, how about Captain B., who may have been known as the "Mad Hungarian," and was married to a Budapest opera star. He occasionally wore a cape with his Dress Blue uniform. At Irwin there was only one day for dress blues and that was New Years when it was required to make a call on the General at home, and leave your calling card. Reserve Officers on two years duty always took leave on the first because they never purchased a dress uniform which seldom was worn.

Camp Irwin's tank battalion was rated as a *Strac 5* (Strategic Army Corps) unit. The lower the number the more battle ready and potent the designee was. Our old tank battalion was a tail end Charlie at five, and we used to kid that in an emergency, old men, women and children would be committed to battle before us! In summation, I would not have blamed my wife for taking the next train home to live with her parents. It was an adventure and she was in for the long haul.

Sharon was a talker, and soon became friendly with our temporary neighbor in the BOQ, Lieutenant Colonel and Mrs. John Prokop, who had just been assigned to the base as the G1, a senior management position. Under his supervision many of the operating departments reported to his office. Our continuing friendship during my service at the base was a definite help in the execution of my duties. My wife's outgoing nature was a real asset as I am rather reserved. As it turned out the base was not expecting my arrival nor had they put in a request for an additional Adjutant General Corps Officer. Still I was there for the next 23 months and the Headquarters had to make room for me on staff. I could not legally stay in the BOQ with my wife so they lodged us in one of two temporary units designated as guest quarters. We could remain there until housing opened up or I was forced by circumstances to move to town. With quarters as minimal as this, it was obvious that guests did not stay very long by choice.

We were fortunate to have the option of living there for a number of months rather than being forced to commute to Barstow. My housing situation was eventually worked out by Colonel Petterson, the Chief of Staff who's ranking sergeant was being temporarily assigned to Alaska for two years and had been living on post in a very nice 60 by 10 foot mobile home. He expected to be reassigned back to Irwin, but if he moved his trailer off post he would never get it back on because of the long waiting list for a pad. Everyone wanted to live on Post to avoid the drive from Barstow, and the inflated local rents. The solution which was good for all of us, with Colonel Prokop brokering the deal, was that my wife and I could rent the trailer for the duration of our assignment. The truth of the matter was that we lived better than the majority of the others on base including the Prokops.

I was assigned to Captain Chambers at Special Services and put in charge of recreational facilities and programs. This was not the military service I had imagined, running the theater, the bowling alley and other recreational facilities for the defense of our nation. Lt. Zephel, who had been trained as an Infantry officer was already assigned there killing time. Our C.O. (Commanding Officer) had come up through the ranks and was commissioned along the way. He was a nice guy but at this point the captain was just putting in his dues, waiting for retirement when he'd become a guard at a Las Vegas Casino and his wife could resume nursing. He had it all lined up.

The first time he had me, Zephel and our wives over to his quarters for BBQ he fixed a round of drinks. After we were served he made a martini for himself and drank the entire contents out of the shaker as we sat. It was quite a show and as evenings go it was an interesting one. The Captain could hold his liquor. I never have seen that done before or since.

Chambers bowling team was looking for a replacement for the new season and I was good enough to join up with the two other old line Captains by the name of Smith and St. Pierre. We had some fun, and custom team bowling shirts to match for the weekly outing at the 10 lane post bowling alley. I must have been 25 years younger than the rest and held the lowest pin average. I also came in last on the number of beers consumed.

It could be pretty slow with my minimal assignment obligations so I received permission to touch up the movie theater which was a pit. We were fortunate to have a private on staff that had artististic abilities, and relished a job that called for creativity. Nobody really checked on what we were doing in this remote building. All the paint had to be requisitioned through the civilian post engineer who had many other things on his mind in his crumbling empire.

Our resident artist painted Parisian scenes on the wall, used red paint conspicuously, especially in the ladies rest room on the toilet seats, and it really looked sharp. We were done before the Post Engineer realized that we had used nearly 100 gallons of paint for a "touch up." The deed was done and he had to eat the consequence sandwich in his budget. He was really fried at me.

Out of boredom Zephyl and I would take different vehicles out of the motor pool just to tool around in. I broke the bank when I signed out a deuce-and- half 10 wheel truck for some marginal errands around post. Unfortunately a Major spotted, and reported my escapade to Captain Chambers, and I was dressed down for Officers are not authorized to drive trucks.

As it happens we were still in the Guest Quarters when the first Thanksgiving rolled around and my parents flew out from Chicago for a visit. They stayed in Los Angeles for a few days enjoying Beverly Hills friends and then flew Bonanza Air Lines DC-3 service to Apple Valley, where we joined them for the holiday and the weekend. On Saturday the four hour round trip to Irwin took up the day, and we showed them our new home. My mother said she would never live under those conditions, and I think you could have taken that to the bank.

After six months I was given a much better assignment as the Personnel Officer for the base with a sixteen man section under my command. At any other installation it would require a grade of captain to be in charge, so I was exposed to a higher degree of accountability in a lesser rank as were all the young officers on base. This occurred because the lieutenant currently in charge of the Personnel section screwed up badly, and he was relieved, and I was tapped as his successor.

It was a good match, and a great section to work with. Sergeant Shipman the NCO (non-commission officer) in charge was a gem, and eventually advanced on to Warrant Officer. The fact that the service runs on the abilities of noncommissioned soldiers is self-evident. Captain Smith, was my new C.O. and also was on the bowling team if you recall. He was pretty provincial in his speech pronouncing Hawaii as Hawaa, and Missouri as Missouraa (sic) and was my new stiff boss. Over him was my friend and father figure Colonel Prokop.

With my position came a "Crypto Security Clearance" as an addition to my Top Secret accreditation, it allowed me to receive and read extremely sensitive information if it was ever transmitted to our Strac 5 base. The other person on post to share this privilege with me was the Commanding General. I am still waiting to receive my first message, and my uniform still fits, so I can.

In summer the khaki desert uniform consisted of a short sleeved shirt, and long shorts, which as previously mentioned felt and wore like tent canvas. It was the duty uniform at Headquarters. When you sat down it almost cracked it was so stiff. The long stockings were made of wool which itched and were extremely hot to wear. I used to sit at my desk with them rolled down around my ankles like a woman with her hose pulled down. The trick was to remember to bring them back up before rising. I occasionally heard Sergeant Shipman, whose desk was across from mine say, "Excuse me Lt. Lassers," and I knew immediately what I had forgotten to do.

Our section cut military orders, dispensed vacation leave, processed efficiency reports, and worked with finance on the payroll. Personnel was involved with the Judge Advocate General's office (JAG), a young lieutenant like myself and an attorney. When it came to post reenlistments I gave the oath, handshake, and took care of the necessary paperwork. I was also assigned as the Recording Secretary for all Court Marshal hearings which every soldier may be subject to. In reality it is the enlisted person who faced charges and penalties ranging from reduction of rank, pay and allowances, incarceration, or dismissal from the service. At the Court Marshal stage of any proceedings few of the accused will escape punishment. By the time a case reaches that level they are already dead meat. Today military personnel can be represented by civilian attorneys where at that time they had an officer assigned to them for their defense. Lots of luck with that!

The air arm consisted of three planes and two officers, both of whom could really tie one on at the Club come the weekend. If the enemy struck on a Saturday or Sunday we were sunk! Our armada consisted of two L19 Bird Dog tandem seating artillery spotting Cessna's and one eight Place L20 De Havilland Beaver.

The base airfield, Bicycle Lake, was a dry bed of sand with a flat surface that ran for five miles. It was also one of two alternate emergency landing fields for the X15 Rocket Ship being tested at Edwards Air Force Base two hours to the west. Edwards was an alternate landing site for the Space Shuttle program later on when it became active. The X15 flew 100 missions over a nine year period (1958-1968) and Scott Crossfield was the poster pilot for this program in the public's eye, rather than the 11 other men that flew the ship. Yet Neil Armstrong of lunar fame did have a go round aboard the aircraft. The X15 is now on display at the Smithsonian Air and Space Museum in Washington D.C.

The Officers Club served booze and food and it was only one of two locations available on Post to eat if home was not an option. It had captive customers as Barstow was 35 miles away. The building stood stucco ugly, had a pool, and was built by the Italian prisoners housed here for safe keeping during World War II. The Club was a good training ground for families with kids to eat before turning the 'Army Brats" loose in the civilian world. The bar no doubt carried it financially and on Friday and Saturday nights it did a land office business.

Each month a reception and dinner was held for the new officers and their wives arriving on post and the old ones leaving for other assignments, discharge or retirement. One of my official duties as Personnel Officer included hosting the event and making the introductions at the head of the two intersecting lines. The reception queue on my right was for those joining or on their way out, while the line on my left was made up of officers remaining on Post.

As military custom demanded, the lines were formed in order of rank, and took some sorting out because everyone was in mufti, and Hawaiian shirts were plentiful. Civilian dress meant no name tags so you can see where this is going! It would be my initial performance and the general was first in line with his Hilo Hattie Shirt, and I can not pull up his name from my memory bank which was on holiday. After a little shuffling of feet he said to me, "Sullivan, General Sullivan, Lieutenant Lassers and I answered "yes sir," and the line started to move smartly as I introduced him to the person next to me.

We eventually were able to move into our "palatial" trailer and it felt like being the king of the hill. Work was only a two minute commute and I came home for lunch every day and usually slipped out of my uniform for the hour. Life settled down to a routine as it always does. The one "Bird" colonel and his flock of underlings were making the best of life in the less than opulent migrant worker homes, while the general lived in a home that was equal to his "Flag Rank.' Two years in those shacks and no career person would ever be faulted if they went "jungle," over the edge, wondering if the service to their country was worth it. Irwin probably had the poorest housing facilities of any Post in the United States, and the occupants were accustomed to far better, especially the higher ranks. That has all changed today as the base is now a Fort.

On weekends everyone that was able, made tracks to get away. San Bernardino was a mainstay for shopping and a good meal. If we were feeling flush a group of us might hit Vegas, and Vegas would hit back in the pocket book but it was the era of the "Rat

Pack" performing on "The Strip," and the incentive was there for us to go.

Aunt Ellen my surrogate mother, was to become more prominent in our lives with the passing of my Grandfather in 1952. She eventually returned to her native California, and lived with her sister Margaret and her family, first in Stockton and then they both purchased homes in Lodi. Ellen was now in her early fifties, and driving around in the first of two classic *Thunderbird* cars, a 1956 and later a 1957 which she enjoyed over the years. Her first extensive trip was down to Tucson when I was in my final year at Arizona, and now she drove to Camp Irwin to visit us, a six hour jaunt. The grey two seated "bomb" could go faster than you dare drive it, and she would many times have the top down and her scarf on her head, blowing in the breeze. Ellen would kid that her snow white hair looked like a blond from the distance and young men would pass her car to get a look and were disappointed. She was a very pretty lady, but older then they expected. I once drove the second T-Bird and punched it up to 120mph on a farm road in Lodi, but I backed off from further acceleration out of prudence for it still had more pep left in the V8.

Conversely we would drive up to her homes in Lodi and also to Dillon's Beach where she stayed at her sister Alice's beach house, eventually purchasing her own. Aunt Ellen was the best and was a good friend and mentor over the years. She never had children of her own, so figuratively adopted me and later was sorry she never legally did. The car was kept in the garage until she passed on as a trophy to her active years, and a trophy to her spirit and zest for life. Sharon called her "Auntie Mame," a descriptive moniker, not far off the mark. As the story progresses you will see how important a guide she was for me, and how I hope I returned her love, and confidence in me.

Colonel Prokop was always interested in establishing a civilian flying club, and we talked often about it. Now he gave the green light to proceed. I held my Private License at that time and I turned to organizing its establishment while he searched the country for a surplus Army airplane which was available and suitable. His efforts located a new L-4 *Piper Cub* still in the crate at an Army Depot in Harrisburg, Pennsylvania, and it was ours for the asking, all we had to do was move it across country. The problem was we had to have the private financing to do so, and we did not. The good news was that the plane had been in storage since 1945, and it probably was not going anywhere until our transportation problem was solved. The Colonel would need to pull a rabbit out of the hat.

Connections help, and it turned out that the Army was running a parachute exercise to Puerto Rico from California with the Air Force and on the way back one of their C-119 cargo planes would divert to Harrisburg and fly the Cub on to the Irwin Airfield. The cost? Zero, nada! Once the craft arrived it was transported into Barstow and driven out to Daggett Field where a licensed aircraft mechanic could uncrate it, and 'glue' it back together.

The Club was a success and we rented the plane for the unbelievable rate of $2.50 per hour and still made money. The reason was the flying club came under the auspices of the government and there was absolutely no cost but gas, oil and repairs. After I was discharged I learned that they received a second plane, a Navion, and it replaced the L4 which was totaled in an accident and written off. Colonel Prokop was able to receive his pilot's license and no doubt he was very pleased.

The Finance Officer on base was an accountant by trade, and he and I became friendly through our work. He passed along his Wall Street Journals when he was finished, and I devoured them. Our location was so remote that the Journal and other publications were a real treat. I always looked closely at the Friday edition because it had two pages of residential real estate ads from around the country many of them with pictures. I kept seeing ads for water front properties at Lake Tahoe, California, with prices far beyond my comprehension, and pocketbook.

I was scheduled to be discharged in another month, so Sharon and I decided to spend a three day weekend at Tahoe, an area we had not visited before, but that sounded beautiful. In five hours the landscape turned from desert tan to mountain green and soon the topaz lake was in front of us. At the next stop sign there was a small building advertising property for sale and I said to her, "let's drop in and just get the drift of what's going on." Knowing me, she refused, and when I pulled in she wouldn't leave the car. Probably my past financial indiscretions in a previous lot purchase was still on her mind, and when it came to risk taking and throwing the dice, it was not always wisely.

The salesman was cordial and we spoke in general terms about properties for sale in the area. I mentioned lakefront, and he said that "... they seldom come to market, but on the other hand I have a scarce two and one half acre parcel for sale". He explained that he had a 'pocket listing.' and a client whose family had passed on and had left him many treasures including a large holding on the lake. Each year he sold off a parcel to continue to live on a very high scale.

It pricked my interest but of course I was suspicious. I mean why was this for sale in the first place, did it really exist, was it priced reasonably, how shady was this guy, plus an abundance of other minor hesitations. Besides where was I going to find the money to do anything at all. At the time I was earning $550.00 a month, and I had $1500.00 in the bank.

He asked if I would like to see the parcel, which was about a 20 minute drive. The answer was "yes." After all no harm no foul. When he got in our car after locking up I could see my wife cringe. The guy never stopped talking and when I asked him that if it was such a good deal why didn't he buy it himself? He said ".... I have all of my funds tied up in other properties and do not have the money to do that." He gave us the old hustle that he had not even listed it yet, "...but when I do, it will be gone fast", a definite 'buyer beware' utterance.

We drove along the North Shore of the lake to Carnelian Bay, considered as one of the most beautiful and expensive locations on Tahoe, and turned into a dirt road that wound its way down to the lake. And there it sat, two and one half acres of prime lake property with a pier into the water, asking to be bought. It eventually could be subdivided into lots within five years. After walking the perimeter we told him, "We are in town until tomorrow, but I will let you know today what our intentions are, on this $35,000 piece of property". Did I say thirty-five thousand dollars?

After dropping him off Sharon and I went to eat lunch at a little cluster of restaurants and stores one being another real estate broker. While she perused the menu I walked over to the office and asked about lake front property. The answer was, "... we have no listings for lake property, and it hardly ever comes on market." A quick check of the multiple listings showed none for sale either.

The last sale of anything touching the Lake was shown as $45,000 for a smaller parcel than the one we were covertly considering. Now we were into a 'two hour meal' as we pondered what to do. There were a million considerations aside of the possibility of being sucked into something that was unaffordable and being taken to the woodshed by a fast talking professional.

After lunch we came to the only conclusion that seemed logical, we would try and buy it! Returning to his office we signed the papers, wrote a check for $1,000 and said we would come up with $2,000 additional in two weeks for the property to be placed into escrow. Meanwhile the broker continued to keep it off the market while waiting for the check in the mail. It was a long and quiet drive back to the base as we contemplated this crazy thing we just did. Buy an unaffordable piece of property from a salesman with a wild story who we did not know, in an area that was unfamiliar. It could be all hat and no cattle. We had big eyes and no bucks to play monopoly at this level.

On my return to base I was determined to find "some cattle," and I immediately put my car up for sale. Station wagons were in demand, sand pits and all, and it sold in a few days. I did not know where my life would take me in the future but I did not need a car to get me there, The North American moving van came the following week and packed up our things for shipment home at government expense. Friends took us and our secret to the Santa Fe railroad station in Barstow to catch the *SuperChief* to Chicago. No more money was due for a year and the big balloon payment was five years off. We had time to skate. If something came up the broker could reach me at my folks, but we could never reveal to them the terrible mismanagement of our funds that had just taken place.

Aunt Ellen previously promised us the money to travel to Europe after my discharge for as long as it would last, which turned out to be a "spend thrift" three months. There was one condition, we could never tell my mother where it came from; she knew what her reaction would be. She and my grandfather never got around to it before he passed on, and she wanted us to have the experience. Indeed it was the perfect time to go between my service obligation and future career. It would be my third trip there in five years. Wow, but now I'd take my wife.

My mother was extremely perturbed that we were going. It was time to get to work. But that wasn't going to fly with an offer to go to Europe on the table. Mother had a habit of interfering in my life and voicing her opinion in no uncertain terms. It came with the territory and would be one of her traits as long as she lived.

A few days before our departure we were staying at my folks' apartment which was a tight fit for four persons even as nice as it was. One night after dinner the phone rang and my mother answered it and said it was some man from Nevada about my land. I was in for it now. I picked up the phone on her desk in the other room, and we spoke for about five minutes. "... sorry to bother you so late" he said in a deep voice, and my hands immediately became clammy, and my mind conjured up visions of financial disaster. The property was not yet in escrow, where it should have been by now. He continued, "I have another buyer for your land at $70,000. Do you have any interest in selling"?

I was so stunned I told him, "I needed to talk this over with my wife. I will call you back tomorrow". To put it in terms of today's dollar equivalent I had put up $21,618 for the property whose total price was $257,425. Now I had an offer to sell it in two weeks time for double or $514,850 (2011 dollars), pretty amazing stuff, all for a $3,000 down payment.

Of course after I hung up my mother became the inquisitor. "Who was that man, and what is this thing about land in Nevada I heard you talking about?" The interrogation had begun. My parents' only real estate holding was the apartment in which they lived and that they were forced to buy when the building went from a rental to a condominium.

When I told her what had happened she was enraged, "You have bought a worthless mountain top or worse, and I will make an appointment for you to speak to our attorney so he can get you out of this shady deal." I could not convince her otherwise and I started to doubt myself. The attorney had his doubts too. By the time Sharon and I left for Europe we both were so on edge that I thought we were going around the bend. In fact, upon our return the property had indeed been sold, and the money was in the bank.

During my life the only thing that equaled this financial accomplishment was a charitable idea for an organization, and the results noted in a letter from the Salvation Army in 1988. Vons Grocery chain had just taken over all of the Safeway stores in Southern California and was disposing of everything that had the Safeway label on it. They were just going to throw it away or try and give it to local charities.

It seemed to me they needed a large organization to take this off of their hands and the Salvation Army was the first place I contacted for possible interest, and indeed they were. They took everything that was being disposed of to distribute in their own programs. I was astounded when I received a letter from the charity thanking me for my interest and that the estimated value of the donation exceeded $20,000,000. It was a good feeling to help others whether it be a dollar to the corner panhandler or millions to the Salvation Army.

Leaving for England on board the great ocean liner *Queen Elizabeth* in July of 1961, we unexpectedly returned from Haifa, Israel on the, 9,000 ton Zim Line passenger ship, *SS Israel* in November. Original plans called for us to sail on the 80,000 ton classic *Queen Mary* and the difference in what was and what could have been was beyond belief.

While in Europe we met Aunt Ellen and her companion and friend Ethel Callahan in Paris, Rome, and Israel. It was a treat and fun to be with them. They were traveling luxe class while we stayed in two star hotels, or homes with rooms for rent. An example was, our hotel in Rome had a coin-op elevator, but only going up, it was free going down.

While in Rome, Ellen and Ethyl wanted to see Pope John XXIII, who was in residence at his summer retreat at Castel Gandolfo, about a 90 minute drive from the hotel. She was kind enough to invite us along and because there were four people plus the driver and a guide we needed a larger car. When they came to pick us up at their hotel the vehicle was a Cadillac Limousine with flag polls on the fenders, *sans* flags. My grandmother and Ethyl rode in the back and Sharon and I on the pull-up jump seats that were so prevalent at the time in this type of vehicle. We stopped for some sightseeing and lunch before reaching the Palace. When we arrived it was a mob scene of people walking from the extended bus park area down the road through the gates and into the large hall where the Pope was to officiate, sitting on his ceremonial throne.

The driver was determined to get us as close to the entrance as possible, and was honking the horn and separating people with his bumper. Flag poles on the fenders brought authenticity to his efforts while the people stared back into the windows, putting their hands on them to better see just who were these important people that were herding them aside. All of us became quite self conscience and for myself I could not slouch down low enough in my seat to avoid their scrutiny. Once inside we waited about 30 minutes and then the Pope made his grand entrance to a joyous crowd of nuns waving handkerchiefs, priests clapping, and the general faithful yelling *"viva la Papa."*

While traveling I had become enthralled with the book *Exodus*, a mega seller by Leon Uris and it turned our compass toward Israel and the Middle East rather than Spain and Portugal as planned. It concerned the great story of how the Jewish people after World War II emigrated to Palestine through the efforts of Chaim Weismann, David Ben-Gurion, Winston Churchill, Harry Truman and scores of others. It became their homeland and the state of the Jewish people in 1948. The book was a page turner, and it changed our plans as now we would head east.

Thus the final part of our odyssey took us to Israel rather than Spain and Portugal, a real deviation. Ellen and Ethel were also headed that way but were flying. We went to a travel agency in Rome and learned that a Greek ship, the *Queen Frederica*, a Matson Line hand me-down was leaving Naples in a few days, and stopping at Piraeus, Greece before sailing on to Haifa, Israel. We would be on it. Amazingly, the ship was full of Greeks, their food and music and we watched in fascination as the men gathered on deck to do the ethnic Greek Kalamatianos dance with their waving handkerchiefs the night before their arrival home in Piraeus.

Two days later, arriving in Haifa, the Jerusalem Post flashed a headline announcing the arrest of numerous dock workers for smuggling transistor radios. I was shocked. The book had created a fairy tale aura of the 'new' Israelites which was not totally accurate for naïve readers. People are people, and never expect anything more or less.

The trip was fascinating and when I am asked which country I liked the best in my travels, I always say Israel as the one with the most historical interest. What other country is home to three different religions, each with its own shrine, whose history is traced back to the early years of the bible and thousands of years before, which has scars of ancient crusades, is the cradle of historic stories, and a modern day landscape of success and stress?

It is a country where the minority religious parties set the rules and the modern majority chaff under their yoke. It is a country of vast political differences, marginal service, mediocre food and brusque impatient and brilliant people. Even in 1961 the secular Jews had it in for the religious Orthodox and their power within the state. Because of their views and political 'leverage' the country shuts down on Friday, the Sabbath night for *Shabbat* and does not reopen until Saturday eventide. The ultra Orthodox spend all of their time studying the Torah, subsidized at government expense, exempt from military service and do not work.

Sharon and I journeyed on from Haifa to Tel-Aviv where we spent a few days and then booked a bus trip south to Beer Shiva and on to the then remote, tiny town of Eilat on the Gulf of Aqaba. The bus carried an armed guard in response to recent Arab attacks on passing traffic in the Sinai Desert. Eilat at that time had one hotel and a small air strip, that touched the Gulf of Aqaba and the Red Sea. It was boxed in by the enemy states of Egypt, Jordan and Saudi Arabia, and the geography dictated that aircraft landing there had to approach from the south over the Red Sea, in international waters so not to promote a provocation. Today it is a roaring Las Vegas look-a-like.

Taking a DC-3 plane that had metal seats with cushions for civilian use, yet could be stripped down in an hour for military support back to Tel Aviv, we then bussed up to Jerusalem to join Aunt Ellen once again. Her escorted private tour to the north would end for us in Haifa and the small boat and long journey back to America began.

The Captain of the *S.S. Israel* was a German Jew, and was onboard with his wife. Frequently they ate dinner only with us. The immigrant Romanian Jews traveling on board were on their way from unhappiness in Israel to a new home in Canada, and they were below his pay grade to socialize with. A 15 day trip with 'three men in a tub' on the Atlantic Ocean in November was an adventure indeed. I might add that sailing on any Zim line ship of the time would be an entirely different experience as to what cruising is all about.

Eating was family style around a rectangular table with platters curtly dumped on the tables by surly waiters without fanfare, or finesse to hungry classless passengers. Mr. Goldberg who was the only other American on the ship, was returning to New York on the fifteen day voyage and he wielded a mean fork and a brutal knife. He was first into the platter and if it was meat your hand should not be in the way as he stabbed his portion as would a swordsman on the kill. Probably the worst luck was that the ice cream making machine broke down and remained so for the rest of the trip. It was good to have dinner with the Captain and his wife, a table where decorum reigned.

The ship's first stop was Naples, Italy and a chance to see the classic petrified ruins of Pompeii. As soon as we tied up a horde of driven vendors ran up the gang plank and set up shop on deck peddling post cards, books, ties and who knows what else. The scene could be a fifteen round championship fight at Madison Gardens with hawkers and buyers chin to chin, bargaining over the price of the merchandise. The last person standing won and that was the price the item sold for. Later that morning the tour to Pompeii started out on a couple of buses. In the midst of roaming the site a tremendous rain storm broke out and most of the tourists were without rain gear or umbrellas. From out of nowhere came vendors selling umbrellas which all went in a nanosecond. Oh those Italians!

When the torrent of rain fell everyone scrambled to find the coach park and board their bus. In the melee Sharon, I, and a few others bounded on to the wrong one which belonged to a German tour group. The silence was deafening, and uncomfortable. When the rain let up we escaped with our lives back to the Zim line bus which returned us to the ship. There obviously were hard feelings and guilt still present when you mixed a volatile cocktail of Germans and Jews on the same bus which today, on the surface, has been mitigated.

One main lounge was used for all social events and entertainment, and all the board games were in Hebrew. Passengers with talent and nerve to show it, did so daily, during the afternoon programs. My memories of the resident pianist from Brooklyn playing his way home seasick as a dog, and other excellent amateur performances, are vivid and unique. The activity director would always hush everyone through the bad microphone and it was like being in the Catskills, or as I picture it would be, having never actually been there. I believe I was a finalist on a quiz team one afternoon and had trouble holding my own against the very intelligent competition.

Marseille was the second and last stop before we crossed the gray and pitching Atlantic. It took us eight days to gain New York and freedom. Midway across in the middle of the night the ships emergency alarm sounded, and people ran up on deck dressed in whatever they could grab, and waited for an announcement or crew members to direct them as to what to do next. I exasperated Sharon by insisting on brushing my teeth and changing into appropriate clothing to meet our fate. People milled around for 20 minutes chilled and anxious, and there never was a clue as to what happened. We went back to bed in our cabin while the others did the same and nothing more was said about the incident during the rest of the voyage.

The closer New York came, the more we wanted to see it. Three months abroad and an Israeli ship will do that to you. It was time to start working, to find a job and a home, but where?

Chapter 5

Go West Young Man

All good things must end and our three months in Europe were now memories of the past, to be occasionally recalled with joy and pondered. I worked for my Dad in Kankakee, Illinois over Christmas season and during that time of snow and cold, Christmas tidings and New Years imbibing I made a life changing decision. I decided to go west with my wife and try and find a job. Sharon was game and the two of us soon would be on our way out of Chicago on the sleek *California Zephyr*, riding the rails on the most scenic train route in America. The grand plan was to head for San Francisco first where as the song says *"San Francisco, open your Golden Gate, don't let no one wait..."* If that did not work we'd go south to Los Angeles, and even on to Phoenix and Tucson if necessary. The choice of last resort was to go home with my tail between my legs if I did not find employment.

The west was in my blood, where the wide open spaces and warm weather reigned. It was a land where you could be you, make your own friends, raise a family and be free to make mistakes without comments from my mother, or working for my father. It would be a different approach, a cheeky adventure to do it on our own no matter how the cookie crumbled. I was fortunate to have money in the bank from the "Great Tahoe Land Caper" to back us up but we decided to live on the cheap to begin with to conserve our funds.

Arriving in San Francisco, it was still de rigueur to take the ferry boat from the Oakland side of the bay to the old ferry building on Market Street which still stands today. We checked into a hotel and began looking for a rooming house situation which would provide meals while I tried to secure employment. We were fortunate to be recommended to a boarding hotel with a great location, a half block off of Union Square that would be home for a month. We were fed two meals a day, breakfast and dinner which was extremely convenient not having to go on the street to eat. Today this same location has been turned into the *Grand Hyatt on the Park* Hotel. Our room was on the first floor, relatively big, and we adapted easily to it, even though it was a complete change of life. Sharon would go out and explore San Francisco, or read in the room while I was clipping the help wanted ads and hitting the bricks. We were in this together after knowing each other for seven years.

It was a tough trick to arrive in a city, not knowing anyone and start looking for a 'white collar' job. I had my resume with me so the next step was to study the phone book for companies to apply for a job. After making a list I would call to see if they had openings for any positions and if so, were they taking applications. I walked, took public transportation or on occasion a taxi cab to go to their place of business to fill out applications and seek interviews. The comment that sticks in my mind as being most prevalent was 'you are over qualified with an MBA degree for any position that is open.' So instead of an attribute it was a liability. Companies that I recall interviewing with were AT&T, Pacific Airlines, Connecticut General Insurance, Southern Pacific Rail Road, the Matson Steam Ship Line, and many more. It was frustrating, tedious and discouraging especially with my cramped handwriting to fill out application after application and wait for a call.

There I was, in the middle of my third week of job searching and the compass needle was hovering on south, while the money was dwindling and Sharon's boredom of being tied to the boarding hotel was creating a vortex and an urge to say good bye to the Bay area.

Eventually, I interviewed with United Air Lines, which had and still does, a giant maintenance and overhaul facility at the San

Francisco Airport. They were looking for buyers of parts, or as they classified the position, 'Inventory Planner.' During the second interview they took me to lunch in the cafeteria and hired me on at the salary of $500 a month plus another $50.00 for my advance degree. At last I was employed and just in the nick of time!

The base was built and enlarged in the late 1950's just a few years before my arrival in 1962 and was expanded to accommodate the new DC-8 jet aircraft and other types such as the French Caravels, and the Boeing 720, This was my element and I was glad to be here. They would also do extensive work on a host of propeller planes that still made up the majority of the fleet. The base employed thousands and the buying department which was divided into four divisions had over 200 people assigned to one giant room. It reminded me of those huge insurance offices with hundreds of women typing away, pictured in old movies.

The Company was in the process of augmenting their buying staff with college educated individuals to offset the mechanic-buyers who were now doing the majority of the work, and doing it well. There were many pretty boy college grads who wore the United Company tie and worked side by side with gnarly old line mechanics who did not have much use for them.

Sharon and I were overjoyed that we would be able to stay in the San Francisco area and were soon house hunting for a rental property near work. This we found on Concord Way in the pretty town of Burlingame which was but a 15 minute drive to the airport and work. It would be a new start in an industry I loved with the added bonus of living in the west.

The job required me to report to Phil Donner, a senior planner who guided and monitored me. The task was to provision the base and major airports with parts that were required for replacement aboard any aircraft in the fleet which might need them. Many times airlines will loan parts out to competitors as a favor if they have a good working relationship with them. I was responsible to buy and stock parts for the constant speed drive, which is a large and expensive unit that creates electrical power from the engine for the aircraft.

I could not believe how many parts it takes to put a drive together and the complexity of keeping the unit running and the fleet in the air. Each day I received a stack of computer card printouts that would indicate the parts inventory which was low across the country. I would have to order replacement parts to avoid creating the worst nightmare an airline faces other than a crash, AOG, aircraft on the ground. This means quite simply that the plane is useless to create revenue until it is fixed and back in the air.

The best part of the job was going down to one of the eight over-haul docks where the planes were brought inside for the "D" check, the most comprehensive maintenance performed. The planes engines are removed and the hull is stripped of paint down to the bare aluminum shell as worker bees buzz all over it performing their specialized tasks of rejuvenation.

United was one of the launch customers (received first deliveries) for the futuristic Boeing 727 transport that brought a whole new dimension to flying. We had special meetings with other departments in the planning stage of how to support the aircraft a full year before it ever touched the tarmac. Twenty constant speed drives were designated for SFOMB, the San Francisco maintenance base, eight to New York and six to Chicago for back up, and so on. If one went bad, hopefully there would be another to replace it.

I was required to wear a suit and tie to work and the work day ran from 8:00am to 4:30pm. The job became quite boring after awhile, unless I could escape down to the docks or over-haul shops to work something out with a technician. Some manufacturers sent reps around on a regular basis and I always enjoyed talking with them.

One Rep fell in love with my secretary and they asked me to be the best man at the ceremony in Reno, Nevada. It involved a late night flight to Reno, a terrible flight in poor weather, and when we got there four hours late the wedding chapel was closed and I paid the cab to plow our way through the snow to Carson City. The fellow being married was a former Air Force pilot and when he got airsick, I became concerned for our safety. The Pacific Air Lines flight was going to bull its way across the Sierra Nevada Mountains after a United Air Lines flight to the same city had turned back to Sacramento because it was picking up ice. The bride had her rosary beads out, as we again boarded our flight after a weather delay in Sacramento which was half way to Reno. She would need those beads during the remainder of the flight.

Sharon and I were very pleased with our small house in Burlingame and after a period of time added to its population by purchasing a dog we named Schroeder. We had been to the Kennel Club show at the ancient Cow Palace Arena in San Francisco and had fallen in love with the Old English sheep dog breed, which at the time was totally foreign to the west coast. The one that was being shown was from the east coast area, and the breed was just being introduced to our nation of dog lovers. We had met a breeder at the show and after we stepped up to the plate to buy one for the exorbitant price of $300.00 plus shipping cost via air from New York, we ended up with one of the few Old English sheep dogs on the "left coast."

We met the cute little fellow at the airport and took him home. The experience of 'what you wish for, you might just get' was starting. Schroeder grew like a bad debt. He was big, unruly and wild and it was obvious that he must be professionally trained in obedience. House training did not seem to be a problem, as much as my ring finger swelling from walking him and that my wedding band would no longer fit. Schroeder tugged on the leash like a bull chasing a red cape! When people came to the door he would stand on his hind legs, put his front paws on their shoulders and they would shrink in terror! If he were to escape the house without a leash the only way to retrieve the dog was to open a car door and he would immediately occupy a seat inside. A simple solution but then it was necessary to carry him back to the house, it was 90 pounds of joy.

One night, Sharon and I drove down the Peninsula to Redwood City to watch a dog training exercise, and then to turn dear Schroeder over to the owner/trainer who would shape him up after two weeks of "boot camp." The trainer spoke with us for a bit before accepting his charge, about how his regimen was the best and that the trick was to preface all commands with the animal's name. Sounded like a good plan. We would have two weeks free from our investment and his patented traits of thumping the wood floors when he scratched, letting out noxious gas in our bedroom at night and terrorizing the neighborhood.

We anxiously awaited the results of "the send a dog to camp" expenditure and in two weeks we were back at the trainers where Schroeder would be transformed into a model pet. The "ring master" had other animals with him and showed off their skills to the owners in waiting, calling them all by their names as they executed his commands. Finally our turn came and around and around the circle he went, not much different than before we had signed up, and shelled out the money as the trainer called out heel, Barnaby, slow down Barnaby, sit Barnaby! Enough said. The training was worthless as the dog's name was Schroeder. In for a penny, in for a pound!

As the seasons turned, the, dog became more unmanageable and our second Christmas would be approaching. Sharon was pregnant with our first child Scott, after suffering a miscarriage, and she was about to lay the law down regarding this magnificent looking beast. "Get rid of him," was all she said. Easier said then done, especially since I actually enjoyed Schroeder and his playfulness, but my wife was unrelenting, and her reasons were valid, the dog did not fit into her pregnancy. Reluctantly I understood. It was time to be a man of action and I contacted my one and only hope, the local breeder who had steered us to the east coast in the first place.

Stan agreed to take Schroeder to his kennel. He would evaluate and also breed him with a bitch that he had and I could have a pup or $100.00, my choice.   Easiest choice I ever made. Meanwhile he would look for a person who would possibly buy a "used" Old English with low mileage.

The results were a litter of nine pups, an unheard of number for a sheep dog, and a lead on a possible crazy person who might be interested in sole and absolute possession of our mistake. Stan felt that after observing him that Schroeder was too closely bred with related family, and that caused this uncontrollable behavior. He did have an inquiry from a wealthy resident of the East Bay, who was known to spoil his daughter, and was desperate to buy a dog for Christmas which was only a few days away. She wanted an Old English Sheep Dog, and there were none locally available. Stan said his contact would call me at work the next day regarding Scroeder.

True to his word his call reached me at work. Yes he was very much interested in Schroeder and was familiar with his short comings. He acknowledged that he spoilt his daughter and he would pay us $300.00 to cover the cost of the original purchase. Wow, was that lucky or not? The conversation went something like this.

"I understand you have an Old English Sheep dog for sale." "Yes I do." "I have promised my daughter one for Christmas and there are none available. I know your dog is high strung but that is O.K., we have a big place here for it to run. I will pay you

$300.00 (over $2,000 in 2010 adjusted inflation rates) for the dog, delivered." "I appreciate that, let me talk it over with my wife and I will call you tomorrow."

That night I told Sharon of the conversation and she asked if I accepted the offer? I told her what I told the buyer. She looked at me like I was an escapee from a spaceship that had just landed at Roswell, New Mexico. Her answer was to accept the offer, the sooner the better. I had my marching orders.

Day two, the phone rings and Mr. Buyer is back, and wants to know what I decided. As you know, I liked the dog and was dubious about his departure. I told him that I did not lean toward selling him He said, "I will give you $400.00." Once again on the 22nd of December, I said "I need to clear this with the wife." He was getting peeved. When I related the latest conversation to her that night she was extremely agitated and called my grandmother, Aunt Ellen to try and get her to convince me to sell the sheep dog. She did call me, and I expressed my love for Schroeder and she let it go at that.

Day three: cold breakfast, cold wife, wild dog. I go to work wondering if this guy is going to call me back, and as luck would have it he does. I tell him about the cost of replacing the dog, training, shipment from the east coast and on and on. For a thousand dollars I would let him go. He roared back that I was nuts and that the dog was worth absolutely nothing to him on the day after Christmas. "My last offer is $600.00, take it or leave it." Sold American. Schroeder was on his way to his new home that night in the back of my station wagon, barking his head off as he was changing addresses. At his new home he would turn their beautiful waterfront lawn yellow and bite his daughter's snow white skin.

Time marched on and I was now into my second year with United Air Lines and not anymore challenged than I was during the first. United had now merged with Capital Airlines, the largest merger in airline history to date and we inherited their old fleet which still included DC-3 aircraft which were soon sidelined. It was here that United acquired its British Viscount turboprop airplanes and a second maintenance base, this one in Washington D.C.

United was the only airline in the United States to buy the French Caravel rear engine jet transport. The first delivery of the 20 ordered started in July of 1961. It was fast, quiet, and fearsome when the speed brakes were deployed for landing and a fuel guzzler. That said my grandfather's Corina Cigars were passed out free to occupants on the 'men only flights' that United ran daily between New York and Chicago, where men could relax, and remove their coats, ties and shoes. This scenario could not happen today without stiletto heels marching the picket line for women's equal rights.

The Caravel drove all the parts buyers crazy. They were French and that said it all. We could not get some integral items that were keeping aircraft on the ground plus slowing down their over hauls. Finally the company threw up their hands and put a expeditor in Paris to find out what the problems were and fix them. The bottom line was that we were dealing with a different animal, and many of the parts were fabricated by small manufacturers, in little towns using makeshift factories. The French were never known for their speed then or now. I was becoming desperate over my job, I just did not like it and I was always waiting for the quitting time buzzer to sound and stream out the main gate like one more ant cascading out of an ant hill.

To stem the boredom I volunteered to participate in a Federal Aviation Agency (FAA) evaluation test to certify a reconfigured Douglas DC-8 for evacuation time. It took place in a darkened hanger especially prepared and monitored by the FAA. The plane was filled to capacity and artificial smoke was pumped into the cabin to simulate a fire. We were all dressed in our normal business attire and the drill started with the doors being shut, the emergency lighting on and the flaps lowered. Upon the command of "go," the doors burst open and the rear and front sections deployed on the slides while those in the middle used the four window exits which require a person to be a gymnast. Once out the window you walked the wing to the lowered flaps and slid down them to the floor where they had some mats to cushion the impact.

The results were adequate to pass even though there was a broken leg, and sprains and bruises to some of the participants. I went out the rear door and jumped on to the slide zipping right to the bottom, and moving quickly out of the way to avoid being hit by the person behind me. I didn't even get the T shirt for my effort but a small plaque as a remembrance, commemorating the exercise. In reality the women employees in their dresses were the ones that deserved a prize for going over the wing and flap,, and down the slides.

I also gave my time, along with two other service minded executives to represent the Company in promoting Junior Achievement. United paid our expenses and encouraged employee participation in local community affairs. We worked with high school students for 9 months over two years creating a company, a product, keeping the books, and selling the item to whom ever would buy it. I do not remember any of the items we sold but it was a good initiation to the business world for young students. The best memory of my years of volunteering is the picture I still have of the three of us with a student posing with our Vice President of the Maintenance Base, "Dusty" Rhodes. He was the first man certified to fly the Douglas DC-8, which he called "the Cadillac of airplanes," and was one of General Douglas MacArthur's personal pilots in the South Pacific during World War II.

As the jets arrived, more and more piston planes were removed from the system, sold to other airlines, temporarily parked on the large apron outside the base, or sent to a dismantler. I thought it would be a wonderful idea if there was a dedicated museum for commercial aviation history which would preserve the old planes for posterity that were currently being sold for pennies per pound. The more I thought about it the larger the brain storm became and now I included a building housing the museum, airline headquarters and meeting halls, Most normal people would have left the idea right there as far too complicated to ever pursue further, but not me, I actually came close to getting it off the ground as you will see.

I created the Society For the Preservation of Commercial Aircraft and sent out hundreds of letters to move the idea forward. The SFPCA was an actual functioning body with airline employees and civic leaders who became interested in the possibility of establishing the only museum in the world devoted solely to commercial aviation. I wrote and prodded executives and Congressional legislators for endorsement of the idea. Each time I received one I trumpeted a news release to the local papers and the New York Times which actually picked it up. I kept the barrage up and the papers must have been desperate for news, they kept printing the releases as written which made me pretty proud. Occasionally I would have a staff writer for one of the papers on my side and I'd write the release and he'd put his name on it. The next step was to corral a group of interested persons to form a board.

The leadership consisted of A.M. Christian, a Douglas DC-6 Captain for United and a distant relation to Fletcher Christian of the good ship *Bounty* which became famous for the mutiny in the South Pacific. He was designated as Director of Transportation and Exhibitions. He always mentioned to me "… flying was not fun anymore today (1961), there were too many rules and regulations!" G.E. McGovern, editor and publisher of the trade newspaper The Daily Pacific Builder was brought on as Director of Publicity and Construction.

P.G. Dobbins, a prominent San Francisco attorney was retained *pro bono* as the Society's legal council. Not bad for a start of a one man show. It was not long before the Society had 250 paying members in 20 states, yet it was the acquisition of political and business leaders that would bring in more interest and move us up the field. By sending out honorary memberships to recognizable names it brought in some high profile results. The appeal letter started with this paragraph.

"Tomorrow is Johnny's birthday and a happy three years old he will be. In 1978 he will be 18 and a proud resident of the western part of the United States. Johnny will probably laugh about the rigors of air travel during the years between 1910 and 1950......"

The closer was;

"Happy birthday Johnny. Through the fore-sight of your elders I hope that you will be able to celebrate your 18th birthday sitting in the pilot seat of an airplane that made history."

In June of 1963 I undertook a seven city campaign to visit 11 airline corporate offices, the Air Transport Association and members of Congress. I could do this because I had free or reduced travel on the airline as an employee. It was rigorous and quite an experience, as United was still flying a mixed fleet of jet and piston aircraft that were running the routes. I was flying a Douglas DC-6B from National Airport in Washington D.C. to Chicago and the stewardess sat on my seat arm to talk for a moment as she did with most of the other passengers. It was de rigueur for the crews to do this on longer flights, for it took hours to get to any destination. Being that we were fellow employees she said that when she transitioned to jets the relationship with the passengers would never be the same and she was right.

Slowly, I was getting endorsements for the project and even the donation of free land located at the Oakland, California airport from the Board of Port Commissioners. All of this was turned into newspaper releases and those hopefully into memberships.

Senator Barry Goldwater wrote; *"Thank you very much for the honorary membership in the Society For the Preservation of Commercial Aircraft. When you stop and think about how transport aircraft, that were numerous just a few years ago, are now extinct, it's disturbing."*

U.S. Senator from California Claire Engle; *"I have read with great interest of your plans to establish on the west coast a museum to exhibit commercial aircraft..."*

U.S. Senator from California Thomas Kuchel. (via Western Union)*"....commercial air Service (sic) immeasurably significant in bridging transcontinental time and distance gap...we must assure preservation..."*

Congressman representing Oakland, California Jeffery Cohelan thanked me for my visit. *"You have a good idea and I want to commend you for this constructive approach to an historic project."* A letter to Richard Daily, Mayor of Chicago brought back strong support and he wanted to enter into discussions. Douglas Aircraft showed interest, but wanted to 'see the beef first.' Boeing Aircraft, Harl Bracken Jr. Administrator of Historical Services; *"This project definitely does interest me and I am enclosing $1.00 for a personal membership in your Society."* The Federal Aviation Agency; *"We are much interested in your letter of July 30 regarding your efforts to preserve commercial airplanes of the past".* The Iowa Aeronautical Commission was *"... favorably impressed with your ideas and objectives,* while the Mayor of San Francisco, George Christopher passed on my letter to the Public Utilities Commission.

The State of Illinois wished to be kept informed of our progress while Victor Rothe, Manager of the Flight Safety Foundation wrote, *"...we were quite surprised in that you are apparently moving along with a project which we have been discussing for some time."*

The trip 'ginned up' support from numerous airlines. President of American Airlines, C.R. Smith, a pioneer in commercial transport and famous for his advertisement in 1934 after a spate of accidents asked "Why Dodge This Question. Afraid to fly?" wrote *"...The purpose of your intended museum is excellent, and I wish you success in this constructive endeavor"*.

" Founder, President and General Manager of Delta Air Lines C.E. Woolman who was an aviation pioneer and noted for one of his favorite quotes, "Running an airline is like having a baby: fun to conceive, but hell to deliver," chimed in *"I believe that your program for establishing a Society for the Preservation of Commercial Aircraft is a most worthwhile undertaking and if successfully promoted can make a significant contribution to the history of commercial aviation."*

Bud Maytag, President of National Airlines, and youngest CEO of a major airline was euphoric; *"I consider this to be a project of outstanding importance."* Charles Tillinghast, President of Trans World Airlines under Howard Hughes was more restrained and in an extended letter said they would watch with interest our progress, while Malcom MacIntyre, President of Eastern who started the famous east coast shuttle between New York, Boston, and Washington considered it *"...a genuine contribution to the aviation education of the public."* Robert Six, aviation pioneer Founder and President of innovative Continental Airlines said the project is *"...extremely far-sighed and worthwhile"*, Frontier, Ozark, and West Coast Airlines all congratulated the idea. I of course working for United, brought them some publicity from the project, chatted up the airline and could not get an endorsement from William A. Patterson, airline pioneer and United's President, who is credited with starting the placement of flight attendants aboard airliners. Finally after weeks of nudging he sent me a letter acknowledging the idea. *"..I admire you for your interest and support. For the present you can use my name as being very enthusiastic about the program."* It was a marginal endorsement at best.

The starting gate was loaded and we would soon be off, except for one thing. The idea was nothing more than that, even with the Oakland Airport offer of land. Not a dime was offered by anyone to move the project forward! Obviously it would take a benefactor outside the industry to travel past this point. It would require a recognized name to sell the concept and engage the heavyweights to move from paper concept to open exhibits, and it would not be me.

In my desire to find other work I even tried selling life insurance and studied hard to pass the demanding and boring state licensing exam. I had read a career book called *"How I Sold a Million Dollars of Insurance a Year,* by Carl Bach who at the time was with Penn Life in Philadelphia. I was impressed by the book and went to the effort to find where he was now located, and it turned out to be right in the Bay Area. He was just creating a new company called San Francisco Life, and I would be his first salesman. Carl was a master of pressure selling and not understanding the word no. I could, and after contacting friends and relatives to try and sell a product nobody wanted unless they died, I gave up and considered other avenues of endeavor.

Sharon had a distant relative who worked as a broker at an old line security firm of good standing by the name of Sutro and Company on Montgomery Street in the City. On the side he had a little business on Market Street that sold hosiery and sundries where Sharon worked a few days each week. Not being the best of drivers, her sister on visiting us at Camp Irwin drove with Sharon into Barstow for the day, but demanded to drive back to camp, one scary ride was enough. Consequently because of San Francisco traffic she took the train in from Burlingame to work and I'd drive into the City after getting off the job at 4:30pm to pick her up.

It was a tangle driving into the City in the rush hour much less driving Home, but when you are young common sense does not come into play. Her one person store front closed at five, but would stay open until I could park in a no parking zone on Market Street and honk. She would then scurry to vacate and fast track out to the car. There are always obstacles to any plan and the one here was a San Francisco policeman who patrolled the area. He consistently waved on or ticketed cars that were illegally parked and he warned me numerous times about sitting in front of the store and waiting for even a minute. I would constantly have to go around the block, and that added another five minutes on every circle.

The table was set for my next trip in to pick her up. I arrived rolling my eye balls back and forth like a Navy lookout during the Battle of Leyte Gulf in World War II. Sharon saw me through the window turned out the store lights and was locking up the front door when the 'Phantom of the Police Department' emerged from hiding in the doorway of an adjacent building. I had him dead to rights. As he moved from the shadows I started to pull away from the curb into heavy traffic. He increased his gate from a trot to a gallop ran along the side of my car and slipped the ticket under the wiper blade. I was road kill!

Through the contact of Sharon's friend, Harold set up an interview for me with the Sutro Company. All went well during the session and the choice was left to me to join the company. After considering the eventual offer of a position based upon passing the California brokers license test, I turned them down. I was not sure I wanted to recommend investments to friends and clients who would be 'mad as hell' if they turned south and became losers. People are funny about money.

By this time Sharon had given birth to Scott Alan, who was the first of three sons, with a bit of Scottish-Irish in their names. Scott had more flights between San Francisco and Chicago in his first year of life then I did in 10 years. Sharon flew on a reduced employee ticket and could always get the bulkhead seat which allowed the use of the planes baby bulkhead wall cribs that had the effect of a personal cocoon, and relieved her from having to hold him the entire flight. Robert Bruce was born three years later and Michael Kevin nine years after that. I have been blessed with six wonderful grandchildren, three boys and three girls who are good looking, smart, talented, and will carry our lineage forward. They are a blessing to both of us.

Sharon's Uncle Max, a part of the family business in Chicago for years, had now retired and was living near us in Burlingame. He was searching for another business to buy and live permanently in California. His brother Danny ran neighborhood ice cream trucks down South in the Riverside-San Bernardino area of California, and was doing quite well. Danny was crazy and a fox from the streets of New York, while Max was crazy like a fox, and he was intrigued with the operation, a simple concept of vending from a truck. The irascible Danny was going to buy the San Bernardino branch of the Good Humor Company, and add it to his profitable existing business and encouraged Max to buy one which he did in San Diego, where he relocated once again.

He thought this would be a good business opportunity and encouraged me to check out the Long Beach branch, one of the few remaining yet to be sold. I was flummoxed as to my future plans so I flew down to Long Beach to scope the operation out. Over on the industrial west side sat the plant (circa 1936) of 60 vending trucks, a small office and two large freezers for storing the frozen product that they were hawking. It seemed like an opportunity and the operation came with a manager, two assistants, a couple of mechanics to keep the fleet moving and a box man who received and distributed the ice cream and popsicle bars. The property on which it sat for the past 30 years was leased and the neighborhood was on the rough side.

It was decision time, for the company was anxious to sell the remaining locations which turned out later were not theirs to sell after all. I forgot to mention one thing. If I bought it the price came to approximately a quarter million dollars which was a staggering figure, but it could be paid off monthly. Never one to blink I bought in using the money from the Lake Tahoe Land Sale, and the 12 year ride was full of twists and turns, of profit and despair, of worry and hard work, and eventual liquidation. There was a great deal of money owed to the parent company, and a big financial commitment on the part of a 28 year old entrepreneur,

My life was moving fast now as I contemplated leaving United Air Lines for "greener pastures," and into business for myself in Southern California. I was unhappy and unchallenged at United, tired of working in an area of 200 other people in the huge buying department, and buying parts in which I had little interest. The chance of advancement remained slim, and I wished I was in passenger service rather than the back shop areas of the airline. It was time to move on.

As to the plans for the museum, I talked with Paul Mantz in Southern California, a legendary figure in the field of aviation who was associated with Howard Hughes and Amelia Earhart, and was known for his aerial movie photography and the ability to stunt and fly old and odd aircraft. I spoke to him about moving the museum idea to Long Beach, California, where I was headed and where the city was talking about a World's Fair on port property. It pricked his interest, but Mantz was soon to die in the filming of the *"Flight of the Phoenix"*, and Tallman, his partner would crash his personal plane into the side of the Santa Ana Mountains a few years later. The museum would die a quiet and natural death.

I returned to Burlingame, and quit my job. We put our newly purchased house back on the market much to my mother's chagrin, and negativism to the new business venture, and started packing. The plan was for Sharon and Scott to return to Chicago and bed down with her folks while I moved into an apartment in Long Beach for a few months and acclimated myself to the world of indebtedness and a new business.

I drove down along the Coast and stayed in a motel over-night, spending the next day with the transitional manager Charley Mosher. That weekend I found an apartment near the plant in a neighborhood of marginal quality, and spent 24/7 learning the business, which happened to demand just that, 24/7. I was to have the pleasure of spending the next 12 years working with drifters, conmen, alcoholics, and the mentally incapacitated that daily took my trucks out into the busy streets of south Los Angeles County. My franchise territory was huge and it ran from the ocean to Orange County and Rosecrans Avenue south. With all its negatives the business was extremely profitable for the next six years. At one time I had over $100,000 in my bank account, part of that due to my slow pay to Good Humor for product. I was three months behind at one point before they demanded payment.

Sharon and Scott returned 6 weeks later, and I found a better apartment in the same cruddy neighborhood where we continued to live for a few months more until she found a house to rent on the east side of town across from California State University at Long Beach, a nice neighborhood.

My life turned into a four letter word, work. I spent at least 6 days a week on site, sharing my time on most Saturdays and appearing on a few Sundays for a look-around. I had found myself a business that was very demanding, time consuming and stressful. I was 28 years old and working with employees who were the bottom of the barrel, except for a relief in the summer when college boys drove for a few months, and this kaleidoscope of characters, some with jail time are who I spent my life with in order to make a living. My rough hewn manager, a fellow named Joe Guerrero did much of the heavy lifting with these guys and became annoyed if I brought myself into any controversy. He was right. I would try to solve it like President Obama, when it needed the hard hand of the Mafia to bring resolution and order. I became so unhinged by accidents that I'd get shell shock if the phone rang at home past 9:00 P.M. The plant never closed down until 10, and late trucks usually meant mechanical problems or an accident.

Scott had now taken up ice hockey, and continued to play until he was 18. In his second year he had been knocked hard into the boards, sliding on the ice and hit his head. He was so groggy he had to sit out the rest of the game. I was really concerned about him since he did not seem to respond well. One of the mothers said to give him a cold bath when I got home. As I did this I prayed that he should break out of this no matter what the penalty dispensed to myself, an allegorical request. The pay off was he did return to normal, and 30 minutes later the telephone rang with the manager reporting that one of our trucks had run a red light, hit a car, careened off it into a gas station knocking over a pedestrian and hitting a pump. I always thought that the whole incident had some biblical significance.

The new owners quickly bonded among ourselves as we fought tooth and nail against Good Humor of Southern California policies. Our vehicles took a beating, the mechanics were Teamsters, the insurance companies bailed out on us like paratroopers because of our terrible driving record, and people were lining up to sue us. I used to facetiously kid that they had to take a number to sue me. A lady carrying a baby walked in one day and served me papers. Normally they would ask for me by name and being younger than what might be expected I always said he isn't here, and force them to try again. But she fooled me completely.

It was with shock and surprise that one day we were called to a meeting of the parent company at their offices on Santa Monica Boulevard in Hollywood. Since our original purchase of the branches the ownership had changed and now we were involved with some high rollers from the east coast, one of whom was prosecuted by Tom Dewey, former Republican Presidential candidate when he was Attorney General for the State of New York, and was sent up the river on racketeering charges. As previously mentioned this Good Humor business was full of unsavory characters all the way through. The news they had for us was shot from cannons.

Good Humor of Southern California was the only franchise ever granted by Good Humor of New York, the parent company. In the contract the franchisee never had the right to sell any of the branches. I believe that they had operated in the Los angles area since 1936 and had always abided by this clause in the agreement. It was now the late 1960's and the parent company has been purchased by Lever Brothers the giant conglomerate, which in turn was gobbled up by Unilever, a multi-national holding company. I never expected to be caught up in such a big mess.

Keeping all this in mind the Southern California privately owned franchise took a gamble, and threw the dice in solving their own cash flow problems and sold the branches and consequently was sued by this heavyweight of the business world who hired O'Melveny and Myers, considered one of the best law firms in Los Angeles. It was no contest and all of us were defrocked of our franchise name, Good Humor. No longer would we be able to use the name.

What now? The southern California company forgave the remaining obligations of each owner that was owed on the trucks and other property. They relieved me of the debt of approximately $200,000, a considerable amount, and we all changed our name to *Melody Ice Cream* which did not seem to make any difference. Later I would change our branch name to Miss Sharon's, which did not seem to resonate with anyone. Still the endemic problems of the business remained, and we were always considered an 'attractive nuisance' by the courts, making us potentially liable for any injured child who was attracted to the truck and its musical call, no matter how he was hurt or by whom. The daily stress was unrelieved whether at work, at home or on vacation. "All Quiet on The Western Front,' meant to me the telephone did not ring that night.

During this period our domestic life proceeded as normal as could be. Raising three boys, all of whom were to participate in the advanced Long Beach School District study programs and move on to college. I spent considerable time in ice rinks for Scott and Michael's hockey practices and games, readopting to the cold that I had escaped from in the Midwest, and on wood bleachers in school gymnasiums to watch Robert wrestle which he excelled in through high school and four years at Ithaca College.

My business was strictly cash and on a good night more than $2000 would cross the counter into the cashier's cage. Keep in mind that the trucks came in anywhere from seven to ten in the evening and the drivers sat in the small central room counting their cash and balancing out. This would eventually be pushed across to the person who would receive it and count it with care, and at the end of the day was dropped into a Brinks safe that only they could open. I was fortunate never to be faced with the situation that Ken Smith did at the Santa Ana branch one night.

The operation was the oldest and the smallest. Ken worked it himself and was a very hands-on business man. On a dark December night he was closing the truck entry gates around 9:00pm as always. That night he was alone and the only one left on site. Out of the dark jumped two men in black brandishing a gun and demanded the cash receipts from the now departed drivers. They walked him into the office and shoved him into the money cage where the safe was. He apparently used a different type of safe that could open without the help of the Brinks service, and they told him to open it. They removed the gun from his back as he knelt down to work the dial and then replaced it against his temple. With that his mind froze and he could not remember the combination. The longer he fumbled the more agitated they became constantly jabbing the muzzle of the weapon hard against his skull.

It was then he found that there was a God! A police siren wailed from a passing squad car, with its red and blue bubble lights going, raced by and they ran away just like that. I saw Ken three weeks later and he still had the shakes and was seriously considering retiring from the business. In a short period of time he did just that.

I realized that eventually my business could not continue for much longer with so many factors stacked against it. I had tried to introduce other off-shoots to diversify in some way and this involved catering large events, including all the football games at Gardena High School and El Camino College. The venture required a 30 foot converted vending trailer and equipment. The schools were in transitional neighborhoods which at times presented a challenge.

Over the years our trucks covered a number of special events like the Dragster Races at the Pomona Fairgrounds and the first Long Beach Grand Prix event. I would vend along with the rest and at the Pomona National Drag Races I had to work the bleachers selling ice cream sandwiches, and in the heat they went fast. The customers would toss a quarter toward me and I had to pick it out of the air or it would drop through the bleachers. Either way I was obligated to toss back the sandwich.

The strangest and most profitable vending event I ever became involved in was held at California State University at Northridge, a 4 day rock concert featuring *The Doors, Jefferson Airplane,*

Iron Butterfly and many more bands. It would be the end to end all, and the County of Los Angeles would never again hold another rock concert at a public venue.

We drove up from Long Beach in a convoy of five vending trucks, a large refrigerated storage vehicle and a supply truck to the Northridge campus. We pulled into the outdoor track facility to scout it out before going to a motel for the night. The event was not scheduled to officially start until the next afternoon but there were many young people milling around and in the center of the grounds was a stage partially set up. Actually the best act of the event was taking place at that very moment as two young Hippies made love on top of the stage, and not really attracting much attention from anyone, except my drivers.

The next day I placed the trucks in position around the large field and handled the supply truck myself. Business was brisk and the weather was conducive to what would become a non-stop event. Like alcohol at a football game, drugs were fueling this event and the crowds were large and the police contingent small. I found that I could even consign young people to peddle ice cream for me, make a commission and return for more, probably using their earnings to purchase more drugs.

The second day the crowd was rowdier and the police had retreated to the entrance awaiting reinforcements before venturing out to control the wild scene. Wood railings around the track were now being pulled up and set on fire and the bands played on while the haze of marijuana, alcohol and other stimulants kept the party going. Ice cream continued to sell like hot cakes and I was collecting money in bank bags which were stuffed into large cardboard cartons and dollied through the throngs daily to where Brinks was picking up the receipts at the box office, including our moneybags destined for the plant in Long Beach the following Monday.

The third day the Police brought a semblance of control to the scene and their job was made easier by the rioters being stoned, blitzed or indifferent in response to the continued beat of the music. They seemed removed, and unaware of the rioting. I was aware of it, but too busy making money to worry about it.

The show was to end Sunday night and I rounded up our men at dusk to make our way back to Long Beach, a tired but richer crew. There were pot heads sitting on the bumper and I told the guy riding with me to ask them to move. When that didn't work he just pushed them out of the way, and they would respond by moving in relation to the energy incorporated into the push. I had him walk in front of the truck all the way to the street to keep from running over or into any of the participants.

Wow, what an event, and we were right in the middle of everything with immunity from the participants and the law enforcement. We worked and spoke with both; it was like being on the United Nations Peace Keeping Force in some violent distant land. All the transactions were cash, and I would make my rounds through the litter and the stoned, and with God's blessing.

During the summer months foreign students participating in college work exchange programs drove the vehicles and we always employed about 15, for seven weeks. They wanted time to see the country before returning to England and I could not blame them, but they were good and also honest. One year I had two Iranian students from Cal State Long Beach work and they told me that the students in Iran would over-throw the hated Shah, and they were right.

At the age of 38 I had to face the bare facts that the business was going south and I tried to expand it to Tucson, Phoenix and El Paso where I took vehicles from Long Beach and started up operations. We tried selling meat products in addition with little success and I opened three ice cream sandwich parlors in Globe,

Casa Grande, and Nogales, Arizona. The idea was to bring a high grade of multi flavored ice cream from Phoenix to the smaller townes and not have to fight the competition of Baskin Robbins. I found out that there wasn't any competition because the towns were not big enough to support what I had in mind. It was also a good lesson of the perils of absentee ownership even though I would make the trek to Arizona, and on to Texas no less than bi monthly, it was not enough.

It is tough to liquidate a business, physically and mentally. What do you do with specialized equipment like old ice cream, single purpose trucks now parked idle in the dry desert heat. What about restaurant equipment that was costly, and now sold for 15 cents on the dollar purchase price. Still a home was found for all the stuff from player piano to the semi-trailer refrigerated unit. When all my downsizing was completed I found a small office near the traffic circle in Long Beach, to continue my property management company. This was America, the land of opportunity and there would be other choices, even for a forty year old.

My career adventures continued and I enrolled in real estate school to procure my brokers license. I joined the first of the alphabet soup companies called HDI (Housing Development Industries). They had set up shop in Los Alamitos and had intentions of building and selling small commercial developments. The group was young and wild, inebriated with ideas which eventually lead to the company going bankrupt. They strayed from building commercial office buildings, and apartments into marketing limited partnerships at Fairbanks Ranch, which left the sales people high and dry with their clients when fraud was involved in the transactions, fraud on the part of the sellers, not HDI, but it was never clear.

My best client lost $25,000 in this deal and forgave me. HDI started to think off the deep end and morphed into grandiose ideas of leasing DC-10 aircraft and super tankers that never materialized, yet the Togo, Africa gold scheme came around full bloom to the investors who were greedy and naïve. The company sent a representative to Togo to see what was up on a trail of gold leading from Senegal south. In fact I believe he went there twice to meet with a sleazy North African "Frenchy," who took the money and ran. We had investors bring bags of cash in to the office to invest in this scheme. Of course if you have that much cash the loss of it is probably payback for how it was acquired.

The image is vivid in my mind of a part-time salesman of limited partnerships by the name of John who was honestly telling an investor on the phone about why the gold partnership was not paying off. Keep in mind he was of Asian birth so his speech was accented. He mentioned that all was in place to smuggle gold from Senegal to Togo but heavy rains are making it difficult. "We expect the courier any day" he said, and believed it. There was a sit-com there somewhere. Well the gold never showed, the company looked incompetent if not sleazy and eventually people were pounding on our locked doors to find out where the owners were. After two years it was time to reshuffle the alphabet soup companies and find another broker to put my real estate license under.

A good friend at that time was taking a real estate course at Long Beach City College. The instructor was brilliant in her estimation and had his own company called CIA Properties. Which stood for Commercial, Industrial and Apartments, yet was a play on the Central Intelligence Agency name. It might be said that a few more letters were added to my alphabet soup business career. Her opinion was one I respected and the location could not have been more convenient in the Bixby Knolls neighborhood of Long Beach, a few miles from my home. I would be soon making a call upon him with my resume in hand.

I set up an appointment to apply for work. Bob Slaton was a big man, in his late forties, with great abilities when it came to making successful 1031 Real Estate Exchanges and keeping the wealth of his clients growing. His great talent was kicking the tax consequences up the road until the final 1031 exchange and sale was made. Capital gains taxes would be paid the government only then, when the client was retired and earning considerably less. He was a genius and he knew it, which made him unpredictable and abrasive.

The office was far from deluxe and as best I could see employed a secretary, a partner-broker, and his son, whose duties to the clients were far removed from selling real estate. He didn't need anything larger for he only had three clients, who all were cardio-vascular surgeons from the same medical group, and all who were getting richer by the year through his expertise and their medical skills.

When I was ushered in to see him in his Plain Jane office with spread sheets of figures covering every surface like oil cloth table covers, he hardly acknowledged me. I explained why I was there and handed him my resume, which after a minute he glanced over quickly with disinterest. I think the only reason he gave me the time of day was because my source was a doctor's wife, and maybe he would expand his clientele.

He made it quite clear that he did not "…have time to nurse maid agents," and maybe I should look else where. It was not easy to stand there, at 43 years of age to withstand his scrutiny and sarcasm, yet I would spend the next 3 years at that location, because something caught his eye on my resume. I was just about to thank him for his time, (his rudeness), and turn to leave when his approach softened and he said, "I see that you are a pilot, tell me about it. I am looking for a pilot."

Chapter 6

Orville Wilber and Gene

A flight of Japanese Zero's at two o'clock, get ready to jump them. I was always interested in aviation and other weapons of war. I read book after book about World War II, built models of anything that moved, and in my mind ran tanks against Rommel in the North African Desert, subs against the Nips in the Sea of Japan and snuggled into a warm and cozy bed at night. Of course now that I am old enough to know better there never has been a 'good war'. Soldiers die horrible deaths and suffer pain which none of us can even contemplate. Civilians are killed indiscriminately and involuntarily displaced from their homes. Millions are spent to keep the world free and ironically our enemies from the past are now our best friends today as we work on new enemies to replace the old ones. Thousands die each day, as we pray for peace, praise and honor our dead, and nothing has or will change.

My family first flew in the 1930's. They were early adventurers of a dubious means of transportation when it came to safety. The trips were on board a Pan American Airlines Sikorsky flying boat round trip Miami to Cuba, and my Dad flew onboard a Lockheed *Boston* to a nearby state for business in 1940. He also flew back to Chicago from his vacation in Hawaii in 1950 when his Father, J.A. had a heart attack, and this was in an aging propeller driven airliner flying the longest over water route in the world.

My first trip aloft was in 1950, during a Hawaiian vacation, and was on board a Douglas DC-3 flying from Honolulu to Hilo, located on the north shore of the Big Island. We flew round trip to see the Mauna Loa Volcano erupt and spew its molten lava into the air and watch it ooze down the volcanic rock frothing into the sea. I was convinced the airlines were stoking the fires to keep the airplanes full, and at 14 I could not wait for the adventure to begin. The main reason for the trip was that my mother wanted to visit an orchid nursery.

The flight was an hour, and it was a thrill to hear the door close and know that we were on our way in an era when a majority of people had never left the ground. Flying was expensive and still considered hazardous, so only the elite, the businessman when required, and the adventurous took to the airways. In the early years the hardy ones flew and wrapped themselves in the mantra, that 'no airline ever left one up there yet'' expressing the wishful thought that everyone would return home safe, with no worries. In reality the number of crashes and fatalities were quite high compared to today.

Over the years, the more I flew, the more I wanted to learn to fly. I can't say I remember anyone that was particularly interested in piloting an airplane in my family. Maybe Uncle Alford, my Dad's brother, who was brilliant but short a few pickles in his jar did, but he never mentioned it to my knowledge. My folks did not send me to the progressive Francis Parker School to become a pilot, they had more lofty expectations, and were probably disappointed time and again.

Although flying fascinated me, I was terrified of roller coasters, and during my two rides, I went brain dead with fear. The fantasy of pulling out of a 3G negative dive after knocking off the German on my wing may not have been realistic, anymore than learning to fly and doing chandelles, spins, stalls and 60 degree steep banks with abandon. Flying through rough weather and bouncing around the skies was not therapy to me, but to fly, one accepted this in the piston engine era where the planes had limited power, and conservative altitude capabilities. It always seemed that the airliners never flew around or over the weather, just through it.

I began flying commercially with the family on vacations, and more regularly to and from Chicago and Tucson, Arizona when I was enrolled at the University. For a kid my age, I was logging considerable flight time. I not only flew domestically, but also internationally to Europe in 1956 and 1958, before the era of jet travel. On a fishing trip with my Dad to Kenora, Ontario, Canada, we flew in a 4 place Stinson plane with a rattling door which I knew was going to fly open. No worries, I was an extremely competent driver and flying was like driving, the more you did it the better you got, or so I thought. Control was everything, and not just being subjected to the vagaries of the clouds or the wind as a vulnerable passenger, I'd find out.

On January 24, 1958 at the age of 21 I was to commit to my dream of becoming a pilot, to soar like an eagle, glide like a sea gull, flit like a moth, and I took my first lesson at McBride Aviation. Tucson was still a dusty afterthought in the Sonora Desert, and the lightly used old city airport with its dirt runway was still in operation. It was located just west of downtown and was home base for a bevy of small civilian planes, which didn't need a tower, only good weather and a St. Christopher's medal for luck.

With that said most of Tucson's airspace lay in the path of Davis-Montham Air Force Base, which today is the largest Air Force bone yard and storage base in the country. Back then D.M. was launching B-47's (some carrying atomic bombs), and other dragon eating birds into the sky. These fast and lethal monsters not only affected the little airports air space but were a disturbance to the town and the local University as well, but a necessity to keep the country safe.

One night at the University auditorium the renowned violinist Isaac Stern was performing in concert and a B-47 flew overhead, drowning him out. He just stopped playing. The airspace around the school was supposed to be noise restricted for concerts except in emergencies, but the plane roared through and eventually flew on. At that point the great Mr. Stern bowed to resounding applause and continued the solo concert. It was an isolated incident, yet indicative of how every activity in Tucson was subjected to the defense of the American skies.

Covered in red and white fabric the Piper Tri-pacer was the only plane that I flew to earn my private license. It was a relatively popular aircraft at the time, and one of the first of a new generation of tricycle landing geared airplanes, and a great advance in technology. The old "tail draggers" (planes with a rear wheel) were harder to fly and more dangerous during the landing and take off sequence. Because of its unique landing gear arrangement the Tri Pacer was dubbed "the flying milk stool," but I always remembered it as the "flying rock." Once you cut the power to descend, it would fall out of the sky like a meteor due to its stubby wings. I never once needed nor was trained on how to use the flaps for take offs or landings, because the Tri Pacer never needed them. It was a skill I would have to hone up on in the future to fly other aircraft.

It was a busy school year to say the least. I was now a senior and still trying to bring my grade average up, and to finish my R.O.T.C. studies so I could be commissioned as an Army Officer upon graduation. In addition I was still working at the F.M. radio station as a disc jockey while darting out to the airfield between classes and on weekends to proceed with my flight training. It was remarkable that I graduated at all much less being able to bring my grade average into the high B zone of respectability, but I just kept trying to do it all, and I did. My class schedule had open periods back to back, three times a week and the airfield was only 15 minutes away. I could get some minor time aloft and inch along to my first big accomplishment, soloing (flying alone) in the Pacer.

There are always stories of those who were *wunderkind,* soloing in six or eight hours and also those dunderheads who did it in 20 hours, while the average student did it in ten hours. Don let me loose at 10.5 hours. After a brief time in the pattern around the field he commanded me to land, said I had it, got out, and never looked back! So on Washington's birthday in the year of 1958, I taxied back to the dirt strip, tried to remember all that I had learned and headed for the sky. I am sure he was watching me from somewhere to know if his one and only plane would return in one piece if at all. It was like walking and chewing gum. You can or cannot, and I could, I soloed and was on my way to my license! It never occurred to me that I would continue to fly over the next 25 years or carry the fantasy as far as I did.

Ground school is required for all aviation licenses and I enrolled at the Tucson Municipal Airport east of town for night courses. It was challenging and I found it interesting. The curriculum had strict parameters for required hours of instruction; and a hard test was given upon completion under the auspices of the old Civil Aeronautics Agency (CAA).

The instruction introduced the student to the tools of the trade, plotting courses, map reading, understanding regulations, and preparing the pupil for the required written exam. It introduced students on how to use the needed implements to figure out mathematical equations and other requirements that got you from hanger to hanger, and tie down to tie down safely. Of course there is a tremendous difference today from the basic accessories available in 1958. Computers and Global Positioning Systems have removed the need for such rudimentary necessities as a straight edge, protractor, and E6B computers which every World War II pilot used, and was manually operated. It was essentially a slide rule with wheels. What took minutes to calculate is now accomplished in seconds if not sooner.

Current day pilots appear to be system engineers that fly with lap tops, multi-purpose instrumentation, and super automation. On the Airbus planes there is no yoke (wheel), only a side stick that is pushed in the direction of desired flight. Figuring compass courses, magnetic deviations, lines of flight wind speed and angle, check points, altitude and fuel consumption, weight and balance, are all inputted by a computer, not so in 1958.

A portly gentleman, K.C. Jones better known by his moniker 'Casey' was our instructor. He was an old airline pilot going back to the days of the Ford Tri-Motor, the first all metal plane, and at the time, a benchmark of air transport sophistication. Henry Ford and Walter Stout are credited for the design, and the Ford Company started production in 1925. Many of the refinements were lifted from Hugo Junkers notebook, the acclaimed German "aircraft wizard' of the era. The Tri-Motor featured roll down windows, wicker seats, three engines, a lavatory and was nicknamed the *Tin Goose*. It was the harbinger of the future, built out of metal rather than fabric and wood, and 199 were manufactured by the Ford Corporation for the airlines to fly.

He was an engaging teacher and a weaver of tales, one which I still recall today. The Tri-Motor was very susceptible to any shift in gravity, so moving passengers or luggage required a frenetic reaction by the pilots to trim the airplane and remain in level flight. Apparently Jones was deadheading that day on company time, and there were only the two pilots and a non-revenue employee on board, who's bathroom needs were very demanding. Back and forth he would go from the front of the cabin to the rear as the mad trimming pilots kept compensating for his movements, while yelling, "…enough is enough already," over the din of the three engines

Ignoring the stern admonitions from the cockpit he tried his luck once to often. The pilots were ready for another journey and when it happened they put the plane into a steep dive and then pulled up into a wrenching climb only to return to a deep dive and level flight. The problem was solved, at least to the satisfaction of the pilots as he stayed in his seat from then on.

In time, McBride Aviation moved over to the Tucson Municipal Airport where the airliners landed, the Air National Guard fighters took off and the use of the radio was mandatory. A novice pilot would have to be on his toes in this congested area. Before moving to the main airport all I had to do was avoid busy traffic areas and keep my eyes pealed for fast moving shadows on the desert floor which was an indication of military jets in the area. Now it was necessary to speak and broadcast aviation lingo by radio and obey the tower, who expected nothing less. The move was good for me if I really wanted to fly in congested areas.

My training involved solo work, and I flew into stark desert towns with names like San Manuel, Douglas, Nogales, and Casa Grande. The big cross-country flight a major requirement was now on the board, and it was a solo triangular affair from Tucson to Phoenix, on to Yuma and a return leg back to Tucson with a landing at each airport. Phoenix was a hub of commercial and private plane activity and Yuma was a shared airport with the Marine Corps, so I needed to be on my game.

The day arrived, I had prepared myself for it as best I could. As I recall it was a clear and hot day in April when I left Tucson on the three stop "hat trick" flight that I needed to make to become eligible for my private ticket. The outbound went so well that I thought I was a genius, the return flight would prove otherwise.

After the second leg of the flight I took a quick lunch at the Yuma Airport and then lifted-off for home on my precision flight plan that returned me to Tucson. The new leg was barren desert with few recognizable places to identify and reaffirm visually to assure my flight track was correct. Worse yet, my to-from indicator to the VOR (Visual Omni Range) was incorrect, it read from rather than to. I knew I was heading east because of my compass but I panicked and decided to call Davis-Montham Air Force Base which had a long distance direction finder, maybe they could help? For whatever reason they could not pick me up, relayed my predicament to McBride Aviation putting them on pins and needles for a potentially lost student pilot and plane. I finally broke away from the small cluster of mountains to the south, and noticed a tiny dirt airstrip parallel to a dusty country road with a few crop dusters parked off to the side of the runway. Best yet, there was a small building right next to it. I hoped that there might be a town name painted on the roof of this wilderness outpost, but no luck.

There was only one thing to do and I did it. I landed, shut down, walked into the store much to their surprise and asked, "...where am I?" They told me in broken English, and I asked for a pay phone, those relics of the past, and called flight service so they didn't come looking for me because of an over-due flight plan.

I cranked up the little Piper and took off to the south circling back to the east and completed the 30 minute flight home. As I shut down and gathered my belongings my instructor Don and the owner of the plane ran over and congratulated me. They had been following my progress on the radio and of course were relieved at my safe return, and so was I, it could have been worse.

As I boned up for my private license Don encouraged me to do some additional cross-country flying so we proceeded down to the Nogales Airport on the Mexican border. This small airport sits on rolling ground, and the runway has an incline or a decline depending on which way you land. If you aren't patient and nurse the landing up hill, the plane will stall out high and come crashing down on the runway, or alternately, produce a hard landing if you failed to keep pulling back on the control wheel as you stretch for the runway.

The trip was flown dual with my instructor Don in the right seat critiquing the flight and boning me up for the CAA (Civil Aeronautics Agency, now the Federal Aviation Administration) license test. For navigational practice he chose to fly the old low frequency network, still in use at that time. I always had difficulty with this since you never knew when you were exactly on course. This was indicated when the A & N Morse code audio signals blurred into one creating a garble of static known as the "sweet zone."

It is only a short flight to wing the 60 miles down to Nogales and after landing we taxied over to the ramp in front of the small administration building and coffee shop. As we did the old Beechcraft C-45 parked in front broke radio silence and asked us to join him for coffee. It was a friend of Don's and the joke he told sitting at the counter remains with me today as one of the funniest I ever heard, though I will let you judge for yourself.

A Canadian farmer had but one daughter of whom he was very protective. He was quite concerned about her going off to a distant college in the beautiful State of Florida alone, and also losing control over her finances. His philosophy was once on campus she should be chaste, studious, thrifty, and stay in touch.

The campus was good sized and the girls in her dormitory were spoiled American Princess's who decided that they would buy bicycles to get around, actually a very logical purchase. The problem was that the girl from the provinces did not have enough money to do so, and wrote her father to send extra funds for what she considered a legitimate need.

Now her father analyzed the request thoroughly, decided it made sense and forwarded the money by return mail. College students are fickle and by the time the check arrived back in Florida the fad had changed, bicycles were out, and replaced by Orangutans. Not wishing to be left behind she tossed caution to the wind and bought one.

Two weeks later she became quite concerned because all the hair was falling out of the chest of the animal and she wrote her father that all the hair was falling out of her Orangutan. Her father wrote back to sell the bicycle.

I did pass my private license examination on May 25, 1958, and was then officially authorized to fly passengers brave enough to travel with me. It was a short list of one, my girlfriend Sharon. Until I entered the service I occasionally flew around the Arizona skies and into its back country airports, but did little more until my Army service where I started a Flying Club.

The little plane that we were able to pry loose from surplus military storage was a World War II artillery spotting tandem seat Piper Cub, the only craft I ever flew without an electrical system. To start up it called for two people, although I tried numerous times to kick start it by myself. It was a dangerous proposition since it was necessary to tie the tail down, crack the throttle, and hand prop the propeller to get the engine running. If this piece of luck happened you should have been at the crap table at the Desert Inn in Las Vegas for it was a long shot, and the propeller raced like crazy if it did since the throttle was wide open. The plane minus the Pilot wanted to take off, but as long as the tie held the tail wheel I was o.k.

Flying in the high desert of California at dusk was dream-like. The air remained still, as the shadows on the mountains began to lengthen, and the outlines of purple hews painted their images on the barren sands below. The sun started its slide down to India, or wherever it goes at night, and the still desert air smothered the snap, crackle, and pop of the mighty Piper engine.

> *When the sun sinks in the west,*
> *There's a place where I go to rest,*
> *Near Cherokee Canyon,*
> *By Tennessee Rock.*
> *(song written by Woodie Herman)*

The right half of the upper window snapped up into the high wing, and the lower door dropped down and clamped to the body if the pilot chose to be exposed to the elements. The heat thermals were now dissipating and I was gliding across the beginning of time. Soon the twilight turned *noir* and it was time to scurry back to the Army Air Field and tuck the Cub into bed. It was hard not to think of Antoine de Saint Exupery, the well known author of *The Little Prince,* describing in vivid descriptions his early days of flying the North African Desert, in the book, *Sun, Sea and Stars.*

Flying took a back seat in my life for a half decade and was replaced by other activities. I only started up again because of my incredible luck that the government would pay me to pursue aviation. I found it incredible to believe that one of my physician friends was enrolled in a flying program under the G.I. Bill. If that was true 90% of the cost was paid for. I could do that, and indeed I did.

Eagle Aviation was established in 1967, just in time to take advantage of the huge up-tick in private, commercial and foreign student flight training. Much of this was subsidized by programs such as the G.I. Bill or foreign governments and the sky was full of small planes buzzing like fruit flies around ripe peaches, and performing the rigors of training. The radio was full of foreign accents as men from all over the world came to America to learn to fly or upgrade their certificates.

I checked out the program offered by Eagle and signed up for the Commercial Pilots License course without hesitation, a big bite of the apple, since I was working and had two kids at the time. It required 250 hours of additional flight time, ten of which had to be on instruments only and five flying after dark. Here again another ground school was required but by flying at six in the morning or after work in the evening this could be shoehorned into my life. The first training flight was on January 27, 1972 thus ending a ten year absence from the skies.

So you might wonder why the government would pay big bucks for Veterans to learn to fly? It's America, it was part of the G.I. Veterans Bill which was still in force 13 years after the end of the Korean War, and probably was extended by the Vietnam War. The requirements were two or more years of service, possession of a Private Pilot's license, and medical certificate. If you could check all of those boxes the government, through an approved flight school, covered 90% of your training.

Eagle Aviation offered 12 aircraft for training purposes, and the qualified instructors to complete the program. Although early mornings were an option I opted to fly after work and into the evening to build up my time. There was not a coffee shop on any airfield in the Los Angeles Basin that I was not familiar with, and if I had an instructor on board, I always picked up his meal. Those guys were starving to death as they logged time for their Air Transport Rating, which gave them a shot at the big time, flying for an airline.

The closest and most popular practice area for Long Beach and surrounding communities was over the water. In the hay day of training in the 60,'s, and 70's there could be as many as 10 "fly swatters" doing maneuvers over or near the Queen Mary. I always called it "Mig Alley," (Mig was referring to the Russian Fighters that were used by the enemy), a reference to the Chinese-Korean border during the United Nations Police Action. It was not called a 'war' but people died with dog tags on anyway. Mig Alley was where the planes from both sides routinely met daily to duke it out along the Yalu River.

Anyway I am sure you get the picture. It was necessary to have a swivel on your neck to clear the airspace that your plane was operating in before commencing any maneuvers. Of course it was a roll of the dice because the three dimensional situation changed by the second. I'd practice pylon eights over the smoke stacks of the Queen Mary, basically tracing a path through the air drawing a tight eight around two pylons on the surface. This may have been frowned upon, but if so, I never heard about it. I remember one or two mid-air collisions over the harbor during the past 30 years. It seems that today, just to see a light plane in the air is a welcome sight.

After playing 'harbor roulette' I always skipped over to the tiny Meadowlark airport to shoot some short field landings on its 2200 foot long runway. This 1930's field with its small plane tie downs and the classic café was a favorite of mine. On the weekend it was crawling with old timers having breakfast and the field was active with Sunday warriors. The two runways were so short that it was a challenge to put a twin engine plane down there. This throwback setting was just on the east end of the posh Huntington Harbor executive home development.

My concentration on the landing pattern needed to be sharp for success. Slip into the downwind, over the luxurious country club, bend your base leg around the corner of the shopping center, and keep up a high rate of descent as the runway in front of you appeared even shorter than it is. Slow down quickly and taxi back for a couple of more go-arounds before returning to the barn at Long Beach.

One day I noticed a message painted on the runway for all to see, Fee To Land, words that strike fear into every pilots wallet, and which made me angry. Checking the scuttlebutt around Eagle it simply meant that there was no free lunch. Either you landed to eat or you paid to land. The hell with that, I thought, let them catch me! I kept pushing the envelope and never had any idea if those words applied to me for I never had any reaction to my normal landing drill. Besides, eating at the café was not on my landing check list. But the sign stayed in place for only the blind, the cheap, and those with an attitude not to see.

Now I knew that the owner of the airport had his offices in a trailer on the field and no doubt he was well aware of what was going on daily at Meadowlark. This particular day I had made two landings and was on the runway to start the last take off roll of the afternoon, when much to my astonishment an old station wagon comes racing down the runway toward me at a very fast clip. There was no doubt in my mind it was one of the four horsemen of the apocalypse coming for the last round up. I debated whether I could clear the oncoming obstacle or force him to deviate and I decided it was too close to try and I just waited there for my tongue lashing which came without prompting. I nodded, made faint promises and he left as did I. Once back to Eagle I reported the situation to the owner who reported it to the FAA as a dangerous incident. I never returned again and eventually the old country strip was turned into a housing development in booming north Orange County.

As I previously mentioned, the commercial license required five hours of night flying, and ten hours of instrument preparation for the final examination. Night flying is different for obvious reasons, some not readily perceived. The good news is that it is easy to see other planes in a dark sky, but it is hard to spot potential emergency landing spots, tough to judge your distances and even tougher to make a smooth landing. With that said, on a cold and dreary night with plenty of fast moving water laden clouds racing by, my instructor and I set out for the short flight to the Orange County airport, it was time to rack up some real instrument time in the clouds toward the rating requirement.

There was not much chatter on the airways because most of the pros were only doing what they had to do in poor weather, and the amateurs sat on the ground with the sea gulls. Now keep in mind SNA, the airport identification code for John Wayne has but one instrument runway which is used by airliners and all other flights with a second short stub designated for light planes in good weather. This training flight was not only at night but under the 'hood' where pilots wear a hinged visor that hides the upper portion of their face to restrict outside visibility, forcing your eyes on the instrument panel.

It could be compared to *Sea Biscuit* with blinders. Because of the short distance between takeoff and landing we were handed off from Departure Control direct to Approach Control to land and Air Traffic Control was left completely out of the picture. Our fly swatting bird was chugging along at the unremarkable speed of a little over 100 miles an hour and although my instructor could peer into the dark of night and occasionally pick up the bleary ground lights through the wet windshield, I only had the instrument panel, and my charts to guide me along with my radio communication.

Approach would now add spice to our life by vectoring a Hughes Air West F27 Fairchild turbo prop behind us as number two to land. The pilots were trying to rein their bird in before it snuggled in too tight. They had no choice for we were number one to land. Approach asked us to keep up our speed and if we could do a little better they would appreciate it. I answered back "unable," we were peddling as fast as our little legs could move. "O.K. Air West you are going to have to back it off some, the Cessna ahead of you is doing the best it can," said the controller. A short interlude of silence and they acknowledged disgustedly over the public airways that they were doing just that. Right over might, we were number one no matter our size.

Meanwhile, back in my corner, Approach Control handed us off to the tower to land, and we were square on the glide path, heading toward the runway. They could see us on their radar screen but our little Cessna was still in the clouds and I remained under the hood. For all I knew my iron man instructor was eating a corn beef sandwich and had his feet on the panel while I sweated the situation. I juggled the cockpit, checking my approach plate for the next mandatory step down and cranking the radios to intercept the approaching fix as to where we were vertically, and meet the required altitude at each radio interception fix. Air West was extended on his downwind leg but still remained number two. So the problem of the two cozy planes persisted, and the Tower told Air West to cut it back more. I believe their acknowledgement indicated they were hanging the plane on the tips of the props now, and this would be it.

My instructor told me to lift the visor, and as I did we were skirting the bases of the lowest weather and the runway came in to view ahead. I advised the Tower that we had the runway in sight. It was too little, and too late for Air West and they were told to go around and shoot the approach again, one of the last things a pilot of any rank wants to do, the passengers want to do, or the airline wants to pay for. They stepped on the gas pulled up over and to the side of us and another road kill was avoided. Since we had the field in sight, the approach was broken off, and we hustled back to Long Beach. After all, I had to go to work in the morning.

I always dreamed of a twin in my family! No, not a sibling, I am an only child and that is not going to change, besides my parents would have left the country with another me in the family. I was dreaming of a twin engine airplane rating. To fly multi engines it takes a special endorsement from the FAA and another flight test by a designated examiner. It's worth it for there are occasions when an extra engine can come in handy. The fact is if one engine quits, it is a blessing. Yet airmen have been known to kill themselves by throttling back and feathering the wrong engine by mistake. But it is sexy to say "clear, starting number one" to the line boy. Now you are one of the 'big guys.' I went for my check ride on November 19, 1971, and passed thus adding a new endorsement to my ticket and some flight time in the only twin Eagle operated, a Piper *Apache,* probably one of the smallest two engine planes ever manufactured.

The *Apache* was an underpowered aircraft that provided economical if not speedy transportation and was adequate as a primary trainer. To me, it was another "flying rock." When you flew on one engine for training purposes it could not hold altitude and started a gradual descent of 200 feet per minute to ultimately become a 'trench digger," if not corrected. So obviously as far as the safety of two engines was concerned, it probably only delayed death not necessarily precluded it. Aside from the bragging rights and a notch on the belt, the *Apache* was the poor man's route to a multi-engine rating, which in my case was nice to have experienced but of marginal value since I could fly single engine airplanes faster, farther and for less, so why bother?

In 1970 Sharon and I departed on a very adventurous trip that began in Australia and continued on to New Guinea, the Solomon Islands, and the New Hebrides, now called Vanuatu. Leaving New Guinea on the thrice weekly Fiji Airline turbo prop with 50 other passengers, we flew east for three hours to our second stop Honiara, located on the island of Guadalcanal. The name of this obscure atoll became a household word in the Pacific campaign during World War II.

Twenty-six years before our actual visit, a vicious battle between the Japanese and the Americans armed forces took place for six months on land, in the air, and on the sea to determine the victor, and was a harbinger of the war's eventual outcome.

In 1970 approximately 2,000 people visited the Solomon Islands. The Japanese were still returning to gather the bones of dead relatives which were placed in burial jars, and sent home for posterity. While Japan ended up with the sorrow of losing the war, the local Chinese community banked a fortune collecting and selling the scrap metal left behind on the beaches, under the sea, and splattered throughout the jungle, thus becoming extremely prosperous. This scrap now returned to the island and the world in the form of vehicles and heavy equipment from a rejuvenated Japan. Nothing was made in America, how ironic.

There wasn't a travel agency in Honiara and we were fortunate to meet up with a young man from the British High

Commissioner's office, who became a guide. The Solomon Islands were a colonial holding on the wane. I was anxious to see if they had a light plane that I could charter to take 8mm moving pictures of the battle fields from the air, and it so happens they did. The Consulate Flying Club owned the only small plane on Guadalcanal, a Cessna 172, and the chief pilot of Sol Air, the islands air carrier, was the man who had the keys.

I met him at Henderson Field which was named after a U.S. Marine fighter squadron commander who lost his life in the *Battle of Midway*. This was the main and only airport, and today the name has been changed to Honiara International Airport.

We checked over the plane, and he took the right seat, as instructor and I the left, as the pilot, and took off for a 90 minute flight, filming the renowned battlefields, and flying over Iron 'Bottom Sound', where it is said that more ships are sunk than any other place on earth. With that finished he turned the plane over to me and I made three touch and go landings at this historic airfield. I will never forget the thrill, honor, and sense of history I experienced during those moments.

On my return to America it was back to work, playing with the kids, and grinding out the 250 hour minimum requirement for my commercial license. Long distance flying was mandatory, and I decided to take extended trips early, to meet the prerequisite. In all aspects of life, for things I was interested in, I pushed myself, and flying was no different. I wanted to fly a variety of planes, as many different craft as possible. The final tally was 15.

Eagle's fleet included a classic V tailed Beech Bonanza model 35S for rent, which was considered the Cadillac of small aircraft. The plane was manufactured for 35 years and production ended in 1982. The model 35 was considered fast and distinctive with its signature V tail and 'ruddervator' tail assembly. Let's just say it was a classic in the world of private aircraft. Powered by a

Continental 285 horse power fuel injected engine it was ahead of its time, and was built for speed, not economy. If one owned a Beech you never questioned the expenditures.

Sun Valley, Idaho was where my wife Sharon and our two sons, Scott and Robert were going to spend some time with friends in the land of the "rich and famous." The country is spectacular and there was so much to do and see during the majestic summers. I decided I would fly up separately and join them for five days and then return home after ferrying the family to Boise to catch a United Airlines flight to Chicago for a visit. What better aircraft to use than the Bonanza,

The G.I. Bill covered 90% of the flight, and I would pick up the difference. Considerable time was invested in planning this adventure that took me over some of the most barren desert, and by some of the more imposing mountains of our country. I had the power to fly above 15,000 feet, but without oxygen I would need to bump along at 10,000 or below.

I took off on a fine day, was already to Las Vegas in an hour and made the turn north toward Ely, Nevada, my only planned stop for fuel and food. Ely was founded as a stagecoach station during the days of the Pony Express, and the Central Overland Route. Its greatest claim to fame was that former First Lady Pat Nixon was born there. There is absolutely nothing around Ely and the mountains all seem to look the same. I had navigational aids of course, but visually, if it wasn't for old State route 93 winding in front of me, Ely would be easy to miss.

Flying in the western part of our great country is a different experience than cruising east of the Continental Divide. The Rockies, Cascades. Sierra Nevada and the Coastal Range are mountains with impressive altitudes, and narrow passes, rough terrain and strong winds. This topography requires extra vigilance by the pilot, good weather, and alternative plans. Turbocharged engines, high tech navigation systems, and oxygen on board are also assets. Weight and balance checks need to be more exacting, and temperature and runway length are extremely important factors. Many accidents are caused by not calculating this correctly, or at all.

It was coming up on 10:00am and I was hungry and needed to stretch, but I had to set down at Ely to do it. The desert haze was fairly thick but eventually the airport came into sight, and I reported in over the Unicom radio channel that is common at all non-tower controlled fields, and planted rubber to asphalt and taxied over to what looked like the only active part of the facility with a few minimal buildings. I popped the door open, crawled out on the wing, and jumped to the ground. Just then a mechanic strolled over and we exchanged greetings.

I told him I needed fuel and asked how to get to the restaurant on the field? Fuel was no problem, but the restaurant was in town, just three miles down the road. Okay, so how would he suggest I get there? Generously he tossed his car keys at me and said "I'll take care of the plane, you take care of the food". It was a great arrangement. I am not sure such trust or comradeship still exists today. The trip on to Sun Valley was another couple of hours but the time with the family was worth every dime of it. As I made my way north the landscape turned to green, and the temperature dropped, as a few cumulous afternoon 'thunder bumpers' began to form.

At the end of our stay in Sun Valley, with the family on board we hopped over to the United Airlines gate at the Boise Airport for their trip to Chicago. I then headed home, picking up some rain and hail that pinged on the metal skin of the Beech and soared over the Cascades, and on into Oregon, then past beautiful Mount Rainer in all its glory, down the Coast through the San Joaquin Valley and across the Los Angeles Basin, mission accomplished.

I finally passed my Commercial test on the ninth of January, 1972, a full year later, although I slipped the multi-engine rating in between so maybe the lengthy process could be justified. The government coffers were still full so I decided to proceed and achieve the instrument rating next. This would make my skills more adaptable to various weather patterns that are encountered when flying.

The instrument training was challenging and different. Then as now, it comes down to a head game of controlling the airplane, knowing where you are, where your next reporting point is, and keeping your cool when you can't see the ground and flying 'blind' in the clouds. This aspect of flying is simulated by the pilot wearing the infamous hooded device which restricts visibility, to practice in real-time weather when present. It requires considerable faith in planes without auto-pilots and computers. GPS was not a reality yet. The flying is by instruments only, keeping altitude by trim or power adjustments, communicating with the controllers, and navigating by radio fixes. Meanwhile, contemplating where are you, where are you going, and what do you expect to happen next! Not much time left over to think of a cold beer, Monday night football, or a steak dinner.

When under the hood the instructor would say "I've got it," meaning he has control, and then would put the plane into an unstable condition for the student to correct. So the plane is diving, banking, climbing, stalling and then he says, "... it's yours," and what you have is a lot of garbage to clean up to get back to straight and level flight, up to speed and on course. This was a simulation of possible actual conditions where a pilot could lose his directional sense in the clouds. If you failed, the instructor was your back up. Before I was awarded my Instrument license, it was necessary to do the obligatory cross country flight, only this time blind.

We flew from Long Beach to Bakersfield, Santa Barbara and return, all under the hood. My dear friend, Lewis Rosenberg, volunteered to go along so to make it as upscale as possible I decided to fly the Bonanza with all its challenges of having obsolete instruments. Lewis had a nice seat in the rear all to himself while the instructor kept track of me in front. All went well during the five hour run until we were on final approach for Long Beach, on the main runway. I was a bit right of course, but close enough to correct when the instructor told me to raise the hood, because we had the runway in sight, and I no longer would be a draft horse with blinders on.

Just then there was a loud bang, the wind started to blow the charts around in the airplane and I was thinking, "there is a problem, Houston." The instructor turns around and says "What the hell is happening?" The problem was, Lewis had inadvertently lifted the control bar on the rear window and it popped open scaring us all. No doubt he was yelling "...it's the window," as he desperately tried to shut it which he finally did. He still recalls the incident to this day, as do I.

If you fly long enough you see it all. Linda, my present wife and I flew regularly in Arizona, using a fixed base operator out of rural Casa Grande. The state has some dust storms that are doozies, and you need to be vigilant because they come out of nowhere without warning. This particular day we took the Cessna Cardinal aloft for an hour of recreational flying and I took off to the southwest after announcing my intentions on the local Unicom 'party line' radio channel. Not more than a minute elapsed into our departure, when Linda points out a huge dust cloud moving quickly over sections of desert and coming our way. She was almost panting, "There is a giant dust storm to your left, and it is moving this way fast. We need to go back and land now!"

I looked at where she was pointing, and Linda was spot on. When the sun is blotted out and the crows and vultures head for cover, it is time for an immediate decision. "I'm going back now," and I made a 180 degree turn and landed on the same runway going the other way. A fast taxi put us back at the tie down and we raced to secure the small plane as the wind picked up and the sand became blistering. Running for the operations shack, Linda and I waited for it to pass and our blood pressure to recede. The next stop was the nearest watering hole and the early start of 'happy hour.'

I was running out of ratings to acquire, still the G.I. Bill had money to spend on me. It was for educational purposes and with the MBA in my pocket long ago I could still pursue education in the field of aviation. A new amphibian aircraft had recently made its appearance at the field. I have talked to professional airline pilots and although their experience and ratings far exceed mine, I have never run across one with this endorsement.

The flight school was having problems finding an instructor pilot for the program. They settled temporarily on a former Navy aviator by the name of Ernie who repaired instruments on the field and had a pod of his own seaplanes nestled near by. Planes which land on water prefer it to be calm and placid, which the Pacific Ocean is not. The only place that was useable was inside the harbor break water and only in the early morning hours before the wind came up and created waves.

Ernie was a grizzled veteran who was not cut out to instruct civilians. He was a pro as a pilot, and a dud and a crab as an instructor, especially at six in the morning. His eventual replacement by a younger man was a blessing and a factor in me sticking with the program. The course addressed the Lake (brand name) as a plane and a boat and the bulk of the training was landing and taking off and control when it sat in the water, where it turned into a boat.

I was awarded my endorsement after the normal test procedure so familiar in the past and I was anxious to use my skills. Scott my eldest son was the guinea pig for my one and only solo flight. The preflight did not take long on a quiet Sunday morning, in the heat of summer. Indeed it was a weekend and I had flown the plane on weekdays only, and much to my surprise I saw that once we were over the harbor there was no place to land. What had been open space on previous flights was now stern to bow coverage. Anchored or moving pleasure craft sat right in our landing zone.

It was time for a back up plan, and that was to fly down to the Belmont Pier and circle back to take in the situation again. This time there was an indication of a thin blue line of unobstructed water which constituted an unprotected landing area if we were to use it. A boat or Jet Ski might move into it without notice, and make the approach a bit dicey. Once around again and I lined up for the blue water strip. It didn't look like anything was different and my son was keeping his eyes open for any intrusion into the space that we claimed, only known to us of course because not one of those sailors ever expected to see an airplane land in their midst. Once we splashed down I am sure many turned to each other and said something like, "..did you see what I think I just saw?"

The landing was a good one, no boats were sunk or animals hurt and I cracked the fold back roof open and quickly taxied on top of the water (aka step) over to the Queen Mary, an area void of pleasure craft. Now the problem was what to do next? How were we ever going to get out of here I wondered? Looking south, out to the oil islands and the breakwater, I felt like Jack and The Beanstalk, in a forest of giant boat masts, I mean we are sitting a quarter inch off the water and the 50 or more boats in front of us were intimidating to say the least. I pondered the situation, there was no sure answer except just do it or wait 6 hours to dusk, and their departure. I made a 180 degree turn back to the bridge crossing the mouth of the Los Angeles River to claim as much room as I could and reached up to shut the canopy and patted my son on the knee and said "here we go."

Next, I moved the over-head throttle (all amphibians have engines mounted high and away from the water) smoothly and quickly forward, the water remained calm and up on the step we came breaking the suction of the hull and I pulled back on the yoke and the masts fell away as we gained altitude, and we made our way back to the airport. It was the last flight for us because the plane sank a week later next to the Queen Mary, due to a malfunctioning gear door opening on landing and it flipped. The two occupants were able to swim to safety. I have always considered this as another second chance in my life.

In1984 the G.I. Bill which dated back to the end of World War II was destined to expire and any aviation benefits covered under it were heading south at Mach speed. Pilots in training were flying late into the night and before day break to get their covered time in. I still had accrued money for my educational benefits and I rooted around for one last stand. Jim's Air was offering DC-3 training, the double catch here was that they were in San Diego, and that the student had to put up his own money and bill the Veterans Administration. As much as I always wanted to fly the Douglas icon it was not to be, but I hated to have money on the card and not use it.

The saying goes, 'if the wing (blade) is flying faster than the fuselage, it is dangerous, and thus it must be a helicopter." I was always wary of helicopters, considering them more like flying lawnmowers. Hughes Aircraft Company made 2,800 or more Model 300 copters during the Vietnam War era. The same flight school that had the Lake Amphibian had a number of these and offered flight training under the generous government program.

I am not sure what possessed me, but I signed on for this curriculum and was accepted. The Hughes is a two place copter of the era and was hot in summer because of its large Plexiglas cockpit, thus it was flown with the doors removed. Flying the 300 demanded that your hands and feet be glued to the controls until you were back on the ground. If your nose ran you were out of luck because it was not possible to remove your hands to wipe it, and there wasn't an autopilot system. Of course the crew was snuggly harnessed in but with the doors off I had a slight tendency to lean the other way when banking to the left and my left hand which was gripped to the altitude and throttle control (called a collective) would rise a tad, and the copter gained fifty feet; a bad habit that I never broke, and could only compensate for it when flying.

I assume that I did not have enough stress in my every day life without flying something as foreign and complicated as a helicopter, which takes a very deft touch and is a totally different approach than flying a fixed wing aircraft.

My instructor was a former Army rotor wing pilot who thought he was still instructing military students. He was said to have flown in Vietnam and I respected him for that and his abilities, but his teaching techniques were based upon "tough love," and he made me so nervous I requested another instructor. I could not take being yelled at, especially in a machine where I was not comfortable. This turned out to be the right move and a better fit as I plowed my way through 21 hours of air time in this unforgiving beast. If you don't believe me, try a simulated auto-rotation for an emergency landing as a starter. The craft drops out of the sky from 300 feet above ground, and responds to increased power and recovers just 20 feet above the practice pad if correctly executed. In a real emergency this one time cushion of energy built up in the rotor is the only hope of a safe outcome when the engine quits.

When the instructor told me I was ready to solo with 18 hours of instruction in, I was sure I was going to kill myself. It was time to "man up," and the noisy contraption with whirling blades, open sides, and incredible noise, was ready to gyrate off the ground, and for me to prove myself. The Tower cleared me for takeoff and a trip around the Long Beach Airport doing the standard pattern and return to the pad. I made it around the airport without mishap and brought it back in one piece, and was glad to have my instructor step back in once again and head for home base.

The G.I. Bill and flight training soon ended for all of us in that the legislative mandate expired and it wasn't renewed again. Boy, did I get my money's worth of Federal tax money back in spades! Those were the good old days, and I was able to participate and accomplish the unimaginable.

My adventures in aviation still had another twist to go, and in 1978 when Bob Slatton owner and real estate broker of CIA properties said to me in a job interview "..I see you are a pilot, tell me about it. I am looking for a pilot." I paraded out my credentials and told him I was current on mandatory flight reviews and had a current medical and radio license. His glacial expression melted a bit and he said, "I am looking more for a pilot than an agent, do you have any interest?" Of course I did, as long as he would also take me on as an agent. It was a handshake deal, I would be the pilot for his best client, a cardio-vascular surgeon with a high profile medical group working at St Mary's Hospital, and Slatton would tutor me in the fine points of 1031 real estate exchanges. One of us fell short on this agreement, as his mentoring was non-existent.

The plane that I was upgraded to was a four year old Cessna 210L retractable gear model with a turbo-charged engine and portable oxygen system. At that time it was considered one of, if not the best, high performance single engine plane in the air, and was in production from 1957 until 1985. Best yet, the doctor would pay for my transition training and testing. It was a coincidence that the aircraft was based once again at Eagle Aviation and I would be back where I started.

So how come a physician, a 'Super Doc,' had a plane, much less one like this? The reason was the Doc, as I always called him, had widespread investments in Utah, California and Montana, and he needed the plane for his workers and family for transportation into remote parts of the western United States. My obligation was to fly when his people needed to go anywhere, otherwise the $250,000 dollar aircraft was mine to use as I saw fit, all I had to do was gas it up. When it came to flying opportunities things just seemed to fall my way, although I stretched my abilities to match the obligations. The Cessna Centurion II would be the fastest plane I'd ever fly. With the turbo charged engine it could easily cruise over 20,000 feet above sea level and grind out 235 MPH as a true airspeed, (still air, no wind). Oxygen on board was a real plus when you challenge the jagged peaks of the western United States. I would have to put my abilities in gear to be equal to the plane.

Soon after I signed on the Doc, the partner of Slatton, and the Ranch Boss wanted to make the trip up to the southern spread near Cedar City, Utah. I had no idea what to expect, and the small unimproved strip there turned out to be gravel which really chewed up the prop from flying pebbles. That would be a no-no in the future. What was not expected was the method of rousing the ranch to come down to the strip and pick up the passengers. This was accomplished by a wide circle over the homestead at 500 feet until they came out and waved a white towel in acknowledgement. Soon a pick up truck with a plume of dust behind it was racing down to the strip to meet us. Remember, this was before cell phones were in existence.

For the five years that I flew for the Doc and his people the routine was always the same, only the destinations would change. We'd always leave at sun up which required me to rise at 3:00 am. Next stop was Spires all night coffee shop for breakfast and a study of the plan and maps for the day. Once the bill was paid the time was drawing down on 5:30 am, and I would mosey over to the weather bureau which was then based on the third floor of the Long Beach terminal. This was a 24/7 operation but many of the times I found the late shift asleep on the floor and I would just do my own research. My cardinal rule was, never wake a sleeping Samoan.

It was just a short drive now over to the tie down area and the simple gate that allowed me onto the field. My, how things have changed since 9/11! Recreational flying was always demanding in high density urban areas before, but now it must be extremely stressful. It will ruin your day to be confronted by an Air Force fighter and forced to land because of some unintended violation. Even though there are more sophisticated tools for pilots, I believe the pressures are too great to fully recapture the ambiance of the days I enjoyed.

After putting my flight case in the back seat I'd pull out a flash light and start my preflight inspections, which included dipping the fuel tanks, draining them to check for water, and compare the high wet mark against the gauges which are always suspected of inaccuracies. Then it was time to file my instrument flight plan. When I was ready to taxi I was required to call Departure Control to pick it up, and be ready to copy the clearance as it was read back. The controllers fed your flight into the flow of traffic, and advised you when to taxi and depart. I am not sure in today's aviation world of the electronic word, that copy and read-back is still used but it was always a challenge because the tower spoke extremely fast and you needed to use abbreviations to keep up, and to understand them when you were done.

Cessna 2049 Delta is cleared to taxi to runway 30 and hold short for further instructions. You are cleared to Cedar City Utah via Vector 23, using the 80 degrees radial of the Seal Beach VOR, crossing Elmo at 1500 feet or below no earlier than...."

The owner and/or passengers always arrived promptly at 6:30 am just as the sun came peeking up over the lip of the eastern horizon, and usually we were first off the field for the day. Traffic was always minimal as we sped across a sleepy basin heading into the blinding rising sun, spreading its severe golden light across a waking Los Angeles. Today we'd pass through Monument Valley, Utah, home to many of Director John Ford's western classics like *Stage Coach, Fort Apache, Rio Grande,* and *She Wore A Yellow Ribbon* to name just a few. Miles ahead we could see the unique rock formations turn pink to red, and then to yellow-orange, as the sun made its ascending arc. We were in God's country, and our Centurion aircraft was but a speck in the grip of the time machine of life.

I am not here to create "hanger flying" drama, but I will relate a few incidents that I will never forget, but surmounted. The Doc worked closely with the U.S. Bureau of Land Management in leasing ground from the government and taking advantages of other services they provided. Although his holdings might total thousands of acres of grazing land, he was leasing the majority of it from the government for a dollar an acre per year. He had made arrangements to pick up an Agricultural Agent in Bakersfield and fly him to Escalante, Utah to check out something to do with alfalfa, which his cattle needed when the grass was in short supply.

We zipped up there, stopped to pick up the waiting agent and proceeded on to Escalante, a blip on the map. Once there I catnapped in the pilots lounge and then checked with flight service on the weather for the return trip. They expected no change except for the normal windy conditions that are a given in the afternoon desert. But indeed what you get in the way of the weather is what you see, and not what is forecasted or expected.

I had filed an instrument plan back to Bakersfield even though the weather was good. I always liked being under the guidance of Air Traffic Control (ATC) if something went amiss, for they would be following the flight on their screens.. I had been handed off from Albuquerque ATC to Los Angeles which was physically based in Palmdale. When changing radio frequencies to report in I could distinctly here thunderclaps in my headset, and on the distant horizon black clouds were making their way up from the south, a sign of a monsoon rain storm that sometimes takes place in this area during the summer months. I asked the controller, "Are you having a heavy rain storm?" "Yes, heavy rain, thunder and lightening." He replied. This was never forecasted before we took off.

Cruising comfortably at 16,000 feet and on oxygen the swirling black mass, dark as a sinner's soul in church on Sunday was making its way toward us at an alarming rate. I don't like thunder and lightening, when I am in the air, nor doing windows for that matter, but the weather was in front of me, not below, and I would have to deal with it. I took immediate action to see if we could climb above the disturbance, but failed to ask permission from ATC to change altitude and receive approval from them. I should have just cancelled the flight plan and they would not have reported on the radio, "...a plane is out of control and going through 20,000 feet." I finally prevailed and reached 24,000 feet, just about maximum altitude for the Centurion and climbed above the storm which was disturbing my afternoon, and I found Bakersfield right where it was supposed to be.

Upon landing we all 'kissed the ground' for the good fortune of being there. The Doc wanted me to continue flying to Los Angeles after dropping the Agent off, but I was rung out. I found him a commuter flight on USAir and told him I was staying the night and I would bring the plane down the next day, and that was that.

I used the plane for personal travel, especially up to Stockton, California to visit my Aunt Ellen, as I called my grandmother who lived 35 miles up the road in Lodi. For many years I either made the six hour drive or flew on Pacific Southwest Airlines into Stockton and rented a car. Stockton was now eliminated as a stop and that left flying into Oakland or Sacramento, so it made sense to fly there myself.

On this particular trip my sons Scott, 12, and Robert, 10, traveled with me and they were pleased to go as I remember it. They had flown in different planes numerous times, but I always took them separately for safety reasons. It was a fine California day as we crossed the Tehachapi Mountains, when out of nowhere the plane shook, and we all were startled by a single miss, a stutter in the engine. "What was that?," Scott said, and Rob echoed his question. The roughness did not repeat itself, and I calmed the boys down. Because they had flown a number of times before in a light plane, they backed off.

Crossing the mountains and entering the San Joaquin Valley, it still was another 45 minutes before being vectored into the long instrument approach for 29, the main Stockton runway. Approach control now handed us over to the Tower and we were cleared to land. Almost immediate they advised us, on the radio for all to hear, "...ah 49 Delta, are you aware that you are trailing smoke?" We were not but *Golly Miss Molly* we were now!

The boys were looking outside the windows frantically, Scott said "I don't see any smoke on this side, how about you Rob", who was in the back looking out the other side. "...don't see any here." I must say I remained calm because this had happened to me once before at Lindbergh Field in San Diego when the Tower asked for a flyby with the glasses trained on the plane for the same reason, but this proved negative.

I felt that the plane was not in danger, the kids weren't going to jump ship, and all was o.k. Then the tower announced that they were going to roll the emergency equipment, and ahead of us down the side of the runway came two fire trucks, their rotating lights flashing emergency red. This really juiced the boys up, but we landed without incident and taxied over to the fixed base operators tie down. No request was necessary to get them to deplane.

I will say, on the return flight, they stood 20 feet away from the airplane as I warmed it up for a period of time to see if it was blowing smoke, but it wasn't. I finally got them in the plane, and the return trip was uneventful, which was good since the cabin was a bit tense as the memories of rolling fire equipment danced through their heads.

The Doc's summer home lay in the northwest corner of the rough and tumble state of Montana, about 50 miles south of the Canadian border. I flew the trip to Libby twice which was the nearest airport, and I passed over some of the most beautiful foliage running along the Snake River in Idaho, a real treat from the air. At this time northern Idaho and Western Montana still lacked continuous radar coverage and it was necessary to report in as we used to do. To say that the weather was unpredictable would be an understatement. We had hail on the Fourth of July, case closed.

The flight was over eight hours each way plus a stop for refueling and food. On one trip I dropped the Doc off at another home he had in Fallbrook, near San Diego and that added another two hours and I was really tired upon returning to Long Beach.

The first time we went up I remember he and his wife as the only passengers on board. The second time I had some of the children and the Doc and his wife, who were already there, came back with me on the return flight. The unique thing is I became part of their family which seemed to fit in with his persona having been raised on a Minnesota farm in his youth. He retained his interest in agriculture and animals during his entire life, cardio-vascular surgeon or not. They were just down to earth people, and it was a comfortable relationship.

I bunked on the front porch and went inside to use the one bathroom. There was no privacy since the porch was also the front door, but I managed. I ate with the family and if they went somewhere, if I chose to, I would tag along. The property was located on a small lake full of logs and stumps, populated with trout and snags that kept any fisherman busy unsnarling his line. It was surrounded by small mountains that were home to hooting owls, honking geese, quaking ducks and silent loons.

The front yard, defined by a few fallen tree trunks, was probably an acre and seemed to be the daily refuge for our own resident moose. He wasn't out of Disney, for he was ugly, bad tempered, huge, and his harsh breath pierced the northern air. We gave him his space and he took it, snorting and pawing the ground to mark his territory.

Occasionally we took an old rowboat out on the log filled, mountain surrounded, rustic lake, and trolled for trout with a spinner or worms. They were easy to catch, the hard part was to keep the line from snagging on the driftwood, and in 40 minutes there were more caught than we could eat. Not only did the Doc haul in the most fish, being a surgeon, he cleaned them in a nanosecond, It was a unique experience, living with a family that was so very different than mine, or the way I was raised, yet feeling very much at home with them in the rustic Northwest.

I could not believe that on the Fourth of July we had hail to welcome the day. I had planned to take the plane solo over to Coeur d'Alene to fill up our oxygen supply for the long trip home but after warming up the engine, and hearing the hail on its wings I decided against this. On the eight hour trip home we passed the oxygen mask around the cabin when the plane flew above a comfortable level in order to breath. It worked, though I am sure we violated some rules on safe flying.

"Eat drink and be merry for tomorrow we will be in Utah," is what our T shirts should have read, for we spent enough time flying over there. Of course this refers to the Mormon dominance in the State, where frivolity and alcohol is frowned upon. The Doc's plane had never visited the northern holding called the Max Tanner Ranch, a property with a swagger to it. It was located in the County of Box Elder on the Nevada, Idaho border, that stretched all the way east to Nebraska.

The Tanner Ranch, which the Doc had recently purchased, was a historic property whose legacy dated back 125 years, when the brothers Alma and Valison Tanner became the first settlers in this vast desolate plateau of the western desert. The property was one of a few isolated homesteads near the hamlet of Grouse Creek, an area bordered by the Wasatch Mountains to the east and the Raft River Mountains on the North, and hidden in solitude at 5,331 feet above sea level. The sun comes, up, the sun goes down, and life repeats itself for folks living here.

The tiny Grouse Creek community is nestled in a valley that was once the route of the original California Trail from the Missouri River to the 'Golden State". It is so isolated that the inhabitants maintain a volunteer emergency ambulance service to evacuate patients over the scrambled dirt roads to the nearest medical facility across the Idaho border. Aside from being a historic ranch the Max Tanner was home to President Gerald Ford's son Steve when he spent a number of months working the range as a cowboy dude.

I researched the, Notices to Airmen Guide to find out about the airstrip that was rumored to be in the area. It revealed a field 45 minutes west of Salt Lake City located next to the Lucin VOR (Visual Omni Range) navigational beacon. What caught my eye was the notation, *land at your own risk*, something I had never seen before in the manual. This got me to wondering.

Bob, his last pilot never chose to take the plane there for whatever reason, but the Doc was hot to fly in and the calculations with a stop for fuel and food in Salt Lake City put us into the field in about seven hours. We made good time in calm air to our Salt Lake City lunch and refueling stop, and then took off for the 45 minute journey west to the mysterious field.

The red and white standard VOR transmitter was easy enough to see from the air and no doubt we were there, but where was the field? I verified once again the Morse code signal emitting from the range to confirm it was the Lucin VOR, but the field remained impossible to find. From the air the ground around it looked like a patch of rough scrub with a hint of a track in the middle saturated with wild tumble weed, brush, and ruts which were evident everywhere.

I commenced a sweeping turn to fly back east and over it again so we both could peer down, but nothing had changed, no field had appeared in the meantime. Our other options were limited to returning to Salt Lake City and renting a car or trying our luck south at the airport in Wendover, which may or may not offer a rental agency.

"I don't see the field, do you," I finally said to my benefactor and passenger, as he continued to peer out the right side of the Cessna. I was set to make another pass from the west when a truck with a plume of dust was spotted on the dog leg of the road that led to our proposed destination. We watched it until it came to the end of the road and stopped. I checked the dust for a wind drift angle just in case we found the field. Two men emerged and stared right at us, a low flying plane looking for a non-existent field which no doubt, was not a regular occurrence. We looked hard back at them for any sign of encouragement, but they were linemen for the county and turned their attention back to the telephone line which ended there.

At this point I said, "Maybe the runway is the road?" or some other nonsensical utterance which has never made sense to me over the many years since. But I can't say the Doc said, "No, it can't be, it looks awful narrow with a dog leg, and planes are meant to land on runways. Are you out of your mind?" No, he did not say that, instead "let's do it, land on the road." My response was brief, "O.K. it's your plane."

The gravel road ran from the north, and half circled a 2,000 foot rise and then doglegged to the south for another mile or so. There was still no indication of any significant wind and the surface appeared to be gravel. The width and length of the road was only a "guesstimate," but would be a huge factor. My hope was that the evening news lead story would not be 'plane crashes trying to land on rural road,' if I were to miscalculate.

I dropped to about 800 feet, and headed north deciding to land toward the south and take my chances stopping before the road did rather then the reverse that presented me with the bend in the road instead. I must say that landing on a road was something I never did before, nor any time since. I really don't remember having any moments to second guess the decision or to be scared. This was certainly the time when I put all my experience and training to test. The decision was made!

The visibility was clear as glass, and it was easy to monitor my progress along the straight part of the road, meanwhile keeping the 2000 foot rise in view, for I would need to make my base leg (90 degree turn) just south of it, in order to line up with our proposed runway. The moment of truth was upon us, as both our lives were in my hands! The gear was down and the flaps were at full deflection as the speed bled off and I made the commitment to land.

All was on track as I swung south and on to final approach. My altitude was dropping nicely and I appeared to be right in the middle of the fast approaching road. It felt good. I adjusted the trim slightly upward relieving the back pressure on the wheel and flared the plane to land at as slow a speed that was prudent because the surface appeared to be gravel.

The plane settled nicely and the wheels touched down, but just after the nose wheel planted the left tire dipped over the unanticipated shoulder of the narrow road, and the plane started to tilt dangerously to the left. I gave a quick right kick to the rudder and it popped up again and as the dust rose and the pings of the pebbles bounced off the cowling, we came to a controlled stop. I immediately shut down the engine and we both just sat there to collect racing thoughts and replace our hearts back in the right place from where they escaped. The linemen were now walking down the road toward us and I asked the Doc to talk to them and find out if this was the elusive airport, the one in the Guide that said '*land at your own risk*'!

As he went to meet them I got out to check the airplane for any damage, and it was then I realized that the road only had clearance of a foot on each side of the main wheels before the 4" shoulder began, truly lucky indeed. The line man came back with the Doc and told us that the field was only 50 yards away and was never used. It sure looked different from the air. They helped us push the plane across a cattle guard in the road which would have destroyed the nose gear if we had crossed it. As we pushed the Cessna over to the unimproved field they kept saying that, "...they never saw a plane land on a road before." I had to agree with them. I did return once more to this fateful place where I was put to the test, but that time I knew where the field was, and it was 'duck soup.'

On both trips I was consigned to the cowboy bunkhouse which was nothing more than a shack; one time with Lynn, the Ranch Boss and over-seer of all the agricultural holdings, and the second time by myself. The Doc slept in the rancher's home as did his wife when she came.

"What's that noise I asked him as we were settling down to bed?" You mean the scurrying around coming from the roof?" "Ya that's it, listen, hear it now," I said? "Oh, what is it with you city guys, those are just rats!" I am still a city guy and never did get used to the rats in the rafters, but a bunk was a bunk, and I was just a crew member.

It was in August of 1981 that I made my last flight from Long Beach to Riverside and return, parked the plane and walked away from flying. The Doc mentioned that his wife had been taking flying lessons for a number of years, and she was ready to take over the work that I did. The upside was I could still use the plane as before if I desired. That was very decent of him but I am not a moocher or a free-loader and it just didn't seem equitable. Besides I was no longer associated with CIA properties so I decided that it just wasn't right to continue. It had been a good run, no regrets and great memories, of the rising sun in the morning and the still air that accompanied it. The desolation of the southwestern part of our country, the golden Snake River running through Idaho, the comradery of pilots and controllers on the radio, the heavy traffic in Los Angeles and Las Vegas, and the unpredictable weather which became the wildcard in the whole scheme of things, who knows, one day I might write a book, I thought.

Thirty-two years have passed and I have not touched the controls of a light plane since. The desire had been met, and the cost was prohibitive to continue. Besides I was raising a family at the time with Sharon.

There has been plenty to keep me busy. Linda and I were in Europe in September of 1991 and we were completely unaware of the following story in the Long Beach Press Telegram until I returned. It concerned the first C-17 giant Military Transport roll-out and it took place on a Sunday on the west side of the Long Beach Airport where the McDonnell-Douglas manufacturing facility was located.

"....However the monumental event (C-17 Military Cargo Plane Roll out and Flight) was tragically disrupted by a sputtering, single-engine plane which lead to an orange colored skyline of

flames, casting most in the crowd...into an all time low." (from a Long Beach Newspaper).

The accident was investigated by the National Transportation Safety Board which described briefly the planes immediate previous history, its pre-flight, take-off and its demise. The cause of the accident according to report LAX91FA393;

"..an undetermined loss of engine power and the pilots failure to maintain airspeed during the forced landing."

There were three fatalities; the Doc's wife and two of his children. I had known and traveled with all of them, and they were wonderful people. Flying in light planes has its dangers and unfortunately they suffered the maximum penalty. The Doc no doubt grieved for the rest of his life and I believe the other daughter continued in the field of aviation. I am fortunate that it didn't happen on my watch.

Airplanes of course are inanimate objects, but it definitely was a dear part of my life at the time and is certainly a very fond memory today. I have but one picture of the plane which was taken at the northern ranch by Mrs. Doc, on our last trip up there. It sits alone on the tumble weed strewn field with nothing in the picture except 50 miles of distant sky; a moving portrait that tells it all.

Those that get a second chance are blessed. We are all just passing through life like trains, and just leave the station at different times.

Gene went to Francis Parker from 1946-1954 and attended all classes in this building. It has been replaced by a newer structure.

My family's beautiful apartment on the Gold Coast of Chicago. Circa 1948.

Family picture aboard the SS *Santa Paula* steamship in the eastern caribbean 1948.

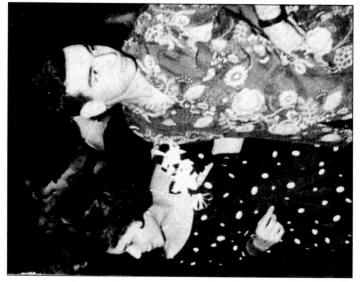

We dated our classmates until we graduated from Francis Parker

The 1947 Harley Davidson motorcycle used during my University days.

KTKT-FM - Classical music studio in Tucson where I worked as a DJ in 1958. Photo by Russ Jackson. CDJ is not identified.

JONES (LEFT) AT END OF QUEST

The "Great Huachuca Gold Hunt". Picture appeared in Life Magazine.

Migrant worker homes which served as base housing for all ranks at Camp Irwin, CA.

ZBT Fraternity House 1956. Gene's Dad was in the same fraternity at the University of Illinois. Gene is third from left, front row.

Gene and Sharon were married in June, 1959, at the Guild Hall, Ambassador West Hotel.

Promotion ceremony to 1st Lieutenant, Camp Irwin, CA, 1961. (L-R Colonel John Prokop, Gene, wife Sharon)

In front of base theater.

Military Flying Club Piper Cub. With no electrical system. It was necessary to hand prop to start. 1960, Camp Irwin, California.

Civilian Air Museum For City?

Old Airliners 'Shrine' Sought

Feeling it only proper that the history of commercial aviation deserves a shrine of its own, 26-year-old Eugene W. Lassers of Burlingame has embarked on an ambitious project.

Lassers, a United Air Lines parts purchaser who lives at 405 Concord Way, envisions a huge museum that will house either actual or large [?] of the pioneer pist[?] aircraft on wh[?] mercial end[?] vanced t[?] tus.

themselves will involve huge sums of money."

Most of the d[?] ble planes, such a[?] able workh[?] er so e[?] that[?]

Talks Set On Aircraft Museum He **Save Planes' Drive Gr**

Seek to Preserve Aircraft

UAL Newcomer Founder of SFPCA

Flight L[?] Back [?] Of Air C[?]

Commerce Aircraft Site Se[?]

The future home of the [?] for the Preservation of C[?] cial Aircraft [?]

Drive Underway

for the Preser-[?]cial Air[?] [?]ablish

at the Metropolitan Oakland International Airport, is conducting a drive for members.

Eugene W. Lassers, founder [?] the organization, said the [?] membership fee in-[?]ription to the [?] publica-

Senators Back Aircraft Museum

Airliner Museum Is Proposed To Exhibit Commercial Craft

U. S. Senators Clair En[?] new Metropolitan Oakland

Air Muse[?] Talks Sl[?]

Eugene W. Lassers, founder and chairman of the Society For the Preservation of Commercial Aircraft, will fly to Washington, D. C., this month with Philip S. Hop-

MUSEUM SPARKPLUG EUGENE lASSERS SHOWS PIONEER AIRLINER
Home for commercial craft would be built here on donated land. (Stor

Bay Area aircraft museum sought

By DEREK SCHOEN

THE BAY AREA MAY SOME DAY BOAST

dled with old, out-of-use planes which they must either put in storage or junk for parts. Both of

craft Museum Plan Gains Sup[?]

Museum Plan Gains Support

Support for establishment of an air museum has been given by California senators Clair Engle and Thomas H. Kuchel to the Society for Preservation of Commer[?]

'HALL OF FAME' AIR MUSEUM

High Officials Lend Backing

Newspaper clippings about the Society For The Preservation of Commercial Aircraft

United Airlines Junior Achievement Program. Seated, V.P. of maintenance, William "Dusty" Rhodes, one of General Douglas MacArthur's personal pilots in WW II.

The "Doc's" Cessna 210T Centurian on a wind swept unimproved field at Grouse Creek, Utah.

Junior high students star in trivia quiz on America's presidents

PERSONALITY PROFILE

Fellow Guest Lecturer Gene Lassers

Gene Lassers has been associated with the field of aviation for 45 years. His extensive aviation experience, numerous published articles and b... have enabled him to b... a highly qualified re... on industrial... Hughes...

...ose and Personal with ...ard Hughes

by Dave Lowe

Gene Lassers never met Howard Hughes, but he knows him intimately. In the many years he's researched ...fe, Lassers has con... ...corded oral inter... ...ople who were ...of this elusive ...genius.

...gly, Gene ...

Gene is the Oral Historian for... green Museum at McMinnvi... which now displays ...

"Spruc...

Gene Lassers

...rian of Evergreen Avia- ...Minnville, Oregon, this ...ughes' life is now the ...Hughes, Mr. Lassers ...ngine and seaplane ...5 different types of ...ored a book, many ...al video presenta- ...l the Island Prin- ...ps and for many ...travel program. ...organization in ...and resources ...rsity. He

Dear Gene.

On behalf of our Board of Directors and staff, I want to thank you for your most interesting and informative presentation today on Howard Hughes and his Flying Boat. All of us were impressed with the high quality of your research as well as the attractive format in which it was presented. As the second program in our Flight Path Speaker Series, your presentation is of major assistance in our establishing the prestige and credibility of this series...

...ion, including never-...
...sound bites of Hughes himse...

Dear Mr. Lassers:
I want to thank you for the marvelous exhibit of railroad photographs! Our staff and library users liked them a lot. I think more people enjoyed this exhibit than any we've had for a long time.

Judith Fraser, Department Librarian
Performing Arts Department

From The ...ublisher's Notebook:

...sted a nationally-televis... program for many years, whic... extensive coverage in the trav... Lassers holds a twin engine C... cial Aviation License, with rati... different aircraft, and his ... include seaplane...

Long Beach businessman Gene Lassers and I serve on a charitable board of directors in ... g Beach. I know him as an astute real estate inv... — and a dedicated non- profit board m... ...ise to me recently ... last year.

INDEPENDENT (AM) *** PRESS-TELEGRAM (PM)

West Side panel re-elects Lassers

By MARY ELLIS CARLTON
Urban Affairs Editor

Businessman Eugene Lassers was unanimously re-elected chairman Wednesday night of the Project Area Committee for the West Long Beach Industrial Redevelopment Project...

I would like to think that our inquiries regarding your suggestion which is estimated to be in excess ... through The Salvation ... has made this donation of food stuffs, available to the needy ...ver want... of twenty million dollars, widely. He an... enjoy the company o...
...ree sons and four grandchildren

Gene Lassers presents today at 10:00am in the Hollywood Theatre.

Some memories in print.

Chapter 7

You Don't Have to Know English to Write

Over the years I have written an estimated fifty articles for various publications. It has enriched my life, introduced me to people that I never would have met, and acquainted me with matters which I knew nothing about. I try to grab a reader's attention by using bold, unexpected and clever verbiage. Here are some brief examples

Western Flyer *The Good Year Blimp*

"It is really tough to look over-weight even if your three sisters, who you seldom see, are confronted with the same problem. I mean, who would like to gross-out at 12,320 pounds...?"

Military Magazine *Eggs over easy with meatballs*

"Charlie Akers went to work on the morning of 7 December 1941. He wasn't looking for a fight, but he found one anyway. This is the story of a Pearl Harbor survivor."

Airliners Magazine *Slow Freight*

"....the two pilots now seated were bantering the checklist back and forth. Flashing hands and barking voices created a panorama of excitement, culminating in the spine-tingling shout: Clear! No. 1 engine cranked slowly,and became a blur as it burst into a smoke-filled roar across the silent airport."

Aircraft Illustrated (United Kingdom publication) *The Howard Hughes Flying Boat*

"This year marks the 40th anniversary of the one and only flight of Howard Hughes famous flying boat...This feature by Eugene Lassers has been crafted by actual interviews with five of the most prominent people..."

Diverse subjects, catchy phrasing or snappy introductions were always what I tried to achieve in my writing repertoire. Humor never hurt, and my thoughts tread through my eclectic mind to find the right word combination to my ear. I never did much with my unknown aptitude over the years, until out of desperation, and engulfed by total boredom it appeared as if a closet unlocked. As an agent in my late 30's, I was working an open house apartment complex for a real estate company when I discovered writing. The first weekend I spent with a table and chair, looking at a blank wall in an empty apartment building with few interested renters stopping by. The next weekend I decided it would be different.

I brought my old antiquated Royal typewriter with me and decided to see if I could knock out an article about the subject which I knew best, aviation. It was a start and from there I would go on to deliver a slew of articles to a gaggle of publications, publish two books and produce a three lecture series with power point presentations on Howard Hughes. All of this gave me entrée into a new world of adventure, and personalities which I never would have known. I found out that people like to talk about themselves, and others are suspicious of what your motives are for doing the story in the first place. Because of my free-lance writing I came across a secret tape recording of Howard Hughes and his New York attorney Chester Davis about the infamous Clifford Irving book writing caper and the specious faux book on Hughes by Robert Eaton, Lana Turner's husband at the time, which was being syndicated by *House Beautiful* magazine.

My introduction into the field of writing was through the doors of aviation, as I was an active pilot, and this was a subject I was very familiar with. One story led to another and the first one published in the *Western Flyer newspaper* eventually resulted in being appointed an Associate Editor. Writing would allow exposure to a variety of interesting experiences and people. One such opportunity was riding the Continental Airlines Boeing 727 simulator when the company headquarters was still in Los Angeles. Because Ralph Reno, a well known race pilot kept his North American AT6 race plane at Eagle Aviation, where I was doing my training, I had the opportunity to meet and see him at times during those years. Ralph was a Flight Standards Captain for Continental Airlines, a position which involved testing other pilots for their knowledge and skills, a mandatory requirement by the Federal Aviation Administration regulations. He was aware of my free-lance writing and invited me to come over to Continental and run through a complete crew recertification which would involve one of the Boeing 727 flight simulators located at their training facilities at LAX. This would be a first and I was excited to get an inside view of airline training.

On the appointed day I arrived for the afternoon session, which was just about to start. Ralph was in his airline uniform and the three-man crew was all dressed in street attire. One even had bib-overalls on. He was in the process of bringing them up to date on new regulations from the FAA, flight directives from the company and current line problems, including recent operational incidents.

In an hour we moved from the classroom to the simulator hanger which contained six of the ungainly Singer-Link monster simulators that by the 1970's had replaced the use of aircraft for flight checks (continued training and educational sessions). Before the simulator a group of pilots would go aloft with instructors who created abnormal and sometimes dangerous situations for testing purposes. Over the years the use of actual aircraft led to a number of training incidents which now were averted by the use of this equipment. Simulators were far safer and less expensive to operate than an actual aircraft. You never read about a simulator crashing, where there were numerous training accidents and fatalities in actual aircraft.

The inside of the Continental trainer was set up just like a Boeing 727 cockpit except that there was room for the instructor's console in the middle that was used to create various conditions, monitor the system, and gave the examiner a means to create normal and abnormal operating parameters during the testing. Once they were set to start up he yelled for me to bring a desk chair on to the simulator flight deck and latch the wooden door. He ran the complete program from missed approaches to engines fires and stuck landing gear. My article detailing the experience appeared in the *Western Flyer*, a regionally syndicated aviation newspaper.

Aero was a sister publication to Private Pilot, a magazine where my stories frequently appeared. When it was decided to write up the brand new Piper Aircraft Saratoga, a six place single engine airplane they asked me if I would like the assignment. So what's not to like? They were going to fly me to Denver in December, but that was changed to Phoenix because of heavy weather. They'd hand the plane over for three days, pay for all my expenses, and the Saratoga would be dropped off back in Long Beach, California. I enlisted a friend to help me with the assignment, he would fly and I would write. It worked out well. I received the byline and the money; he went on to be a Captain for American Airlines. Things are not always equitable in life. The story opened like this.

Aero Magazine *The new Piper Aircraft Saratoga*

"Only mad dogs and Englishmen would travel to Denver after that city was paralyzed by what has been called the "snow storm of the century," but that is where we planned to pick up a brand new Piper Saratoga...."

Interviewing people and writing stories creates the opportunity for introductions and insights that are unexpected. A story about an Executive Lear jet which was being tested to confirm that a mechanical 'squawk' was addressed and corrected before it was put back into service brought a surprise revelation. It really turned out to be a "double lucky." The two pilots I rode with, also flew the *Lady Barbara,* Frank Sinatra's private jet based at the Long Beach Airport. This was due to the fact that *Old Blue Eyes* Budweiser Beer distributorship was located nearby.

The 45 minute test ride took place over Catalina Island and involved raising the nose of the aircraft into a stall position (where the airflow over the wings is diminished and lift eventually bleeds off) to see if the "stick shaker," a mandatory tool in modern jet powered aircraft reacted appropriately to indicate a stall to the crew. They told me that with jet aircraft a tail slide can occur during this maneuver where the plane starts sliding backward because the angle of attack is too high, that this can be hard to break out of and could be fatal! Did I still want to go? You bet!

On our return I sat down for the interview with the two pilots who would help me sketch the story that appeared in Private Pilot Magazine. Yet the most interesting part was the insight that it gave into Frank Sinatra, and his entourage. Sinatra let the pilots alone to fly the plane with complete authority, and would rely on their judgment as to fly or not to proceed in poor weather, not bad for a controlling, and dominant personality. The Captain shared a story with me about the famous singer.

When they flew back to Palm Springs late at night, which was often, they had to depart out of the North Las Vegas Airport due to noise abatement procedures. Not only was this further away from the Sands Hotel on the Strip where he performed, the runway was a long distance from the terminal. Eventually after about eight minutes of rolling along the ground he would stomp up to the flight deck and yell," Are we going to taxi all the way to Palm Springs?" It never failed to happen.

Sinatra's travel ran like a Swiss watch. In Boston they had arranged a motorcade of the city's finest to speed him from the airport to the performance. On one-nighters at various cities, the plane glided to a stop as the limo rolled up to the stairwell. The door of the Lear would open and the passengers spilled out in less than a minute, the car doors would slam and they would be off and racing to the engagement. The car stopped next to the stage door entrance and the guard would open it as Sinatra was straightening his tie, brushing back his hair with his hands and disposing of his cigarette. He'd appear in the wings of the stage just as the announcer would be saying, "..and now The Sands Hotel is proud to present the star of our show, Frank Sinatra."

"When you have been to the moon and back, it is a priority to establish a tranquil base on earth. Charles "Pete" Conrad and his wife Jane have done just that." Long Beach Review

It's not every day that you get to meet and speak with one of 12 human beings that have walked on the moon (Apollo 12). The opportunity arose when the *Long Beach Review,* on which I served for many years as an Associate Editor, arranged to do a piece on the Conrads and their lovely historic home in the magazine section called *Hearth and Home.* I was chosen to write it. Doing a home feature required a portrait photographer to spend the day shooting appealing or unusual rooms which would be featured.

Quite frankly my knowledge of architecture, furnishings, coverings and accoutrements is limited and I received help from some of the other staff when it came to describing what I was writing about, but that was secondary. I was to meet Pete Conrad, Navy pilot, famous astronaut, a man known for his adventurous participation in the Gemini, Apollo and Skylab space programs, and for having walked on the moon.

Conrad, a former Navy pilot was now working for McDonnell Douglas as Director for Marketing, and lived only minutes away. He was dressed in a sport coat and tie, and briefly showed me some of his awards from the space program, and then shook hands and departed for work. I am sure I didn't wash my hand for weeks knowing that it had touched such an illustrious person. I passed the day with his wife Jane who told all and showed every crook of this home designed by the prominent architect, K. Cutter. It is ironic and disheartening that Mr. Conrad was killed years later in a solo motorcycle accident in nearby Ojai, California.

Stories are everywhere if you keep your eyes and ears open. Our Kiwanis Club in Long Beach had a long time member by the name of Charlie Akers, a career Naval Officer and World War II veteran, but if you looked further he was special, for he was stationed on board the *USS Ramsay* on the morning of the bombing of Pearl Harbor by the Japanese and the start of World War II.

An unassuming guy, he was one of three brothers to attend Annapolis and make a career out of the Navy. He retired as a Captain and was commander of a destroyer squadron during and after the war. The remarkable feature story was published by Military Magazine, and his picture was on the cover.

Charlie graduated from the Naval Academy, and after the mandatory battleship tour of duty he was assigned to an old four stack destroyer from World War I which limped across the Pacific Ocean to take up station at Pearl Harbor during the first days of January, 1941. Charlie was the junior Engineering Officer on board and he called the 1919 built vessel "A woeful old ship." He and his wife Becky would live ashore in a small apartment near Waikiki Beach in Honolulu.

On Saturday, December 6, 1941 he had the day off, and was required to report back on board dressed in his uniform at 08:00 hours Sunday morning. Coming on board he stuck his head into the wardroom to order breakfast from the steward, ham and eggs over easy. A bit later the Captain returned from shore leave and retired to his cabin to change into uniform. By this time the clock had struck eight and the Japanese had started their infamous attack on Pearl Harbor and the island of Oahu.

A moment later there was an explosion on Ford Island in the middle of the harbor and home to *"battleship row."* The Captain rushed back out and hollered, "What was that?" Nobody was sure until one of the younger officers stuck his head out of the port hole and said, "The Japanese are bombing Ford Island sir." The Captain didn't believe the young ensign so he asked Charlie to assess the situation. He looked out just as another fighter plane with the Japanese rising sun on its wing, commonly called a "meat ball" was attacking, its guns blazing. There was no doubt the kid was right! The Ramsay was the first ship in line to witness the initial attack from the west by the Japanese, and the start of World War II. Well he never did get his eggs over easy but he did receive Japanese "meat balls" in spades, and he spent the entire war aboard those pesky destroyers in the Pacific Theater.

One day we had a speaker at Kiwanis from the Toyota Motor Car Corporation which had its North American headquarters nearby. During the question period Charlie asked "why the hell should I buy a Japanese car?" In his case it could never be justified and he never did.

Two articles I penned were quite memorable for me and covered the act of flying the freight to Catalina Island. They were about two different companies, during two different time periods, flying two different type of airplanes, and published many years apart. Although the article for *Airliner* magazine gave my bi-line greater exposure, the story about two beat up World War II vintage C-45 cargo planes and their Chief Pilot and owner Cliff Forrester, in *Private Pilot Magazine,* was the most bizarre experience I ever had as a scribe. He operated from the west side of the Long Beach Airport which at the time was a bone yard for dismantled, scrapped, and work in progress aircraft. If Forrester's 'twins' did not have fix and repair tags all over them from the Feds then there was no doubt that he was on their watch list for flying rule infractions . Cliff was a former 'bush pilot' who had come in from the wilderness and was not totally adaptable to the rigid ways of high density airport areas. The story was titled *"Flying the Fast Freight."*

The day of our flight together, to and from Catalina, in order to deliver and pick up the freight, dawned cool and windy. In order to land at the Island it would require a rare back course approach, thus reversing the direction of the runway, to down hill after dropping steeply over the mountain. Cliff and his yappy, arthritic little dog which always rode with him appeared to be up to it. We ground to a stop on the relatively short runway, and taxied back to be unloaded by his ground crew, then reloaded with a bunch of furniture destined for the mainland. On the trip over, there was no conversation due to the twin 900 horse power Wright engines that made such a racket that even the dogs barking was moot. It comes as no surprise that Cliff was practically stone deaf, since the engines were mounted right next to the cockpit and he flew daily.

I was glad to be heading back on the return since the Santa Ana wind condition was strong and the dual tail rudders were slapping back and forth against the stops on the ground, like a base drum beating in a marching band. Taking off in the same direction we landed, Forrester gunned the engines and we lifted off easily into the air and he made an aggressive climb to the normal cruise altitude of 2,000 feet that pilots use between the two airports. Once stabilized, he leaned over, and face to face yelled did you ever do a barrel roll (a 360 degree wing over wing) and I shook my head. He obviously was going to do one with a full load of furniture so I put my pad under the seat and my pencil in my pocket, and he rolled that plane like a clock making time; it was perfect, flawless and nothing moved it was done so well. After leveling off once again he wanted to know what I thought of it and I gave him two thumbs up. He screamed, "Better not put that in the article, they (FAA) will take my license away again!".... and it never was.

When interviewing the Long Beach City Treasurer on behalf of the *Long Beach Review,* he asked me point blank if I was an investigative reporter. If I was, he was out of there. I wrote a story about the Long Beach Harbor Department and Joe Prevatil, the General Manager at the time, and handed it to him for his factual review. He proceeded to severely edit the whole story in red pencil, and returned it a week later. While writing the Howard Hughes series, I interviewed former prominent engineers that had worked and flew on the "Spruce Goose" flying boat and to my surprise was privy to hear some venting against one particular person years later.

I eventually published two books, and crafted the one that you are now reading. *The Famous and the Infamous,* a book about our American Presidents, was an idea that germinated from quizzing my sons on presidential trivia at the dinner table. I wrote down the questions on 3 x 5 cards and eventually had a box full, which gave me the impetus to do something with them.

The next step was to put the questions into a form with the answers following, and my editor from the *Long Beach Review,* Mary Lee Chambers, was kind enough to mold it appropriately for publication. While she was doing this I put together a few quizzes and puzzles for the back of the publication and contacted the post office department for their permission to use presidential stamps that would be placed as graphics in the book. I also designed the cover to make it stand out among other publications where it would compete. Red, white and blue never hurt anything for sale in America.

I now needed to find a printer, which I did, and he ran off 2,000 copies that sold in about a year and a half. The publication was marketed in bookstores, Presidential homes and Libraries, Mount Rushmore, the Statue of Liberty and similar places. In fact if you were to look for the book on eBay or Amazon .com, there are always a few offered for sale. Two years later it was time to update it for a second edition run of 2,000 with a cosmetic change to the cover, new questions and some new answers to old ones which were no longer accurate.

To help promote the sale of the book I sent a copy to five of our past presidents, Richard Nixon, Gerald Ford, Jimmy Carter and Ronald Reagan plus the one that was in office at the time of publication, George Herbert Walker Bush. The process of sending a letter and a book was a long one indeed and a complete round trip could take four months or more. There are some interesting back stories to the five acknowledgements that are framed and hanging in my home today. These are highly treasured albeit a few of the signatures are fading.

My letter to Richard Nixon, then living in New Jersey, was answered with a thank you from his secretary. No luck there, so I put it on the back burner for a while. By the time the second edition came out I had written an article entitled *Return to Satiwan* which was published in *Air Classics* Magazine. During my interview with Dick Showden, a survivor of the heroic bomber mission in the Caroline Islands during World War II, he mentioned that where they were based, Green Island "...Nixon was up safe in the control tower of the airfield." I always remembered this, so when I tried again to generate publicity for the second edition I sent the article along with the new book to the President. This initiated a reply from him which appears to have been written on an old style typewriter, that addressed the magazine story but gave no mention of the *Famous and*

Infamous second edition. It is an interesting bit of insight into Nixon's naval service, something you do not read much about.

November 3, 1990

Dear Mr. Lassers:

Since I was officer in charge of the SCAT detachments on both Bougainville and Green Island, I am sure I was in contact with members of the VS-115 squadron.

I vividly remember incidentally meeting Pappy Boyington on Bougainville shortly after he had shot down a Japanese plane on the way to becoming one of World War II top aces.

With best wishes,

Sincerely,
Richard Nixon

Gerald Ford followed Richard Nixon as president, becoming the only person not to be elected to either the Vice Presidency or the Presidency. I received the following letter from his home in Palm Springs where he now resided.

February 14, 1987

Dear Mr. Lassers

Thank you for forwarding your trivia book on United States Presidential history, which will be a fine addition to my library. I am most grateful for your thoughtfulness.

Warmest, best wishes,

Gerald R. Ford

The first letter I received was from President Carter, signed Jimmy, and was complimentary.

February 16, 1987

To Eugene Lassers

Thank you for sending me the <u>The Famous and The Infamous</u>. You are to be commended for providing our nation's young people an education in history.

With thanks and warm best wishes.

Jimmy

I was able to put 3 of the letters in the front of the second edition which I hoped would have an influence on its sales. As I mentioned I wore all the hats in writing, producing, promoting, collecting, and shipping the book. It was a a matter of pride that people were buying it, and that retailers were stocking my work.

Ronald Reagan retired to California when he stepped down, and maintained an office in Los Angeles, near his home in Beverly Hills. His secretary had originally replied with a thank you for the birthday present which it was not. I forgot how it was straightened out but it did generate a letter. President Reagan was known to always include his wife Nancy in his letters.

January 31, 1990

Dear Mr. Lassers:

Thank you for your thoughtfulness in sending me the most recent edition of the <u>Famous and the Infamous</u>. Indeed it is a welcome addition in the Ronald Reagan Library where it will be enjoyed by many.

Again, thank you. Nancy joins me in sending our warm best wishes.

Sincerely,
Ronald Reagan

As most people know George H.W. Bush, the sitting President, at the time of my second edition was the youngest U.S. Navy pilot to fly and fight in World War II. His actions were most heroic, and a number of books have been written about his exploits which included being shot down twice and rescued. In the first edition there was a question which asked who was the only President to have earned a pilot's license? The answer was Dwight Eisenhower who received it while taking flying lessons during his active duty tour in the Philippine's in the 1930's when he served as an aide to General Douglas MacArthur. When I revised the second edition I knew that President Bush held a military flying license, but did he also have a civilian ticket? His answer was surprising and a unique treasure even though it was only a Xerox copy of his license..

November 14, 1989

Dear Mr. Lassers:

Many thanks for the copy of your book, The Famous and the Infamous. I look forward to reading it.

I've enclosed a copy of my commercial pilot's license. Needless to say, it's been a while since I've piloted an airplane.

Best wishes and thank you for thinking of me.

Sincerely,
George Bush

If I do say so myself, I received a lot of mileage out of one little trivia book! Twenty five years later I published my second book entitled *Steams Up*. It was totally different than my first effort and was a coffee table picture book of steam locomotive photographs that I had taken since an early age. I was always fascinated by steam engines and the men that operated them under extreme conditions. The noise, the danger, the haunting hours which ran around the clock in all kinds of weather, came with the job. They operated subject to the elements with the driving cabs partially exposed. I drove all over Chicago to take pictures, and have been privileged to have a number of them published in enthusiast publications. Rail fans are nuts about their hobby and I was no different. I was maybe 16 years old and the year was 1952. I always tried to meet my dad at the 12th Street Station with the family car when he came home each evening from work. I had to tangle with the downtown Chicago rush hour traffic, find a free, but illegal place to park, all the while praying not to receive a parking citation, then make my way to either the platform or stand on the bridge over looking the tracks if I was going to take pictures, before meeting my dad.

As I remember it was summer and I was on the bridge snapping train photos with a policeman standing idly below clearly identified later in a few shots. The Korean War was in full swing and rail stations were considered a potential industrial target for the enemy, that is, if they had the plane fare to fly from North Korea to attack the station. The railroad cop looked up at me and moved away, and I paid no more attention to him until he was standing next to my side. "Come with me" he said in a stern voice, "it is against the law to photograph vital installations," and he was right as rain as I look back.

In his custody, I, the 16 year old spy was led away to the sergeant sitting in the office inside the station. The officer explained the circumstances and I was out of there in one minute, free as a butterfly, and flew like a bird back to my perch on the bridge waiting for Dad's train, and to tell him what had just happened.

Rich Boy Rides the Rails

My family rode the rails during the great depression and after, but we rode in style. High varnish was where we sat, in the bedrooms, compartments, and the plush drawing rooms of Pullman sleeping cars, not on the "rods." And that was just the way it was.

The fifty page soft covered coffee table book is full of railroad pictures that I had snapped over the years. There are black and white photos as well as Kodachrome slides from locations stretching from Columbia, Mexico and Germany to New Zealand and America. I started to do this when I was 12 for it seems I never passed a steam engine I didn't love.

The picture from Columbia was taken in 1951 on a drive from Barranquilla to the interior, while the ones from Germany were done in 1956 during my first trip to Europe. Steam was still vigorously in use. My earliest pictures from America were snapped during the late 1940's, featuring a public display in Chicago of the Santa Fe Railroad's newly equipped *Super Chief* all-deluxe train.

My most unusual picture was snapped by chance when I arrived upon the scene inadvertently while driving in Arizona in the early 1950's. I was threading the back dirt road over the Catalina Mountains outside of Tucson to Benson for a Sunday excursion. Upon arriving at Benson there lay a Southern Pacific engine and auxiliary unit on their side while the rest of the consist remained upright and on the track. The track was ripped up and the dirt was plowed as the capsized engine unit had chewed up the ground to a stop. It was a train wreck and I shot away to record it.

I have used my writing to venture into making a three part lecture series on Howard Hughes from material that I recorded in interviews as well as to become a volunteer Oral Historian for the Evergreen Aviation Museum in McMinnville, Oregon. It is here that the *"Spruce Goose"* once an attraction in Long Beach, is on exhibit along with other memorabilia related to aviation. I have been pleased to give lectures on Hughes to the passengers of three cruise ships, and to numerous organizations around Southern California, based upon my findings.

The stories also led to an eight week teaching assignment at the Adult School of Education at California State University Long Beach. Lecturing adults is fun for they are there to learn and the class was full and vibrant and something I enjoyed very much.

So you don't have to know English to write and I believe I have proved it. Either way I have enjoyed recording history, and have carried the ball up the field further than I ever expected to. In doing so I have met some very diverse people, written about numerous interesting subjects, and enjoyed the insight, the adventure and the perks that were made available to me.

It was Howard Hughes, the eccentric billionaire, aviator, movie producer and aero-space manufacturer that fate would allow me to better understand up close. He was considered a genius by some, a spoiled kid, which he was, by others. His life would turn 180 degrees, from very good to outrageously bad during the 71 years he lived. Hughes lost both his father and mother before he turned 20 and outfoxed the remainder of the family for control of his father's estate which was turned over to him before his majority by a Texas judge.

During America's economic depression of the 1930's he was making movies while depleting the Hughes Oil Companies balance sheet of its profit margins. Only through the genius of his accountant, Noah Dietrich, was the company able to survive and make billions from the oil drilling bit his father had patented world wide. It cut through shale, would not break and was for lease only to oil companies and 'Wildcatters."

His motion pictures received both acclaim and scorn, often pressing the limits of decency of the times. In the end some were just poor, or out of date, because of his perfectionism and meddling. *Hell's Angels,* a story about two American World War I aviators cost a fortune, was remade from a silent picture to a talky for millions more in 1929 dollars, and astounded people with the crash scene of the German dirigible. The movie, *The Outlaw,* stirred up great controversy and made a considerable box office return on sex, a flimsy story, and astute marketing. His best effort was *Scar Face,* a gangster movie of the 1920's. At the end of his career he returned to making aviation fluff that took for ever to produce and was outdated when it hit the theaters.

He was a natural seat of the pants aviator who listened to few, and seldom read the flight manuals. He would fly when he wanted to no matter what the time was, day or night, or if the weather was good or bad. While doing this he was bedding a bevy of Hollywood starlets, adopting odd behavioral habits, producing movies out of his own pocket at phenomenal costs, and building aircraft that would set world records. The Hughes Oil Company which was started from scratch by his father became a giant corporation, with the purchase of Trans World Airlines.

Originally Howard Hughes along with industrialist Henry Kaiser, joined hands during World War II to build what originally was Kaiser's idea, a flying boat that would cruise high above the German submarine menace in the Atlantic Ocean. In 1942 and 1943 the enemy U boats were sinking ships faster than the United States could build them. It was devastating, and Great Britain was slowly starving to death, while the Allied military effort was in danger of vast shortages of everything needed for victory.

The idea was just that but it never happened in time to help the war effort. The one flight of the aircraft, also known incorrectly as the *"Spruce Goose"*, took place in the Los Angeles Harbor on November 2, 1947, two years after the war had ended, and for which it played no part. With Hughes at the controls, a pack of engineers, technicians, and a few reporters on board, most sitting on orange crates or standing, he took the aircraft to task and hopped it off the water, and up to 70 feet for a one minute flight of only a mile before splashing down.

From that day on for the next 33 years the plane was locked up in an enclosed hanger in Long Beach under guard, constantly ready at a minute's notice for Hughes to return and fly it again. The cost to do this was staggering, and he never did return.

Through the efforts of Jack Wrather who had the lease rights for the liner HMS Queen Mary now located on the Long Beach waterfront the plane would be exhibited under a specially constructed dome as an additional attraction. Private Pilot Magazine, one of the publications that I was writing for as a free-lancer, requested that I cover the media event that was held one day prior to the public opening. On the designated date I scooted down to join the flock of obscure and known personalities such as T.V. newsmen Chuck Henry and Hal Fishman, who were there reporting the mega happening.

It was a first for me, and I soon found out that there was a predetermined pecking order for entry on board the exhibit. Television channels first, followed by radio stations and then the 'lowly' print media. On that basis I could have probably come to the event without a tie and suit, positioned as I was at the bottom of the list. Once on board reporters had access to the huge two deck interior and the chance to sit in the pilot's seat, and imagine you were Hughes at the controls. It would be a three hour wait to get the opportunity.

I sat down and waited. Soon I noticed a portly gentleman dressed in a blue blazer and striped tie, who minute by minute, was becoming extremely agitated, mumbling to himself, loud enough for most to hear. "...I am a busy person and if the television stations want to interview me the clock is running..." and he would be too if they did not hurry up. Sitting near by, he appeared to be addressing his remarks to me, and I was sympathetic to his problem knowing that my place on the food chain was much lower than his.

It was like two men on an island, we started to talk. He was Rae Hopper, the Chief Engineer in charge of the H-4 (Hughes model 4) during its planning and construction. He was a treasure trove of experience, information, opinions, and memories. I felt lucky and honored to make his acquaintance. Soon Chuck Henry came and took him for his T.V. interview, but before he left he gave me a business card, and I was thrilled when he said "...if you are interested in learning more about the plane give me a call and we could get together." What a great opening for the assignment!

My turn came to board and I took pictures, made notes and plunked by self down in the pilot's seat as if I were Howard Hughes himself. A few weeks later I called Hopper at his Brentwood home near Beverly Hills and he offered me an invitation to come out and interview him, with permission to use my trusted tape recorder. It would be a marvelous opportunity to look at the flying boat and Howard Hughes from the inside out.

His home was a fine one and came with a barking dog and a noisy gardener who was trimming the hedges and mowing the lawn. The interview lasted for over an hour with an invitation to return which I never did. Hopper was a dominant personality and a known aero-space executive who belonged to the *Los Caballeros* insider club whose members were the top dogs of the aviation industry. He revealed many memories and had strong feelings about Hughes, and the people who worked on the project. He related numerous incidents and stories of his tenure at the Hughes Company and how he became a vice president of the SUMA Corporation, its final legacy.

He spoke about how Hughes always wanted employees to be available to him day or night, holidays or vacation time. Finally Hopper told him he was not waiting around anymore for his call, because if he did not go on vacation and attend the Los Caballeros function he would be kicked out. From that time on he never told his employer when he was leaving because Hughes would always cajole him to stick around.

Hopper maintained that Hughes never read the manuals, and never listened to advice regarding flying. He considered him as a good seat of the pants pilot, but you couldn't tell him anything when it came to flying. You could not even tell Howard a joke, but he would occasionally tell you one. Hughes would argue a point to exhaustion and was most comfortable with his aviation staff, many who addressed him as Howard, not Mr. Hughes.

He emphasized that "....if Howard had meant to fly the plane that day, he would have told me." It was a reference to the controversy about Hughes intentions to fly the giant flying boat which never moved outside the dry dock until the flight. He claimed to have stood behind Hughes on the final run calling out the speed over the water while touching Hughes shoulder, something that Howard avoided like the plague. It was his only recollection of ever having physical contact with his boss. He remembers calling out "..60, 65, and then there was total silence, we were off."

By now the article was written and submitted, and soon to be published by Private Pilot Magazine. I still had the curiosity bug about the invisible and legendary Mr. Hughes and I would follow it up with vigor. I drove the Los Angeles basin to meet with others who were suggested by the historian of the Queen Mary-*Spruce Goose* attraction.

Dave Grant was the Hydraulics Engineer on the project, hailed from The University of Michigan, and graduated from the school of Engineering. He told me that "...one of his aeronautical engineering professors always proclaimed that if you put enough power on a piano it would fly." The huge H-4 was designed to accommodate the biggest piston engines in existence at the time, eight Pratt and Whitney 4360 horse power Major Wasp radials. It would be aviation's "flying piano."

Grant had a very prominent part in the hydraulic system engineering, and was asked by Hughes to sit in the co-pilot's seat during the taxi runs. He had no flight experience in piloting a plane, but he was closely affiliated with the mysterious Mr. Hughes when it came to the flying boat, and would meet with him in the evening at work or, in his home.

Dave maintained that the flight might not have happened if he had not been sitting in the co-pilot's seat during the last taxi run. Hughes called for 45 degree flaps, and as his only flying responsibility, Grant lowered the lever, only nothing happened. Grant nervously glanced back to the electrical area of the plane and caught the attention of the mechanic standing next to the command point for the flaps, who made a manual adjustment to an obvious error, and they then deployed as commanded. Apparently Hughes never noticed, he was too busy flying the world's largest airplane. That was the only time it moved or become airborne. His take on whether Hughes meant to fly it or not was like Hopper's. He felt that the famed pilot was surprised by the plane taking off so soon after the flaps were lowered and he immediately reduced power, and then reapplied it, before bringing it back on the water.

Dave made an interesting statement on his personality when he said "..Hughes never asked how much anything would cost, only how long it would take to get it done."

By Hughes placing Grant in the second most important location on board, he froze out his long term associate and pilot Glenn Odekirk from any of the limelight. He was assigned to one of the chase boats filming the entire event as it took place in Long Beach Harbor.

The 405 Freeway bisects the Santa Monica Mountains as an artery between the Los Angeles Basin and the San Fernando Valley. On top of the ridge, in a country setting, lives Bill Barry and his wife. He was the Program Engineer on the flying boat project.

Bill took care of many things beyond calculations and was eventually in charge of the storage and upkeep of the plane as it sat for 33 years in its hermetically sealed hanger in Long Beach Harbor. When the plane made its final taxi run there was an iconic picture taken of Hughes at the controls and a group of engineer/crewmen sitting or standing, and Barry is quite prominent.

It was his opinion that Hughes intended to take the flying boat up because of all the reporters on hand and the throng of bystanders along every inch of surrounding ground. Also the lengthy production delays and the prominent Senate hearings on cost overruns the past August were a prickly thorn in his side.

As we talked the door bell rang, and Bill said, "…oh I forgot the State of Texas Auditors are coming to depose me regarding Howard's will." As you may recall three states were trying to establish his residency so that they would be entitled to tax the estate. Indeed that is who it was and he showed them into another room as we spent another fifteen minutes to close the interview. It was ironic to me since Howard Hughes never paid any tax if it could be avoided. He never owned land in California in his own name except when he first was married to Ella Rice (a wealthy young lady from the family that endowed the creation of Rice University in Houston, Texas). Eventually in his declining years he escaped to Nevada and other places around the globe, and disappeared from sight. In the end he protected his estate by the brilliant move of creating the Howard Hughes Medical Research Institute, which took control of all his assets and expenses. It was the ultimate charitable gift, or the world's greatest tax dodge. In this way he protected his wealth. Howard no doubt was looking up or maybe down on the two luckless agents, and Texas would be barred by the court's decision from any of the inheritance tax.

Glenn Odekirk was a graduate engineer from Oregon State University, and migrated south to Burbank where he was introduced to Howard who was in the midst of making the movie, *Hells Angels.* Hughes and "Odie" became inseparable for over 15 years when it came to aviation matters. Not only was he a good mechanic, he could conceptualize aircraft construction and design, and was also a pilot. He is given credit for overseeing the construction of the famous H-1 Racer that set two separate land speed records and he traveled with Hughes constantly for a period of time. By the way Richard Palmer is credited with the design. Both are mentioned in the Air and Space Museum exhibit at the Smithsonian Institution where the plane, aka *the Silver Bullet,* is on permanent exhibit. By the time I had interviewed him in his small apartment in Anaheim, California he had fallen on hard financial times.

He mentioned that "when he was in Miami with Howard during the early 1930's, Hughes was racing a modified military plane in the All American Air Race. The performance of the plane was unsatisfactory even though Hughes won, and he told him "...go back to California and design an aircraft that will break the speed record." And that is exactly what he did.

Howard was notorious for not returning anything and once was billed a year's rental charge by the Hertz company for a car he just left on the street. In fact when another person I interviewed talked about borrowing a plane for the boss from the now defunct Eastern Airlines. The man on the other end of the line told him "..no, Hughes never returns anything."

Howard Hughes had promised a number of key employees that they would be rewarded in his will. The road to hell is paved with good intentions and there was no will discovered as it turned out, and it may have been hyperbole to begin with. Odekirk was still waiting for the 'check in the mail' which would never come.

Merle Coffee lived over in San Pedro, just a stone's throw from Long Beach in a nice neighborhood with a view of the Pacific Ocean. He was an electrical engineer and was aboard the day of the flight coordinating the complex electrical requirements of the huge ship. He reminisced about the many nights he put in while the Flying Boat was being prepped and tested. "When it came time for lunch at midnight, for we worked nights to accommodate Mr. Hughes demands, he would pull up a table or chair, break out his brown bag and have his sandwich just like everybody else. …..the 'boss' was always very courteous to everyone." Coffee was convinced "…..that Hughes was under the control of his Mormon keepers who were feeding him drugs!"

The main office of Howard Hughes was a bunker like structure on Romaine Street in Hollywood. Here a staff of workers handled business for RKO Pictures which he owned, and a myriad of other matters, but none having to do with the Hughes Tool Company which was headquartered in Houston, Texas. While a young man, he had left Houston for Hollywood, returning only once to his birth place.

No Regrets

I interviewed Dorothy Phillips near the end of my quest. She was employed in the executive secretarial pool at Romaine Street, the fortress-like building of the Hughes Empire in Hollywood, and had many encounters with Mr. Hughes during that time. It would be safe to say he never came to the building except at night when no one was present. Groucho Marks, the famous comedian, once said to her "There is no such man as Howard Hughes," referring to his invisibility in public. Phillips would take work to his Beverly Hills home which he rented from Cary Grant for meetings. She was amazed to see him sit there eating chocolate chip cookies with his shoes off and holes in his stockings. One time she was there and heard some one rattling the door. Howard finally went upstairs to check it out and it was a young starlet who needed to leave the bedroom for the bathroom, that he forgot about.

Although he was always respectful she didn't consider him much of a businessman the way he wasted the staff's time by repeating the same work over and over again to his perfection. He would not allow women to wear lipstick or use powder for fear it would tarnish the paperwork, he was tyrannical in that way. She always wondered how he made any money. As we know, if it wasn't for the huge profits of the Tool Company and the deft hand of Noah Dietrich its chief executive, he wouldn't have made very much at the rate he spent it. Her feeling was that he had been done in by the 'Palace Guard,' and Bill Gay, the supposed heir apparent.

It seems whereever I turned I would yet run into another intriguing person of the Hughes story; My banker introduced a customer standing in front of me, and his name was John Tucker, the son of Preston Tucker the industrialist best known for manufacturing the Tucker automobile. Hollywood made a motion picture entitled *Tucker, The Man and His Dream,* based upon his father's calamity in regards to money matters and the Security and Exchange Commission (SEC). Too late, and after his financial ruin, the decision the Commission reached was that no laws were violated.

John agreed to an interview. He told me that his dad and Howard Hughes used to hang out at the Indianapolis speedway together, and had a friendship which went back to the twenties. During the period of the company's financial collapse Tucker was living in the tony Gold Coast area of Chicago while Hughes for the moment was holed up near by at Chicago's famous Ambassador East Hotel.

Tucker was scrambling for financing and spearheading an effort to raise money through a stock offering. This had resulted in an indictment by the SEC for irregularities which turned out not to be true, but the die had been cast. Tucker knew Hughes was in town and phoned over to his hotel to see if they could get together. They argued over who would come over to meet who and they never did get together. Tucker had bought out a company to manufacture the motor for the automobile who also produced the Franklin Airplane engines. He considered that Hughes might be interested in producing his own helicopter engines, but the thought was dead on arrival. The two stubborn men could not agree on something so insignificant as who would come over to the other person's residence to meet.

During the first of two encounters with Vince Kelly, I found him to be very outgoing and garrulous. He became the ultimate interview in regards to the mysterious years where Hughes disappeared from the outside world, as he played cat and mouse to evade observation. As an indication of this, Robert Maheu worked as his right hand man for fifteen years until there was a 'palace coup,' and he was frozen out, while Bill Gay, the interloper, and Chester Davis, his brilliant and infamous New York Attorney turned the tables on him, and took control of the Empire. They renamed the company SUMA while a disgruntled Hughes who hated the name was still alive. Maheu worked downstairs at the Desert Inn Hotel, one of a number of Hughes properties in Las Vegas, while Howard resided upstairs behind heavy window coverings on the penthouse floor. During their entire relationship they communicated by memo and telephone and never met.

Kelly was on the outer lip of the inner circle seeing Hughes on a regular basis, and acquainted with the "Mormon Mafia." As the 'wireman' for Hughes, a term I was not originally familiar with. Mr. 'K' recorded all of the conversations that Howard had on the telephone since Hughes first took up residency in Las Vegas. He was witness to the boss's treatment by his keepers who shielded him from outside scrutiny, and in the end spoke on his behalf, cared for him, and secretly moved him from country to country.

They would also line their pockets with perks and "toys" during this time. Hughes went into seclusion the last 20 years of his life. They had a meal ticket for as long as Howard Hughes lived but he was by no-means an easy patient.

Kelly started to work for the billionaire while he was still a full time officer with the Los Angeles Police Department. He was recommended, and joined the private security detachment that was being formed to jump over the cashier's cage counters and into the back counting rooms to seize the gaming operation back from the crooked people who were operating the Desert Inn casino for him. The people involved were outsourced for this caper possibly by Robert Maheu's office, an ex FBI Agent, and CEO at the time.

He would continue to moonlight in various capacities, but mainly as an electronics expert until he retired from the Police Department. He then joined up full time and was one of the few people who saw Hughes on a regular basis. At the time he was involved with the 'traveling circus' that moved the recluse from country to country in the strange odyssey that would play out as the boss 'tripped out' on morphine and codeine. The pilgrimage took him to the Bahamas, Vancouver, Nicaragua, London and Mexico.

Kelly knew reams of highly personal information about his employer, and more. He is mentioned in a number of books on the billionaire's life as a man of 'gray,' an undefined person behind the scenes. He was considered a prime suspect in the famous Romaine Street break-in where stacks of highly confidential information about the secret mystery ship, the *Glomar Explorer*, which was clandestinely trying to raise a sunken Russian submarine in the Pacific Ocean for the CIA, while using the Hughes Tool Company as a cover, were stolen.

I had first heard of Kelly while I was showing property to a client. How that came up beats me but it did. I was told he was sequestered at the old Hughes Helicopter Division which was now owned by General Motors. I proceeded to call the Company and established he was working there and wrote down his extension number so not to have to go through the operator in the future. It was a wise move for it took me about two years to finally reach him directly. When I called he never returned any of my messages.

One day I hit 'pay dirt' when he picked up and said, "This is Vince Kelly." I identified myself as a freelance writer and told him I was working on a story on the lost Howard Hughes will, and that I very much desired to interview him. At this point started the 'world's longest pause.' Finally he said, "…if Hughes was still alive I wouldn't even acknowledge that I knew him…." but he was now gone. The hook was set and he took it, and a interview was set up at his modest Culver City home.

I found him home alone, affable and not the elusive figure that I had imagined him to be. Once we started the interview he was eager to speak about the hidden side of Hughes, the many exploits he had with him and his thoughts about the 'Palace Guard." He revealed insights into the Romaine Street warehouse which most people didn't know even existed under the office complex, and the myriad of items from Hughes life including his films that were stored in the vaults lining the walls. Furniture from his original house, cars hanging from the ceiling, and wine that probably had now turned to vinegar were stored in a cellar. Documents in neat piles littered the tops of tables. Hughes never got rid of anything.

Kelly was an inside man to the insiders club. He was fond of Hughes, disdainful of the "Mormon Mafia." Bill Gay, and Chester Davis did not fair well either. He felt strongly that all of them catered to Hughes to satisfy their own needs not the demands of the man who employed them. They tried to keep him drugged, and he was not declining the shots. He never got off the morphine or the heavy pain killers ever since he was burned in the horrific crash of the experimental XF 11 reconnaissance plane in 1946.

Except in rare instances he was a prisoner in his own room. How ironic; one of the wealthiest individuals in the world, locked up. Kelly spoke of being with Hughes in Managua, Nicaragua and going through the penthouse after the great earthquake to destroy drug paraphernalia, and sensitive items. He has always thought he burned the will and other documents with a fire in the bathtub as the hotel swayed back and forth. The will was being worked on while they were in residence there.

The surprise though was when he asked me if I had ever heard Hughes speak. "Only on newsreels I answered." With that he left the room and came back with a recorder that had a cassette in it. He laid it down on the coffee table next to mine which was already recording. I captured Hughes telephone conversation on my set, a 17 minute diatribe from the Bahamas to New York City with his lead attorney Chester Davis. It concerned two books which were more than a thorn in his side. The more notorious one was Clifford Irving's faux autobiography that Time-Life and McGraw Hill paid over $600,000 to Irving, supposedly royalties to Hughes for his personal story. This promptly went into Irving's bank account and made Hughes liable to pay income tax on money he never received or knew about. As you may remember, Hughes never paid taxes, ever! The Eaton book was a complete fabrication written by Robert Eaton the husband of the movie star Lana Turner.

From the material, I was able to produce additional magazine articles and a lecture series with video presentation for service clubs, air museums and cruise lines. If I couldn't be Howard Hughes, at least I could talk about him with authority. After all, he was one of a kind.

Chapter 8

Ladies and Gentlemen, the Lassers of the Touch of Travel Show

We were on the beautiful Island of St. Lucia in the southern part of the Caribbean, working, though others might consider it vacationing. They were wrong, travel was our business. Eventually when the green runs dry, the wallet thins, and the credit card company lets you know you have exceeded your limits, its time to go home.

Linda and I were just boarding our American Airlines flight to Los Angeles in Miami, the third flight of the day to make it home. The door of the Boeing 757 opened right into our section and as we entered one of the two male flight attendants announced in a loud voice to the cabin;

"Ladies and gentlemen, the Lassers of the Touch of Travel Show!"

As heads turned our way, we were astounded. It was not the first time that we had received recognition from folks that had watched our television show. It had happened in Phoenix and Honolulu and certainly locally. I told Linda when we originally started the program that we had to be very careful in public because people see us on television. She scoffed, but it turned out to be true, we were always on camera.

To start a travel television program we really needed to be in the business, and with an unfortunate beginning, we were smack dab in the middle of owning a travel agency. Our previous livelihood was real estate development, but the available land for purchase had become priced beyond reasonable, and now our associate builder was moving to Colorado. Real Estate was not the brightest crayon in our occupational box.

On our honeymoon Linda and I superficially talked about doing something fun with the rest of our lives, why not own a travel agency, which was similar to the utterance during my aviation days "I don't see the field, it must be the road...," crazy. We had no idea about how one operated, all the scams that are associated with the industry, as well as the long hours and low profits, but we loved to travel.

By coincidence the agency which booked our honeymoon had a partner that wanted to sell and after spending about two months looking it over we took the bait, not coming close to imagining all the heartache it would bring and the perils of partnerships with a really strange woman. But for all the problems, there were many perks and bennies, most of them coming through our own ingenuity and good luck. From the start we had always been a great team.

We began by purchasing half interest in an agency called *Touch of Travel*. It had a variety of clients from business to leisure, and a separate category known as the "Community," which translated in the vernacular, to gay and lesbian travelers. The latter was a mixed bag of life, and included doctors, lawyers, professional people, police officers, and Fed Ex drivers, a rainbow of occupations. They were courteous, affluent, intelligent and loyal. To service this clientele there were two "significant other" gay men that were employed by the agency, and were responsible for us being a player in this market.

Al and Chuck were an Irish couple who lived openly together. One was a black sheep from an extremely prominent corporate brokerage family and the other a "music man" who at one time hawked piano's off the back of a truck in Missouri. They had worked for Trans World Airlines for many years, and I believe were terminated by the Airline. Al, the black sheep, as he referred to himself, was the nicer of the two, while Chuck did not take kindly to us and had an anger management problem. Down the road they would leave Touch of Travel and secretly establish their own agency with a copy cat name, unfortunately taking with them a goodly number of our customers, while leaving some debts behind.

Our partner, Staci, was as odd as a three-dollar bill, still we needed her knowledge in this highly complex business, where selling airline tickets produced the cash flow that kept the agency in business. In the beginning we just considered her odd, uncommunicative, secretive, but down the road her behavior turned bizarre, deceitful, unlawful, and harmful to the business. We would eventually have to buy Staci out for a small price to be free of her. She already had done the company severe harm financially by her irresponsible actions.

The airlines were constantly on our back about debit memos as was true with any other agency. D.M.'s were normally issued for mistakes in selling a ticket, or not paying the airline through the Airline Reporting Corporation for a transaction. The leverage they had was to take your "plates" (metal plate used in an imprinter for airline tickets) away so you could not sell their tickets.

It all started with a debit memo, and then constant calls by their accounting department, or worse a collection agency. Northwest Airlines always used the latter approach and they called weekly as we stiff armed them because we thought we were right. After a number of months of this nuisance I asked the account collector to wait a minute, "I'm busy on another call." He said "I have all the time in the world, I am calling on your 800 number from Minneapolis." I eventually got rid of him once again and immediately called AT & T and removed Minneapolis from our 800 call free plan, and I never was bothered again.

American aka the "Air Nazis" to many in the industry, were always on our back, We sold more of their tickets and tried to steer our clients to them because there were incentives for us to do so. But American or United for that matter took no prisoners. I was handling one debit memo situation with American's main office in Dallas, for about a month. I felt we were in the right and had been assured by our partner that we had paid them for our obligation. I was at the point of yelling at them over the phone "… I am going to have our attorney sue you for harassment." After work we searched our partner's desk and found the hidden unpaid outstanding notices for several thousand dollars due the airline. She had never collected the money from the clients but gave them the tickets anyway. It was very strange, but the agency had to pony up.

On one day just after we had opened for business a nicely dressed man in business attire walked in and asked for the owner. Unfortunately I qualified. He was there to collect $5,000.00 in unpaid debit memos, or he would pull our "plates." when he returned in the afternoon. This kind of money could only come from our personal savings and when he returned I was able to strike a deal for half cash and half advertising on our television show. If nothing more it added some class to our normal commercials, and saved the 'right to sell' Lufthansa Airlines.

As an example of our partner's ineptitude she sent 20 Navy wives to Hong Kong to meet their husbands' ship when it docked. She had made a mistake so she never charged them for the trip, and was hoping we would cover the loss. At this point we had paid thousands of dollars covering her errors. We forced her to go to her mother who held her personal purse strings, and ask for the money, it was one for the good guys. She never did ask for the money from the clients. It was a constant problem. Our partner promised things she could not deliver on and expected the agency to pay for it.

The biggest debacle and the one that ended our partnership after fighting a lengthy legal action on behalf of the company was an unbelievable flow of events and the disappearance from view of our partner until we could settle with her and go it alone. She stonewalled, denied, wouldn't talk, and laid low, but there was no place to run. Financially this situation was killing us. We had made our bed, now if we could just avoid sleeping in it.

There are American and Eastern Samoa islands in the Pacific Ocean, and a large Samoan community living in North Long Beach. These are the humongous football players that go on to play at major colleges with names like Ukufanuasegee, Osofaalave, and Leaisetupa that are hard to pronounce. The church is the center of the community, and many of their parishioners' lives revolve around its steeple.

Now keep in mind that each agent did their own work, handled their own clientele, and collected the monies due. Information was not divulged to others unless it was necessary. I had overheard our partner Staci, talk with the pastor and his wife during the last year about the church sending a group of dancers and musicians to the South Pacific, but that was about it.

We always filmed our television show (more on this later), on Tuesday morning, but on this day our partner did not show up for her part which was very odd. There was no word, nor was I able to reach Staci. In fact she would never return to the agency, physically, or contact us, and the last we heard was she had suffered a stroke and was in Los Alamitos Hospital. It was pretty bad news, but it got worse.

Around 10:00 A.M. here comes her client, the pastor's wife asking where our absent partner was. "Staci is sick, could we be of help?" She was there to pick up the airline tickets for 60 Samoan dancers on four separate flights to the South Pacific and back, for this coming Friday, four day's away. To say that I was stunned, flabbergasted, terrified and mystified would be laying it on lightly. I was mystified because I had not the slightest inclination of any such trip that was in the works, nor did Linda or anyone else, and our partner was in intensive care.

I questioned if she had any paperwork regarding the trip, any receipts for payments made or anything from our agency that I could look at to try and figure out which side was up. She had nothing, only our partner's word that it was taken care of and that 60 members of her church, who had been saving for two years, and were booked for concerts in New Zealand, Samoa, and Hawaii were ready to leave and perform. All was arranged, the tickets had been issued, and the church was packed and ready to travel, except *Touch of Travel* had nothing to confirm this by payments, tickets or documents.

I asked how she expected to do this if nothing had been paid for. She said that Stacy, was taking care of it and that it was "...a culmination of a dream." When could she have the tickets, she wanted to know. The only tickets I could think of were on the *Titanic,* and we were going down. I said I needed to check around and that I would meet her and the elders of the church at 1 p.m. to update them. All I got from the two gay agents who had a bit of a relationship with Staci was an attitude that said "....got you now 'pork chop,' you are really screwed," and they were right. The task of getting 60 Samoans on a complicated four leg limited space itinerary at this late date was next to impossible, but it was our company on the hook, and we had to try!

At one o'clock, I went out to the church with a heavy heart for I had nothing to say that was encouraging. The elders sat in a sad-faced circle as I told them our side of the situation, that they had paid nothing in, and although I knew nothing about the situation, I had little to encourage them that this trip was going to happen. Their mood was grim. I said I would see if there was anything I missed and that the chances were small that they could get to where they expected to go. Meanwhile I needed money. I had to have the price of the ticket that was promised to them, and it had to be brought to the office. I would start to see what I could do in a limited flight market during a very late inning of the game. The following were the cards I was dealt to try and make a winning hand.

- 3 ½ days to departure
- No money in as of yet
- Limited flights from New Zealand to Samoa
- Last minute pricing that would not come close to the original quote which was inaccurate to begin with
- Finding flight times that would coordinate with the groups scheduled performance
- 60 angry Samoans waiting for tickets

It was time to get creative so I called the Air New Zealand Sales Manager who was a friend to see if there were 60 seats left on the daily Boeing 747 to Auckland that Friday. He sent a teletype to headquarters to see what they could do. The flight from Auckland to American Samoa was a smaller plane and was the cork in the bottle impeding our success. Hawaiian Airlines could accommodate our group from Pago Pago to Honolulu and after their performance, home. I came away the first day with three confirmed flights, one impossible situation from Auckland to Pago Pago, and no idea what price I was going to end up with.

At midday Wednesday I had a thread of hope, but no solution to the leg on Samoan Airlines. The plane on this segment held only a hundred fifty passengers, and was sold out. I did not have a hint of a solution, and I mentioned this to the pastor's wife who was in the Agency regularly with suit cases of cash and dragging along other Samoans bringing cash in over-flowing paper bags. I believe we took in over $50,000 in currency before the deal came down. I told her I could not find enough space on the Samoan Airlines flight, and at that point she said the granddaughter of the Prime Minister of the islands was a member of her church, she would call him. May be this would be the key log to break the jam?

On Thursday morning, Air New Zealand confirmed a miracle, there were 60 seats still available, but they required that the passengers had to have ongoing tickets to leave New Zealand or they would not issue their own flight coupons. The country had enough Samoans and did not want any more jumping ship.

Meanwhile the Samoan Government which owned the money losing airline, agreed to fly an empty airplane down to Auckland, pick the group up and take them to Pago Pago. Good old grampy came through. Happy days were here again, well not quite. Even though the money was all in, Air New Zealand needed to physically examine each Samoan Airline ticket, and these had to be hand written by the airline's office in Los Angeles. We could run the tickets of ANZ but they weren't any good without the Samoan Airline coupon.

Although hand written tickets were rare, they could be done with the proper plate applied, each one taking about ten minutes to write. Friday, the Church was on the move and ready to go. Our agency was issuing tickets on the New Zealand carrier and Hawaiian Airlines, and the airport office with the instructions of the Samoan Prime Minister, was issuing 60 hand-written tickets without a dime paid in for any of them.

My son Michael came in after school, and along with the Air New Zealand sales rep. sat on the floor of the agency trying to match up Samoan names that all sounded very similar. The flight to Auckland left at 8:00pm and it was now four in the afternoon. I collected all of our tickets and went to the airport where the Air New Zealand counter was starting to show activity. The Samoan Airline was still issuing tickets from their office across Century Boulevard and running them over to the International Terminal by car.

The Samoans were lined up, and processing started early due to the fact that they had huge drums, batches of spears and hanging bags of costumes that had to be boarded. The final batch of handwritten tickets came to the check-in area around 6:30pm and we had a go.

I waited to make sure the plane took off and went home and took off my tie and suit, and felt good about the whole outcome. The only kind word I ever got from our "chippy" gay piano hawker was, "I never thought you could do it." If you are familiar with booking airline seats this was a miracle, and I was proud that I saved this dream for the church and at the same time Touch of Travel.

The ticket price already subsidized $200 per ticket by Touch of Travel came out to $75 additional but they were going. They were happy, I was happy and Touch of Travel looked like a champ. We were home free, maybe not. When they returned from a glorious trip that could never have happened without my tenacity they gave us our reward and sued the company for the difference in ticket price and damages for errors and omissions. The judgment requested was $25,000.

For all we knew our partner was on "Mars", and the merry band of gay guys was snickering at us when we were not looking, it was time to get legal representation. The first choice, an acquaintance at a large law firm in town was not the answer. In three weeks time we had run up a bill of $3,000.00 and nothing had happened except a few phone calls and his office generating a blizzard of paperwork that we could ill afford. So with a stroke of brilliance I contacted a friend of mine who had retired as an engineer and had became an attorney. Joel Rattner was a smart guy who worked from his home and was not over-loaded with clients which was his choice. He took the case and it dragged on and on, but the question was where was the church getting the money from to hang in there, and then I found out.

The pastor's wife worked for one of the largest trans-ocean shipping companies in the world. Their local office was across from the Port of Long Beach, and one of the corporate attorneys was handling this affair pro bono. As it turned out there was still a tooth fairy. Once Joel ramped up the case, and generated paperwork and meetings the shipping company attorney blew the whistle, called time out, and told the pastor's wife that there was too much work to continue doing it at no charge. End of case and we paid them $5,000 to settle it.

Our partner finally came to the table and after numerous meetings signed over her share of the agency to us at a nominal price. Free at last, Martin Luther King knew what he was talking about. After this debacle, the 9/11 terrorist attack, and the stock market nose dive, all coming one after the other, it didn't look like the agency was going to make it.

Money was in short supply, and the travel business wasn't Wall Street gone wild! To make these payments to the attorney, and the church I needed to come up with money from somewhere. My son Robert had given me my dad's watch which at one time belonged to my grandfather Lilienfield. It was a nice gesture and I appreciated it, but I was not the type to wear such an expensive watch so it lay in the safe deposit box for a number of years. I had seen ads offering to buy expensive watches and this was a Patek Phillipe, 1940 vintage. I shopped a few places after researching the archives on line to verify which model I had. Upon calling I received a quote of $14,000 to $15,000 dollars, both out of Beverly Hills. I went for the higher offer; it saved the agency! I would have to give up the only item I received from my parents' estate.

This is a story of "I'd rather be lucky than smart," because by nature I am trusting and naive. The person who answered gave me his background and the way he operated, take it or leave it. He came down, authenticated the watch, opened it up to look at the works, and if it was what I had described, he would then write a company check for $15,000.00 and walk out the door, watch in hand. What's wrong with this scenario? The check and its bounce could have made bungee jumping look like a minor sport. I said I wanted a cashier's check, and he said that is not the way he has operated for the past 30 years. So indeed he comes to the office, authenticates the watch, makes out a check, leaves me his card, and walks out the door. You know what, the draft cleared and the problem was solved, like the luck of the Irish!

During our first year in business I came up with one of my daily ideas, a television program involving our agency which would expand business, a logical conclusion not considering the time, knowledge and money that it would take to do this. Very few if any agencies in the country had their own T.V. program, much less commercials on the air because of the cost. I called the local cable station and set up a meeting with the Marketing Director to discuss the impossible dream. Simmons Cable was serving the 34th largest city population in the country, and channel 3, the local broadcast outlet sat on the dial bracketed between CBS and NBC. Channel surfers would definitely see us even if they weren't looking for our travel program. She turned it down out of hand, even if we were paying for it, no harm, no foul,

In October the telephone rings and it's the Simmons Cable female version of "Doubting Thomas" on the other end, the one that said, "No way Jose." She had thought about our idea some more and they would be willing to try it if the costs can be worked out. Oh, by the way the program, "would need to start the second week of December," the year was 1990

So on the plus side I believe I had a good idea. On the negative side, I had no idea how to produce a T.V. show, no format to fill an hour slot, and my time was short to start filming. Also there was more to my life than the television program. My wife Linda thought she had married a dreamer, a dangerous person, but eventually she would become an important part of the program, and a supporter. The impossible has never prevented me from making a pass at it.

The affordable deal gave us three one hour play dates each week, which actually turned out to be many more, and a studio with a director to make it happen. Ron Petke, our man in charge was great, and became a friend during the 10 years that the program was on the air. We filmed almost every Tuesday and used occasional updated reruns.

I would call the program, The Touch of Travel Show, and in two weeks had the format down which revolved around free films from the tourist bureaus of different countries and interviews with their representatives, plus a segment called best hotels of the world where Linda did the voice –over track. Soon I was able to get private travel purveyors to come on and trade out trips for the T.V. time and exposure. So programs might be on Fiji, the Cunard Line, or Las Vegas. For the first show I secured the manager of the Hawaiian Tourist bureau with a great film about the islands narrated by Cliff Robertson.

The big day was upon us. For the two live segments that would be filmed our partner was still on board and we both went to the studio in our Sunday best. It was a medium sized two story room with lights and wires hanging everywhere, and three cameras that were ready to record the pictures on the set while those appearing would be lobed with a mike. Two people were in the control booth and there were three cameramen and a floor director, who would give silent cues to start and stop talking and flashing the count down for the last minute of the segment, with a cut sign at the end. The best thing, it was on tape and could be redone, but nobody wanted to do that. Real performers do it in one take, and the three cameras recorded the good, the bad, and the gaffs.

One take could be hard to accomplish because we were reading off of a 20 year old teleprompter that if President Obama had used it he would not have been reelected. The small screen displayed gigantic letters that allowed only three or four words to appear at a time so the person in charge of the scrolling had to be on their toes in keeping pace with the reader. When the floor manager pointed to me the first time to speak my lips quivered, my mind went blank and the results sounded like something from the movie *The Kings Speech*, which was about the terrible speaking impediment, that George the VI, King of England had to live with during his life and his public appearances.

The program ran its course for 10 years, and during the last three was edited down to a one half hour show for the national Nostalgia Cable Network. Aside from destination programs I interviewed sea captains, customs agents, port and airline pilots, antique suitcase refinishers, consulate generals, and bartenders that worked the cruise ships. I had the opportunity to talk with guests in our "green room," Ron's office, for about 15 minutes, to brief them and loosen them up before filming. Ha, me loosening anyone up is worth a chuckle. I am not exactly the "life of the party."

The lady from Tahiti Sales said she drove around the block three times she was so scared to be on television. I could identify with that. The Consul General from the Netherlands answer to my question regarding his retirement, "Would it not be in Holland." He was incredulous and said "...what are you crazy, the south of France."

Even the well-known author and celebrity, Arthur Frommer, came on the show and ended up recording a commercial for the program which we used extensively at no charge. He was a very nice gentleman, and we established a bond when I told him that on my first trip to "Europe I had used his guide (*Europe on $5.00 per day*).

Each guest was different and most I met only for the short time we had before we moved downstairs to film. I never knew what to expect. The lady from South Korea was an American who would answer my questions with one or at the best two words, which surprised me and made my mind spin for more questions than were written on the yellow pad on my lap.

China had just opened a legation office in Burbank during the early 1990's and they had begun to promote tourism. I called to see if they would be interested in participating in the show and the young man speaking flawless English jumped at the opportunity, but he needed to check with the Counsel. A few days later he called back and asked me to write out the questions and fax them over for his boss to read and memorize the answers in English. Only Chinese was spoken there and being a proud man he was going to be on camera no matter what. This was a definite dilemma for me. A person giving memorized answers to stilted questions certainly would not be very interesting about a hot new tourist destination. I thought about the request and called back and suggested that both of them come down for the interview and be on camera. It turned out they did, and it was the way to go, for the consul would have been a one trick pony.

I invited the United States Customs Department to do a show and bring their 'drug sniffing dog' with them. I thought that would be interesting to our viewers. They mentioned that there were two different types of canines, aggressive and passive, which one did I want? "What's the difference," I asked? The passive one is the dog you see on a leash at the airport with a customs officer that you want to pet. The aggressive one is of a Pit Bull variety that they turn lose in a warehouse and it races around sniffing, jumping, growling and tearing into crates. It was a tough choice, but I suggested they bring the passive one for obvious reasons

Five agents and one dog came for the filming session and they showed the viewers how the dog is trained by putting a simulated bean bag with the smell of narcotics in my sock. When they brought the dog in from another room it went directly to it and sat down next to my chair. So if you are waiting for your bags at the airport and this nice dog comes by and sits down next to you, make sure you have your affairs in order, you could be in for a long night.

I had watched the PBS television program, *Washington Week,* with Louis Rukeyser for years and always looked forward to the New Year's show where the host and guest wore formal attire! Why couldn't I do that? I invited top people from the travel industry to sit at the "round table," and discuss what they expected to see in trends and prices for the coming year. I wanted it to be representative of the industry as much as possible and of course the people needed to be based in the Southern California area.

I was able to book an appearance by the west coast manager of Swiss Air, the manager of the English Tourist Bureau, and the Vice President of Passenger Sales for Princess Cruises. Tuesday at eight in the morning all of us came dressed in tuxedos like we were going to the Emmys with the business day still ahead of us. The show went well and was interesting, and the most memorable part were four guys in the men's bathroom changing into everyday business attire to go to work. It could have been the walk of the penguins, and there was lots of kidding going on. The program was a one-timer. It was too much of a hassle for all concerned.

The Touch of Travel show had a long run, produced great publicity for the agency, and super perks for us because we were now considered the media. Sales from the show did not respond accordingly and bookings price wise were in the bargain basement. Three night cruises, a week on the island of Oahu in a cheap condo, or Europe for ten days in two star hotels on budget tours was the best we could do. The big money either wasn't watching or stood on the sidelines with their hands on their wallets. It did not really matter for Linda and I received free travel for appearances by companies on the show, many of them to become repeat customers. Here are some examples of the loot and booty we collected.

- Three Atlantic crossings on the Cunard QEII 1st class
- Numerous trips to visit and stay at Sandal's resorts around the Caribbean.
- A Seaborne cruise to Canada, one of the world's best luxury cruise lines and a 3 week cruise London to New York
- Private tour in Monaco by consulate limousine
- Eight 1st class flights to and around Chile by LanChile Airlines
- Free flights from Los Angeles to Bali, Indonesia and up to Bangkok and Singapore on Garuda Airlines, upgraded to First Class of course.
- Free hotel accommodations at various 5 star hotels throughout the world.
- Free air to Amsterdam
- Free stays in luxury hotels in Hawaii

Egypt still had a tourist bureau in Los Angeles and they were on the program a few times and of course we used their fascinating film as a rerun every few years. Unfortunately the country was engulfed in terrorist incidents against tourists which were flagrant and magnified by the press. Throwing bombs off over-passes of the Alexandria-Cairo freeway is certainly one way to create havoc and make the news. The situation was starting to affect tourism, which was and remains the number two industry in Egypt. The situation forced the Minister of Tourism, a member of the 21 man inner cabinet under then President Mubarak, to make a tour of the United States to reassure the media and the public that travel to Egypt was safe. He would hold a luncheon and press conference at the Beverly Hilton hotel and I was invited, being a television host.

Upon the day of the briefing I was one of the first to arrive and talked for a few minutes with the Director of the Egyptian Bureau and his lovely wife. As more of the media in attendance arrived they turned their attention elsewhere. The Minister finally arrived and took to the podium and spoke in halting, and stilted English about all the joys of Egypt and how safe and rewarding it is for people to make the journey, really boring stuff. I was seated in the back row and I could see the 75 others in attendance were getting restless, and what did get my attention was that they were setting up a lovely buffet luncheon behind me and not only could I see it, I could smell it! He finally droned to an unreassuring end; answered some tepid questions and the captives were now let loose and broke for the buffet offering with me in the lead. It was a reenactment of the Charge of the Light Brigade, without the horses.

Carrying an over-flowing plate I parked at one of the distant empty tables and addressed my 'feast." I did not know anyone there aside from the local Egyptian Tourist Bureau Director and he was nowhere to be seen. As the tables filled the two places to my right remained open and who should sit down there, but the Minister himself and another media type he was speaking with. I can listen and eat at the same time and that is exactly what I did. But before I knew it he had turned to me and asked what I did.

"I produce a television program on travel that reaches a potential 400,000 viewers and we feature a program on Egypt about every 18 months," I said. His face lit up like a Nile sunrise and he said very sincerely, "If you ever travel to Egypt let me know, and I will take good care of you." That was a great offer since I would be there in three weeks! When I told him this he seemed incredulous but made some notes and said he would have his office contact us with arrangements, and indeed they did.

Linda and I were only there for two days since we were traveling on a small cruise ship of foreign registry which over-nighted in

Alexandria. Upon arrival a guide and driver picked us up for the two hour drive to Cairo where we spent the day. We were not sure how to dress so I wore a suit and tie and Linda a dress and boy did we attract attention going through the Pyramids at Giza. We were a target for every ragged vendor peddling at the historic site. Linda was the only woman crawling through the Pyramids in a dress and high heels.

The next day they again picked us up and this time our guide was a professor of antiquities from the University of Alexandria, what a treat. Travel agents are about one step above house siding, used car or real estate salesmen. It's the media stupid, that get the best rewards.

Early in the program we had the Moroccan Tourist Board on the show and we faithfully did reruns of the program over the years. They had provided a great film on the country that included the famous La Mamounia Hotel with its turn of the century design and opulence, and the themed suites portraying the *Orient Express, a* Turkish Kasbah, the Winston Churchill quarters and others. It was described as "...a palace, a mirage with enchanted portals, a legend that is unfolding." The director of the bureau always said they would take care of us with a free stay at the renowned La Mamounia Hotel in Marrakech, one of the most fabled watering holes in Africa, if not the world. Winston Churchill stayed here many times after World War II to relax, paint and write. The bureau closed in Los Angeles as did many others in the 90's and the show had ended by the time we ever got around to traveling to Marrakech.

We sailed on one of the Silver Seas luxury ships which stopped over-night in Casablanca, Morocco and laid-over giving us time to take the two hour train ride to Marrakech. There are no victims of lost opportunities, only volunteers and I recalled his offer of putting us up at the hotel free. I e-mailed the manager and told him the whole story and asked what he could do for us even though the program was long gone, but of course, the

Touch of Travel Agency was still in business and remains so today.

I received a reply a few days later that the lowest price room went for $400.00 per night and as a courtesy they would wave the charge to honor the verbal six year old offer. That was great, so I e-mailed him back that this was wonderful, and dropped the hint that I was an admirer of Winston Churchill, and was always enamored with the pictures of the themed Churchill Suite as shown in the film, I put the whole thing aside not giving it another thought.

By chance, when onboard the ship we met some acquaintances who had done some business with us previously, but not this trip, and we decided to eat together each evening. We told them of our planned adventure and invited them along. They bought in and Linda made a reservation for them at the hotel. With friends in tow we took a cab to the train station and were accosted by a hawker in the parking lot to buy tours of Casablanca we did not want. After telling him our destination, and hoping that he would get lost he said his brother lived in Marrakech and would pick us up at the rail station, and before we could tell him no, he was on his cell phone to arrange it. Beware of merchants selling rugs, fezs, or making travel arrangements from parking lots, but in for a penny, in for a pound and we were in. He drove us to the rail station. I had been to Casablanca once before in 1968 and not much had changed. Take my word for it, the movie Casablanca is better than the city.

We arrived at the station carrying only an over-night bag, and fumbled our way to the ticket counter where we purchased first class tickets to Marrakech. The train originated in Casablanca, and it was impossible not to board the right one. The assigned seating was in a dingy compartment with a capacity for 6 travelers. Already sitting there was a young Moroccan dressed nicely in white short sleeve shirt and slacks. If he spoke English we might learn something in the two hours we would spend together.

The train jerked to a start and crept through the back streets of the city and Humphrey Bogart did not appear anywhere as we scampered into the monotonous desert sands of North Africa. We finally made an attempt to communicate with our fellow passenger, it wasn't hard. He lived in New England, owned a pizza parlor, and was on his way home to visit his parents. This made the two hours fly by and we exited the train at Marrakech, and the brother was there holding a sign with our name on it and transported us to the hotel.

Upon checking in the clerk found our reservation and immediately pushed a bell to the interoffice. An assistant manager appeared who was quite cordial. After the formalities he said that he would personally show Linda and me to our room while another receptionist would guide our friends to theirs. We asked about touring the property (a relatively common request from travel agents), and after going back behind closed doors he returned and said that the General Manager would take us on a tour at five o'clock.

Our friends went one way and we trailed the gentlemen to our quarters which was a long walk and turned out to be the Winston Churchill Suite. How sweet it was! He showed us around the three room, 2 bath complex with its balcony overlooking the glorious gardens with the majestic Atlas mountains in the distance. There even was a Churchill original painting hung on the wall. "I hope this will be to your liking" he said, and left, stage right. When the door shut Linda and I did high fives and hoped that there wasn't a secret camera taking it all in.

The suite had two dozen roses, a buffet set up of delicate cheeses, meats, and hors'doeuvres with wine and chilling champagne. Just then the phone rang and our friends with great excitement told us of their good fortune to be upgraded to a deluxe room, but they were concerned that we were in the least desirable room as described in the original e-mail. We assured them that things were better than they pictured, and invited them to come on over to see for themselves. After spending an hour in the crème de la crème digs they agreed we had no worries. They would meet us for a late dinner in the magnificent Moorish dining room, meanwhile Linda was going to take a long bath using the fine toiletries which were at our disposal. We still had the obligation to meet the G.M. for the property tour at five.

While she luxuriated in the marble bath tub, I was in the living room reading an article in one of the magazines on the coffee table. It was about the hotel and devoted mainly to the suites, especially the most expensive one, the *Winston Churchil,* which billed out at $2700.00 per night. Cold tingles ran up my spine as I realized I never heard anything more via e-mail from the hotel about the arrangements or if they were going to put us up in this one of a kind lodging. When Linda emerged I told her about my fear. I said "I am not staying here at that price. We will go back to the free room. I will just ask the General Manager what the deal is when we meet". The afterglow of a luxurious celebration was fading fast

At the designated hour we were downstairs awaiting our rendezvous with fate as both the assistant and his boss were soon to arrive. After the initial introduction we were handed media kits for the hotel and it was then and there that I decided that if they did that they would not have the brass to charge us for the suite and I was right. It was on the house, a phrase I would like to frame and put on my mantle place.

That evening at the manager's weekly free cocktail party and buffet held in the magnificent gardens for guests, was when we saw the G.M. again as he greeted every person entering. I passed along the little gift we carry for just such occasions when we were reintroduced. An American Eagle silver coin in a presentation box. When he opened it he said, "When Hillary

Clinton was here just a few weeks ago she gave me the same thing". Good shopping pays off I thought!

One of our most rewarding journeys was to visit the Normandy invasion beaches, and the nearby towns of Cannes and St. Mere Eglise to name a few. The good citizens of the Provence of Normandy, and for good measure throw in Brittany, are different than those in the rest of France. They remember what Americans did for their country, and the liberation that the Allies brought to the French from the repression, and deprivation of the occupying German forces.

Linda and I arrived at Charles De Gaulle Airport in Paris via Pan American Airlines from New York. The car rental was waiting and we circumvented central Paris on our way to the Chateau where we'd stay for three nights, which was just miles from Omaha Beach, made famous during the Normandy invasion. The road was clear and the police with white gloves, no doubt for us, seemed to be everywhere, at clover leafs and in vehicles on the top of over-passes. Working it out in my mind as to what was going on, I came to the conclusion that this was the way the French caught speeders, timing them as they got on the freeway and then matching it against a second clocking as the car passed under an over pass. Clever those French!

As we approached the end of the road where it emptied into the famous town of Bayeux, home to the renowned eleventh century tapestries of the Norman invasion of England, it was necessary to pass through temporary barricades. They were manned by hand waving police, waving frantically as it happens with frustration lined on their faces. It turned out that we were just minutes ahead of the motorcade of Prince Charles and Princess Diana of England, who were on there way to make the one thousand year dedication of the historic tapestries that would be commemorated by a plaque for all to see in Bayeux.

Our chateau was located near the seaside town of Port Besson and it was a throwback to a World War II black and white movie. It had a long driveway through worn wrought iron gates twelve feet high, lined with towering trees which ended before an aging chateau with squeaky wood floors that had seen better days. It was one of the most interesting experiences of all our traveling years. We had planned to eat dinner there the last evening, an option generally offered by chateaus that accept guests throughout France. Our host was a widow, who lived there with her nephew and an elderly maid who rode her bicycle to work daily. That night the lady cooked and served us by herself and we asked if she might not join us for coffee when the meal was over, after all, we were there to meet the locals and she might have something interesting to say

We were sitting in the dimly lit living room when our hostess mentioned that her father, who was an aviator, had escaped to England during the war and flew against the Germans with the Free French who were now operating from England. The family owned two Chateaus, the second one not far away from this one where she lived then. Let us travel back in time to her devastating story.

The German soldiers had been around for a few months but did not bother them until around May of 1944, when they moved a detachment of SS troops into the woods on the property. She described them as very polite when they would come and ask for things or talk with the household. Soon the Normandy Invasion started and the chateau was located in the British zone. The gliders came over but some flew too far and dropped the Canadian paratroopers into the German hands, where all 25 were captured. The Allies pushed inland, and the Germans were being forced back. It was at this moment that they lined up the Canadian captives and shot them in cold blood as the household looked on in horror rather than sending the prisoners to the rear as POW's.

291

This left such a negative impression on an 18 year old girl that when the British came, she volunteered to become an informant, and disappeared into the countryside still held by the Wehrmacht, unfortunately only to be recaptured by them. She would spend the rest of the war imprisoned at Ravensbruck, an infamous concentration camp for women where her head was shaved. Eventually she was liberated a second time by the Russian Army, a very unique experience, having been liberated twice.

Linda asked her if the Allied bombing of the cities and countryside where she lived was a mental and physical problem for her. She said "...no, they were bombing the Germans!" Linda followed up with "...when German tourists stay here is it a problem for you?" To that she said "yes," the hatred lingered on, over 50 years later. It was indelible on her soul, and even time would not bleach it out.

We returned the car to the rail station in the nearby town of Caen, and took the train to the south of France. When we arrived they asked if we had filled the petrol tank up which I never thought of doing. Avis told us that a few blocks from there was a filling station and we had plenty of time before our train arrived. We circled back and the gas station was easy to find. It was huge with many pumps with different names on them, all French. We chose one that said "Gasol"and proceeded to fill, even topping off. As I was putting the cap back on the tank a little nondescript man ran out waving and yelling "Non, Non", no idea why he was doing this but he had a uniform shirt on so we replied *"no parle' Francais."* With that he walks over to another man filling his car and drags him over to where we were standing. His broken English translated into the fact that we had unfortunately just filled our vehicle with diesel fuel, when it burned gasoline, and if we left the car they would drain the tank and get it back to Avis. The Frenchman with the tiny car offered us a lift to the rail station, only in Normandy! Wow!

We took him up on it and with our three suitcases stuffed into a tiny trunk, the empty seat and riding freeboard on top we made like refugees back to the rail station. As we drew closer I said "thank you", and he said "Non, non, thank you." I wasn't getting through so I tried it again with the same results. I made a third effort as we slowed to a stop and he held up the palm of his hand and said once again , "thank you," and with his finger drew an invisible 1944 on his palm, Thank you for invading, setting us free from the Germans, giving us our land and lives back. It was an unforgettable spine tingling moment that I shall always remember.

In my pocket I was carrying an American Eisenhower dollar to give away, which I did. He looked at it and said "Ike, Ike." recognizing General Dwight Eisenhower on the face of it. The strange thing is that 10 years later we inadvertently stayed at the other chateau that our previous host lived in during the war and which still belonged to the family, and walked the forest where the killings took place. Freedom lives in the memories of the people of Normandy, they have not forgotten the sacrifices made by the "Greatest Generation."

The British seemed to enjoy put downs, doing it extremely well by looking down their nose with disapproval. Michael, our youngest son was always a go getter and interested in aviation. While at Denver University he worked for Great Lakes Air Lines and through his own initiative and speed aced hundreds of other prospective applicants out of a job at British Airways when they opened and inaugurated the Denver service to London. After graduation he was one of three sales representatives for the airline. Before he left their employment he was stationed in Seattle and Los Angeles, We were booked on B.A. to England in coach with a prayer that he could get us upgraded to business class. This is an exercise like moving the Rock of Gibraltar, for the Brits are very class conscience, and a coach seat ticket is nothing but a coach ticket for life. When we checked in, the stiff upper lip lady agent sniffed, "... that for some reason we had

been upgraded into business class and thus were very fortunate."
I wanted to yell "here's to the Queen," but I didn't.

After her formalities were completed I asked for passes to the
business class lounge and she curled her lip and said, "You don't
get a double lucky!" My son eventually rescued us later from
sitting with the common folk, and we did rub elbows with the
upper crust in the lounge until the flight was called, and
proceeded on board to claim our business class seats. Indeed a
"double lucky!"

Cunard was a regular on the television program and for each
appearance they would trade out for a free trip on the Queen
Elizabeth II to England. The QEII was a two class ship and we
would be blessed with a lovely first class cabin and dining
privileges in the Princess Grill, the second best eatery on the
ship. On our third crossing Captain Warwick was still in
command only now he was Commodore of the fleet, an honorary
promotion. On a trans-Atlantic liner the Captain gives a private
reception to a very special small gathering of the noted on board.
This is held in his large living room suite attached to his cabin
and I thought it was worth a try to be one of the invited on this
crossing.

I was carrying a prepared letter with me that was informally
addressed to him saying it was "nice to be back on board and we
looked forward to meeting him again". Fortunately our cabin
accommodation luckily matched the boldness of the letter, for he
did not remember us from Adam. I would see if I could gin up
an invitation to the elite cocktail party that would be given for
the rich, the famous and any four-flusher (a term used to describe
a poker player bluffing on four cards to a flush when five are
required), who made it through the screening process

Sure enough, the second day out a note arrived inviting us to the
affair. It was a formal night for all of the first class passengers
and it brought out a wealthy looking society group hiding behind

their penguin suits and fancy 'Needless-Mark Up' dresses. We arrived fashionably late and were greeted by the hostess who introduced us to the Commodore standing next to her. "Mr. & Mrs. Lassers," she announced as he extended his hand and said, "… glad to see you again, thank you for joining us, and sailing on Cunard." Mission accomplished.

Moving on we were immediately served champagne by a liveried butler and offered wonderful hors d'oeuvres on a silver tray by another. We moved around in the quarters which now had become a bit cramped due to the turn-out. At that moment my not very patrician wife, who knows a wealth of information about British history, says there is the fellow we see on television who is a "Royal Watcher" and popular author, Robert Lacey. He was just finishing dazzling a dowager of grandeur with his gossip and about to move away when my wife yells, "Hey English Guy, over here!," and sure enough he came over to chat about the Queen, the Duke, Prince Charles, and Princess Diana. After 15 minutes of gossip Linda could stop buying People Magazine for a few weeks, she had all the tidbits she needed. Also I could get up from behind the couch and reappear after her cockney "Hey English guy." As you have guessed by now I'm a rather reserved fellow, and Linda is the opposite, saying exactly what she thinks. It makes for a relationship encompassing a pallet of rainbow colors.

It should be noted here that we sent our formal wear on the ship back to our home through a UPS counter on board, a service provided by Cunard. It would be on the return trip to America, and it just so happens the ship encountered a 90 foot rogue wave which Captain Smith met bare knuckle on the bridge as the news media recorded the incident. It was providence that only our 'good duds' were on board at the time.

Indonesia is one of the more difficult places to fly to, and remains so as I write this. Most of the time it is necessary to travel through a third country to reach it's shores even though it is home to the world's fourth largest population. At one time Garuda Airlines flew directly from Los Angeles to the island nation in about 23 hours elapsed time with stops in Honolulu and Biak, New Guinea for fuel and replenishing.

The Garuda representative stopped by the Agency occasionally and encouraged us to visit Indonesia on them, as a trade-out for their appearance on the television program, but we never did. When we remembered the offer we had a new rep, but at least there was one. Soon there would not be any sales representatives to call upon agencies, and airline ticket offices became a thing of the past, as did airline ticket commissions. We were looking into a two year old offer to visit Indonesia and it turns out we could still resurrect it.

Not only did we travel there, we would cruise the island nation for seven days on a 30 passenger expedition ship, fly to Bangkok and catch the Eastern and Orient Express luxury train to Singapore, and stay at the renowned Raffles Hotel on arrival. We made our home base in the beautiful tourist region of Denpasar, on Bali, home to luxury hotels and night life. We traveled through Bali three times staying at the same Sheraton five star resort which began to actually feel like home, with its beautiful landscaping, and waterways, comfortable hammocks and beaches.

We were ready for the adventure when the day came, and checked into the Garuda business class counter early for our seats. We certainly didn't want to miss the flight or have any confusion over our free tickets. No sweat, we were in business class and were entitled to go to their lounge where they had a nice offering of pre-boarding food and beverages. Soon the plane was announced and the premium passengers were escorted to their seats. The pretty flight attendant put her hands together, bowed, and that was that, or so we thought as departure time was almost upon us. Just then an elderly couple stood by our seats, with a Garuda escort, and said they believed we were in the wrong seats. After comparing boarding passes it turned out Garuda had assigned us both to the same set of seats. The Chief Gate Agent came back on the plane, surveyed the scene saying "Just a minute," and got off again. It turned out these folks were Christian Missionaries on there way back to Biak, New Guinea and their jungle ministry.

The supervisor returned, told us to get up, and tells the missionaries that the seats were theirs, and asks that we collect our belonging and come with him. I thought we were about to get kicked off the flight. This was a Boeing 747-200C, one of the few planes that was built as half passenger and half cargo. I hurriedly looked around, and saw that all the seats appeared to be taken. Fortunately that was not the case. As Bob Uekcer used to say in the Budweiser beer commercials, "I must be in the front row," for we were now upgraded to first class, which on Garuda was like going to heaven. Only the Gods and the Board of Directors got this privilege unless you paid for it.

Our seats were across from the well-used prayer mat on the floor by the bulkhead for crew and passengers who were Muslims, a worn piece of tapestry. Only on Garuda can you be uncomfortable in all three classes of seats. The seats had fold out wooden leg rests that the occupant had to manually extend, and they looked and worked like a beach chair. Not much luxury here after all.

In Hawaii where we stopped at one in the morning, American coach passengers were lying on the terminal floor during the long stopover, stretching their backs, legs and probably their minds. When we arrived in Bali, our imprisonment on the plane was momentarily forgotten, as we enjoyed the beautiful hotel and looked forward to the small boat we would sail on. It would be a new adventure to the remote islands of Indonesia.

The expedition ship left from Bali with a multi-national list of 30 passengers. Included were a brother and his two sisters from the

Netherlands who were returning to Indonesia for the first time since World War II. They had been interred there for the duration of the war by the Japanese and suffered greatly under their occupation. Indonesia was a Dutch Colony before the conflict, and oil rich, one of the commodities Japan was always in need of. On board were a guide and historian who held class every day speaking about the next port of call. I use "port" loosely, since at least three times we used the Zodiac rafts to go 'hit the beach' in remote areas.

Before our arrival I remember the lecturer speaking about the island of Komodo, famous for its large Monitor Lizards better known as Komodo Dragons which are found only in this part of the world and mainly at this remote spot. She spoke of the one documented instance of where a human was attacked by a dragon, its powerful tail subduing the visitor and then dining on his remains. The lizards feast on every part of the kill and there is only a spit ball of bone left as they leave the table. Well she had our attention now.

It was a warm morning that greeted our early arrival at the island and there were no other vessels in the small harbor. Komodo Island then and now is off the beaten path for cruise ships, We boarded our Zodiacs, rubber life boats where passengers sit on the raised side, and motored the short distant to shore where we assembled for the trek inland. We were met by two guides who lived there with other full time rangers employed by the National Park Service. They led us on a two mile hike to the 'people pen' where we would be enclosed to watch the creatures do whatever they did. After the enlightening stories the naturalist had imparted the night before, the long wooden pole with a two fingered prong on the end carried by the Rangers as a deterrent did not seem like the Maginot Line of Defense against such a ferocious creature which consumed all it killed and digested it. Needless to say we were in for an adrenalin fueled hike.

Off we went on the trail and passed enormous spiders in hollowed out stumps with prey in their webs. There was no talking allowed and the escorts were placed one in front and one in back. We soon descended into a dry stream bed, when the lead guide turned around and put his finger to his lips. Up ahead was a six foot lumbering dragon making its way toward us. The guide motioned to move close to the bank, and the Komodo kept walking as we did without even an acknowledgement. Soon we were at the enclosed people watchers pen where we could view 50 or more dragons of all sizes, as they slept in the sun or moved around us lethargically. It was a rare chance to visit their habitat, and indeed a pleasure to return to our expedition ship which swung on its anchor off shore in a calm sea. It was quite an experience to be in a cage with the animals watching you!

On this trip we both had the opportunity to represent the ship in what we have called "the patrician and the little brown hen." The island of Flores is a medium size island in the archipelago chain that is called Indonesia. The ship's passengers went ashore in our faithful Zodiacs to meet a tribe of natives, dressed in different costumes including UCLA sweatshirts and baseball hats with various logos. Aside from selling us their craft ware which was laying out in the blazing sun on well prepared tables, they welcomed us with a traditional native ceremony that involved two passengers from our catamaran. Dumb Americans will volunteer for anything so Linda and I stepped up as the representatives for the civilized world.

The Chief stepped forward with his assistant and first held out a bottle of homemade brew which probably could have fueled astronauts going to the moon, and then a live chicken that was relatively tame if not drugged. Being that I was not overjoyed to have a live chicken for various reasons I snatched the wine and backed up two steps, while the Chief with a sweeping gesture bestowed the chicken on Linda. Now coming from a patrician family I knew how to coddle the wine, and I had it under complete control, while Linda, from metropolitan Los Angeles, was fumbling with the chicken. The ceremony took about 10 minutes and we both escaped unscathed. I did not have to taste the wine and the chicken did not require an eventual change of clothes.

Linda and I flew back from the island of Timor, spending the night once again in Bali and then continued up to Bangkok where we boarded the luxurious Eastern and Orient Express train which over three days wound its way down to Singapore. A night or two at the famous Raffles Hotel was next, and then we flew back to Bali.

Unfortunately, it was now time to leave for Los Angeles and the memory of the hard seats and the benefits of first class danced like sugar plumbs through my head. How could we ride up front on the way home? The PNR (passenger record) said business class and the only thing I had otherwise was the two first class boarding passes from the flight down from Los Angeles. It was worth a shot to try a little subterfuge and persistence to see if I could reclaim the seats in the privileged class section on the plane.

We checked in and as the agent looked at the computer record I said that we were on complimentary tickets and it was in the passenger record that if first class was available we were to be placed in it. The agent scanned again and read every word but did not see anything close to what I was referring to. He said I had to go to the manager's office and talk to him.

Linda waited with the luggage, since we were not checked in and I found the office which had one busy individual working in it. I told him my story and he said that only the manager could handle this, and he was out with the flight at the moment and would return. As the time ticked down toward departure I asked again, but the man deferred to the manager who still had not appeared. Finally with 15 minutes to go he relented and ran first class boarding passes for us, and the 23 hour trip home would be a bit more comfortable on Garuda than anticipated. On one of our first trips to Hawaii after buying the travel agency I found out that sometimes you should just keep your mouth shut.

On the return trip on Hawaiian Airlines from a free stay on Maui at the beautiful Hana Maui we boarded a DC-10 aircraft. Traveling in coach we were fortunate to be in the two seat exit row next to the right rear door, where there was a wide swath of room, making us feel like "the chosen few." The flight attendant was standing by the door ready to give the safety presentation which included over-water procedures for obvious reasons. I thought it would be cute to ask him in a smug way if we had to share the life raft stored at our entrance with others, and without blinking an eye he said you better, this exit does not have one. Touché!

A grand journey from London to New York ended far different from how it started. It was Tuesday and the Seabourne Pride, a small 10,000 ton luxury passenger ship was sailing, actually bouncing from London, England to New York City. It was a grand voyage to begin with as we acquainted ourselves with the small contingent of upscale passengers. Linda and I love the game of trivia, and our team was locked in solid for the three week voyage and included Y.A Title, the great football player who sat on my right at every session. Y.A. still holds long standing records is an icon of the game, and we figured if he could call plays in the huddle, lead his team to championships on the field and wore his championship ring we would take his answers without question.

So the question asked at one game was (...how many states were there in the Confederacy when it was formed when the American Civil War broke out?" Linda said 11 and Y.A. was sure it was 13. They tussled back and forth over it and Linda deferred to the football legend and it cost us, the right answer was 11. It was a treat to make his acquaintance.

On the 11th of September we were a day out of Reykjavik, Iceland, the weather had calmed down and the passengers were emerging from their cabins for the morning activities. At this moment in America events were taking place that would change our country and the world for ever. It was stunning!

- American Airlines Flight 11: Left Boston's Logan Airport at 7:59 a.m. in route to Los Angeles with a crew of 11 and 76 passengers not including the five hijackers. The hijackers flew the plane into the North Tower of the World Trade Center in New York City at 8:46 a.m.

- United Airlines Flight 175: Left Logan Airport at 8:14 a.m. in route to Los Angeles with a crew of 9 and 51 passengers, not including five hijackers. The hijackers flew the plane into the South Tower of the World Trade Center in New York City at 9:03a.m.

- American Airlines Flight 77 Left Washington D.C. Dulles International Airport at 8:20a.m. en route to Los Angeles with a crew of 6 and 53 passengers not including five hijackers. The hijackers flew the plane into the Pentagon at 9:37a.m.

- United Airlines Flight 93 Left Newark International Airport at 8:42a.m. in route to San Francisco with a crew of seven and 33 passengers not including four hijackers. After the passengers revolted the hijackers crashed the plane into the ground near Shanksville, Pennsylvania at 10:03a.m.

On this horribly tragic day 3,000 people perished in the attacks, the Twin Towers were destroyed in an inferno, and a wing of the Pentagon was damaged with fatalities. As this was happening we were benignly playing our daily game of ship board trivia when the Countess of Napoli (I kid you not) rushed into the room and said, "The Twin Towers just fell down."

Our ship was able to receive intermittent transmission by satellite of CNN and the catastrophic news quickly circulated with disbelief as everyone went to turn their cabin TV's on or go to the lounge where the trivia games were dropped and there was a big screen set. We were stunned as the scene unfolded and confusion reigned as assumptions changed and disbelief spread. Soon the Captain was on the ship's public address system (P.A.). He knew nothing more than we did, but stated that the following was going to take place.

- He was going to stop the ship in mid ocean.
- Divers were going over the side to inspect the hull for anything suspicious per company orders.
- The French balcony sliding glass doors which certain decks had, would be locked down until further notice.

Linda and I returned to our room watching the unthinkable depicted as the "crawl" or moving scroll at the bottom of the screen brought up to date the passenger fatality lists of those on each flight. I was watching it carefully and by afternoon I saw a familiar last name go by. The Long Beach community had lost an expatriate who was on his way to visit his family in town. I worked with his mother on the *Long Beach Review,* and we felt very down over his death and over the entire situation.

Obviously the entire atmosphere on board changed and we were in limbo except for the television and the ship's announcements. The *Pride* was due to dock in New York City in just five days and the Captain told us that this was not going to happen as scheduled. Meanwhile everything ground to a dramatic halt in the United States as its transportation system came to a complete standstill for the first time in history. People hunkered down. A new directive from the bridge stated that we would need to present identification every time we boarded or left the ship. This was not required before because of a capacity of only 200 passengers. Updates would follow. A Rabbi traveling on board held non-denominational services to a large audience in need of comforting.

The next day we cruised into a fjord in Greenland, passing a tiny cabin and numerous ice flows, and then reversed, once again heading for North America, but where would we land? This had not yet been determined. The mood of the ship was somber and concerned, but activities continued, and televisions remained on everywhere as the horror unfolded, the passengers jabbered, and some wept.

Now came word that the Port of New York was closed to all traffic, we would terminate in Boston, and because of new procedures to enter the harbor under gun boat escort we would be two days late. For those desiring to leave the ship early our first North American port was a tiny fishing village in Newfoundland where going ashore would be by tender. Although most passengers continued on, a group hired a light plane to fly them to a major city in Canada, in an attempt to try and get home. People were desperate to travel and without any public transportation a few people were able to rent cars at phenomenal expense and made the drive across country to return to their families.

Only two public phones were located on shore in this tiny village, and people had to wait in line to use them, and they better have a telephone card or Canadian money or they were out of luck. We were fortunate in that our Travel Agency 800 number was good for Canada also. Before boarding the small tender we now had to show I.D. even though after three weeks on board the crew knew who we were. Our next stop was the major port of Halifax where the city was functioning quite well. We birthed across the way from a Royal Caribbean cruise ship. It had just arrived from New York prior to the incident. The passengers from the ship whom we met on the streets and in the shops were as bewildered as to where the world was going as we were. A private security officer was now standing guard by our gang plank onto the ship, a minor defensive gesture at best.

We sailed north overnight to kill the extra two days at sea and landed at Cape Breton, to visit *Beinm Bhreagh*, the home of Alexander Graham Bell and a local lobster museum. We had time to visit both and the same security guard was once again there, having driven over from Halifax. it was now time to land in America and face reality. The ship was scheduled to dock in Boston by noon on the 15th. It was an understatement to say that there was now considerable concern and apprehension among the passengers.

The next day, four Coast Guard Gun Boats positioned themselves around the *Pride* to guard it as we docked. The harbor was jammed with ships that could not enter the closed down port of New York. Upon disembarking strict procedures were in force and armed policemen with automatic weapons at the ready were in evidence everywhere including the taxi stand. It was like the third world, the 'Banana Republics' had been welcomed to America.

The ride to Logan Airport was over deserted streets and upon arrival there was no activity in front. There were no cars or people where normally it is a cauldron of activity. The American Airlines check in counter was the first one inside the door and it was empty as was the airport. Linda expressed her sympathy to the agent and asked if they were taking the situation hard. He started to cry and wondered if they could have done anything different to spot the hijackers. Walking to the boarding area we passed few passengers and numerous police and National Guard troops patrolling the concourses, some with dogs, sniffing every bag and parcel on the floor. I felt like it was the last flight out of Vietnam after the fall of Saigon, but the saga wasn't over.

As expected the plane was late and we cooled our heels in the empty terminal with just a handful of fellow passengers and a phalanx of police and soldiers. Two hours behind schedule the flight was loaded and ready to go, but yet another mechanical problem held it at the gate. Twenty minutes later the authorities boarded and escorted a middle-Eastern family with a baby off the plane and into the terminal, and we all sat. It was now six o'clock and dark. Thirty minutes later they were escorted back on and placed in first class. The pilot came on the p.a. system and said that this was a very nice family, that we had nothing to fear from them and American Airlines apologizes for the incident. Boy, were people paranoid, but the folks got an upgrade and AA might hear from their attorney again when they got home.

Yet once more the pilot was back on the p.a. to explain that the plane was now ready to depart but we had lost our slot in the air traffic control queue and that the flight must again wait for an opening. It is 7:00p.m. and folks are getting grumpy and the flight attendants have to take it on top of mourning their brethren that died and the immediate daily threat of terrorism.

After sitting for awhile the captain is back on the horn and states we have our slot now and orders the doors closed to get ready for 'push back.' We are buttoned up and the flight attendant gets on the mike with the normal departing instructions. All seems normal until half way through she is over ridden by the Captain before we have even moved. He announces that the entire airport has been shut down due to a terrorist emergency! An American Airlines flight is currently being escorted by fighter jets, and is landing here momentarily, and will be parked at an isolated part of the field. We can already see the flashing blue police cars race out into the dark to meet it.

A black comedy of errors had produced an emergency; it is now 10:00 p.m. The 9/11 catastrophe has been so monumental that it has created a labyrinth of problems, tensions were high, and new permanent procedures had yet to be in place. Because the airline system was up and flying again a procedure on each airline had to be temporarily established for cockpit entry by the crew.

American Airlines' temporary answer was that the flight crew was to establish a password between them on each flight. On the intercepted flight one pilot went to the lavatory and quickly forgot the password, and the remaining one would not let him back in. Not only that but he flashed the digital numeric sign on the transponder to indicate a hijacking, and that was the circumstance that created another delay. Every one was on edge throughout the country. We finally arrived home at 3:00 am with the additional stress of a stormy flight, and a changed world.

This last tale could have been right out of a sit-com television program, and it happened on a trip to eastern Europe just recently in 2010. We spent a week touring countries we had never been to before, the Czech-Republic, Slovakia and Hungary, which were all worth a visit. From Budapest we flew to Venice, Italy and boarded our Crystal cruise, touring the Greek Islands, the Black Sea and ending in Istanbul, Turkey. Consequently we needed some extra formal clothes for the ship still featured formal dress nights.

Because we had flown British Airways business class into Prague, we were within the required luggage weight limit, but we were booked on a small turbo prop flown by Carpathian Airlines, a Romanian gem that bumped and grinded its way once a day From Budapest to Venice, this was the only non-stop daily flight.

Prague was a busy and lovely city. The last Day we went on a day long visit out to the site of the infamous Theresienstadt Concentration camp which has been left as a memorial to all who perished there. It was a deportation camp for Jews, gays, Gypsies, Communists, and others to 'death camps,' and was converted into a model Concentration Camp to fool the

International Red Cross on how the prisoners were treated. The first prisoners arrived in November of 1941, and the camp was eventually turned into a crematorium in the end.

Our 88 year old guide had been a prisoner and was a teacher at the 'model' school in which children permanently enrolled, or were just passing through the antiseptic classrooms studied. The Germans even had a prisoner performing orchestra that gave concerts in the beautiful park as a deception. Our guide wrote a book about his experience and I bought one from him to share this gruesome tale. What a privilege to have spent the seven hours with him and I marveled at his energy. I asked him that if the horrific action of the Germans in their persecution of the Jews and others, could ever make any sense, and he said "none what so ever." He autographed the book which certainly made it more meaningful.

From Prague we trained with our luggage over-land to Bratislava, and then on to the beautiful city of Budapest for three days. The day of reckoning though had come with the suitcases and Carpathian Romanian Airlines, but not exactly in the way we had anticipated.

We arrived early at the airport for the 8:00 am departure looking like displaced persons from a war torn country. We carried our breakfast in a paper bag to eat at the airport since we had left the hotel before they served, and were dragging our gaggle of luggage. Once inside we were faced with 40-some ticket counters most of them belonging to the Hungarian carrier Malev, and none saying Carpathian. No one spoke English so I sat with the bags while Linda trooped upstairs to an area of private airline offices and sure enough ours was one. She was told that they would open in a half hour at the first stand to the left. This was pretty good information from a land that speaks 'goulash." and we became the 3rd party in line, waiting for our turn to be processed.

Right on time a bureaucratic little man walked briskly up to the counter and slipped his sign Carpathian Airlines over the Malev name. He busily arranged his papers and whatnot at the counter and eventually turned on the light, he was open for business. The first person, a single man took about five minutes to get his passage in order, apparently the agent was not in the groove yet. The second couple in line was Hungarian, with Crystal Cruise Line luggage tags on their menagerie of bags, and got into a heated argument with the agent. Eventually with disgust they handed over some Hungarian Forints, the coin of the realm to settle the debt.

"Next," he bellowed and we stepped up with our two large bags and two over-weight carry-on's, that we had hoped to skate by the scale with, but the idea was dashed when he demanded to weigh them. As he checked the weight it was obvious he was becoming more agitated, and maybe he noticed the line behind us was growing like Pinocchio's nose.

"You have more weight than is allowed free," he barked. "You Americans never follow the rules." It was not a very good start to our journey. Linda was standing in front of him and I a few feet behind, and she told him that we were going on a cruise, that we had no option, and that we would have to pay for whatever the excess came to. "How much would that be," she inquired?

"You don't have enough money," was the gruff answer, which he repeated a second time in case we missed it and he reached for the phone. "I must call my manager!" O.K. what are they going to do, make us buy a 30 year old Fairchild turboprop (at least it wasn't a flimsy Russian airliner) or have us flogged? This guy was from the old bureaucratic Communist world that once ruled Romania, and he stayed on the line about five minutes with his boss, who was upstairs in the office that Linda had been to earlier while the passengers behind us shuffled their feet over another delay.

He hung up briskly shaking his head and scowling as he mumbled that the manager said to let it go and not charge us. Wow, what a pleasant outcome. He proceeded to finish with us like he was touching dirty laundry and as Linda was thanking him I edged up to the counter. I still had in my pocket a 100 Forint bank note worth about $10.00 American and I said as I laid it on the counter, "Maybe he and his manager would like to have a beer on us." What a shock when he jumped up from his chair, his face turning red and yelled loudly, "corruption, this is corruption" as the area hushed around the counter and no doubt people's attention were drawn to the spectacle. "I can have you put in jail for this!"

My wife said "we were sorry, very sorry" and nudged me to start walking away as I was trying to do a David Copperfield trick and make the non-bribe disappear. Who knew, maybe the airport cops were on the way already. So at a brisk pace and dragging the carry-ons we made our way to the boarding area where they started loading 30 minutes later and who do you think was there also? You guessed it, our friend, the one and apparently only agent of Carpathian Airlines, but he never said a word, and we did not have to use the 'get out of jail card' after all. Thinking back, it maybe safe to assume that only the three Wise Men can proffer gifts, and if you do, it better be at an airport in Bethlehem!

The business generated from the television program was insignificant, but it did not matter. What we got instead was worth much more and certainly created some wonderful trips, great experiences, treasured memories and unusual stories. Come to think of it, we should get a gold medal for even attempting to produce a television show to begin with, but 'fools rush in where wise men fear to tread.'

Chapter 9

Wedding Bell Blues

I remember as if it was yesterday, sitting on the couch in the living room of our lovely home on Bouton Drive. I had my pajamas and robe on and our good friend Susan Stuhlbarg was sitting right next to me, and talking to Sharon as if everything was normal. It was a seminal moment in my life, and no doubt Sharon's and Susan finally caught the drift of what was going on. I would be spending my nights in the back room until I found a place to move.

It was hard to believe that my marriage had reached this point. We certainly had put enough time and effort into trying to bring the union back together again. Continuing to stay married was beyond where I wanted to go, for that time had passed. We had tried numerous marriage counselors. I was surprised when one of them told me flat out that I had a shell as hard as a turtle. Apparently my position did not allow for any more namby-pamby make believe, that everything could be fixed by therapists and counselors when it was obvious that those days had long passed.

After 29 years of marriage and a 35 year relationship it all would be severed and I would have to take the heat from Sharon, my mother who sided with my wife and became vitriolic, and my friends who chose sides, and my side came up short. Some wondered why this happened, others were surprised it took so long and of course I am sure there was the gossip which comes with such events albeit the Jewish community does not use the divorce card often. Some folks just didn't care one way or the other. Many of our best friends were long time marrieds, and had not experienced the trepidation of traveling the long lonely divorce trail of tears

311

No Regrets

Sharon Joyce Banowitz was born May 10, 1940 and used to say that *"she fell when France did to the Germans in World War II"* Her Mother Faye was actually born in Russia, and came over to America as an infant, while her Dad Morris was brought into the world on the east coast, and either due to financial hardship or death was raised by the Banowitz family, and not his parents. They were nice people with Faye always being the business woman as was her mother who had founded and still worked in the Howard Juvenile Shops which supported the five families. Her grandfather was taken to an early death during the great influenza pandemic that swept the country in 1918.

Faye was a dynamo, engaging, pushy, kind and well meaning, but with her hand in everything. She was ahead of the times with a portfolio of wild land investments, which were dubious, and she dragged the family in as investors which annoyed them, especially when the leaking dykes of speculations kept requiring additional capital with no financial return in sight. The money was put into vacant acres of desert land that someday would accommodate housing in the Tucson, Arizona area, just not in that century. They had endured some financial setbacks but Faye was always an optimist and plowed straight ahead in buying vacant parcels of sand with some success, but to continued complaints of the family that it didn't have any cash flow.

Morris owned a bakery, and made a good living at it. He rose at 4:00 am six days a week to start the ovens and raise the bread for the coming day. He was not a sophisticated man, and was frugal in his spending ways. He left the family investing to his wife, who held the purse. It is interesting to note that all three of his step brothers were extremely successful and Sam was a nationally known entrepreneur, a financier catering to the high roller business community that finds and markets gold plated speculations to the 'top hatters.' Sam was a bit of a rogue and

312

was known to sell more shares in his properties than were authorized to unsuspecting gilded risk takers.

My mother-in-law was cajoled by Sam into some good and bad investments and I suspect the judicial system was at Sam's door at the end of his life, if not inside of it when he died of mysterious causes in his sixties. He sold to the Hollywood crowd, the likes of Director Hal Wallace, and Faye was out of her league, no matter what the property was.

He ran with the Grandees and was well known as one of the original investors in the huge Huntington Harbor complex in Huntington Beach, California and was also made an honorary Chief of the Palm Springs Indian tribe after he leased dirt from them and built the landmark Spa, a pioneer venture. He was written up in Time Magazine, and the article included a picture of him wearing a full Chiefs war bonnet on his head. Sam went by the name Banowit in case you are confused like many of his investors were.

His estate in Beverly Hills was of such stature that when he divorced, the property was sold to Harry Carl, the shoe magnet who at the time was married to actress Debbie Reynolds. Oddly Sharon and I ate Passover dinner with Sam and his new trophy wife just weeks before he passed away mysteriously. There was some nonsense that she had poisoned him but no autopsy was ever called for.

Faye and her husband Morris were as different as night and day, but at the end of their marriage they were still together. They would separate for months at a time in the winter, one in Chicago and the other in Tucson, before joining up again. Morrie was a nice man who had lost confidence in himself and was afraid that they would run out of money. I know the feeling.

Eventually they retired to Tucson with the rest of the Zee, clan, (Faye's) side of the family. He was always gentle, loving, and stubborn while Faye was dynamic, and kept her feet skipping into wild investment schemes, some which came home a winner. She probably viewed more desert property than Cochise, and never did trust her brother-in-law Sam, yet was in bed on some of his investments, so she had to live with him and him with her. They quarreled constantly, but seldom talked to each other, a good solution.

Morrie did not marry until he was 38 and Faye's age was always a mystery, but she had to be near thirty. Always a business woman, she started out as a secretary on the West Coast as a young adult. They married during the *'depression years,* and were hard nose to the grindstone workers. As mentioned Faye's father had died in 1918 so being the oldest of five siblings, she and her Russian mother carried the burden of raising the family. Her oldest brother attended the University of Illinois and became a successful pediatrician after serving as a Doctor in North Africa during World War II. The family paid his way for a college education, but there was not enough money for any of the others to earn a 'sheepskin'.

Ruth, the older of the two sisters was smart, attractive, an excellent student, and independent of mind. She received her diploma from Wellesley College around the same time as future Secretary of State Madeline Albright, and continued graduate work at the University of Chicago. Ruth became a successful psychologist working from her home on the North Shore. Sharon, her baby sister was born four years later.

Dating at Francis Parker was very insular. We stayed within the halls of ivy, and our lives centered around the school and the children with whom we associated daily. Talk about inbreeding. My first date was for a hamburger at O'Connels on Rush Street. It was a hangout for many Parker kids, and I asked Caren Meyer from our grade to join me and probably others for a lunch date.

I enjoyed the company of girls, and I believe they felt comfortable with me. My sense of humor was a plus, and I was a good listener. Our class beauty was a lovely young lady who could sing, act and charm a brick. We spent a semester year of informal dating until she left me and started seeing the captain of a yacht that belonged to the family of another girl in our class, and all I had left were fond memories of my sophomore year.

My long time friend, John, with eventual degrees from Brown, Harvard and Yale once mentioned that he acted as a matchmaker in our Senior year and fixed Sharon and me up on a date. I was almost 18 and she was a freshman pushing 14. It sounds like a Tennessee Williams play, 'Kitty on a Hot Tin Plate', or whatever, but the relationship held like gorilla glue for more years than I can count.

We were married at an early age, not unusual for the times, having known each other for five years, which was an eternity for young people. Sharon was now 19 and I just 23, a college graduate, and facing a two year hitch in the Army after we were married. We both looked forward to the military posting which took us first to Indianapolis, Indiana for training at the Adjutant General School at Fort Benjamin Harrison for 3 months, and then on to permanent duty in the high desert of Southern California.

I was quiet, introspective, and shy compared to Sharon who made friends easily, and her words flowed like wine. That and her sparkling personality paved the way for my good relationships with my superiors during my tour of duty at God forsaken Camp Irwin, located just 30 miles south of Death Valley. I must hand it to her, she adapted to our desolate post as few others would have, and made the best of it by taking a job as an assistant at the Camp nursery school. We lived in Spartan quarters to begin with, but eventually moved into a nice trailer which we both enjoyed and felt privileged to be able to rent for the duration of my posting. Trailers were superior to any other housing on post except the General's.

While at Irwin we traveled to various places and occasionally visited my Aunt Ellen up in Stockton. We were just breezing through life on a Lieutenant's salary of $500 per month plus allowances. Still we were concerned about money, what the future held, and Sharon's relationship with my mother which had put her under considerable pressure from the beginning. Mother did everything possible to break us up before we were married.

She was a good sport and companion. When we decided to seek our fortune out West and move to the golden state of California after my discharge, she was on board. We packed our belongings and took the train to San Francisco and squeezed into a downtown boarding hotel for a month before I was accepted for a position working at the United Air Lines Maintenance Base, and we then moved south to Burlingame on the Peninsula. We were happy to be out West and have never left California since then.

For a while Sharon worked three days a week at a little hosiery shop on Market Street in downtown San Francisco and commuted to work in the mornings by train. In the late afternoon after work I would drive into the City and pick her up. Once we had moved into a rented house in Burlingame, she became friendly with ladies her own age and was the only Jewish member of a WASP cotillion of young marrieds. It was similar to the Army where I was the only Jewish Officer on post, and Sharon fit in with this group quite well. Under both situations we survived comfortably.

The move to southern California would change all this 180 degrees and Sharon assimilated with Jewish couples. I believe this happened because there were Jews where we were living, and before they were not present or known to us.

Our first son was born in Burlingame, the second in Long Beach and the third in Los Alamitos. I worked hard at the ice cream distributorship which I had purchased and Sharon did her own thing with organizations and her friends. She was the second Jewish lady asked to become a *Rick Racker*, a prestigious ladies charitable group in Long Beach, and knew everybody in town. My wife was a joiner and a talker, like her mom.

A mutual friend called her *Goodie Two Shoes*, a reference to the children's story, but directed specifically to her personality as being too good to be true or realistic. It was given as a compliment I am sure.

During this period we were known as creative party givers, and some friends still remember what went on over 30 years ago. Themes involved treasure hunts where instructions were delivered by a flying owl (a man dressed in a owl costume) who deplaned from an airliner at the Long Beach Airport. In the confusion he handed out the game instructions to each group of participants, with directions which led to treasures best not mentioned here.

Another grand bash involved a conference call in French, a wet suit diver jumping into the water from a Catalina Airlines amphibian plane, who swam ashore carrying instructions to the invited who were waiting on the beach for him to arrive. It ended with a dinner at a fine restaurant where checks were issued to each of the astonished attendees. You see no one knew who was giving the party (for years), and there was great consternation at a bill being left to each distinguished costumed couple who jabbered, complained, and slunk off into the night without paying. Of course arrangements had been made with the restaurant that we would pick up the tab.

As the children grew older, Sharon and I grew apart. Through years of marriage counseling, separations and returns it was becoming evident to me, and no doubt Sharon that our marriage could not endure. But how to end it? I was very close to our boys, and I certainly did not want to alienate them or lose them. I did not look forward to the infighting and bitterness that usually surrounds all divorces no matter how our situation strongly encouraged me to do so. My mother eventually aligned herself with Sharon and it became quite nasty, not really a total surprise.

Father who was in declining health told me that if I divorced, and married another woman that we would never see each other again. I was incredulous that this could happen, but he went into a full care home for the infirm and refused to see me for fear of verbal abuse from his wife. How she applied this quarantine, I still puzzle over.

For two years I spoke weekly with him by telephone, yet it was at the insistence of his nurse that encouraged a visit, and I agreed to do so. Making arrangements after such a long separation was a concern that a snap appearance might cause him physical harm from the shock. I decided to see him upon my return from a cruise that was earned by the travel agency from the *Seabourne Cruise Line* as a trade-out *for* an appearance on our agency television program. The port of debarkation was Quebec, Canada, and it was a convenient flight from there to Chicago for my surprise visit about which I remained very nervous.

This entire scenario was not to be as I received a call while still on board from his nurse that he had passed away, two days before my arrival. I was devastated, but said I would come as planned, and at least I could attend the funeral. That did not happen either. Upon my arrival in Chicago I was flabbergasted that my mother had buried my father, her husband, before my arrival and without the presence of a Rabbi for the service; there was no service! Mother didn't get mad she really got even. When I arrived I called the family Funeral Director, and asked if he knew a Rabbi I could hire to come to the family mausoleum with me in attendance and give the traditional prayer for the dead, the

Kaddish. One was found and my Father's proper burial in the echoes of the still family crypt of the mausoleum was completed.

Although my mother had avoided speaking to me for a year, and had not seen me for two, I went to her apartment to express my condolences. I could have saved my time for she accused me of coming to town to see what my Father had left me and didn't even believe that I had hired a Rabbi to go to the cemetery to perform a proper religious service.

She need not have worried about me receiving anything, for my father's estate went to her, and rightfully so. It would be another year before I would see her again, meanwhile her letters of anger and hate grew worse, her writing deteriorated into scribbles. Mother was in such a mental state, all over my relationship and conceivable marriage to Linda Johnson that she became highly unstable.

The strange twist to this surreal tale is that on a visit to see Sharon in Long Beach, a visit I was not included in, she tripped and hurt herself. Sharon stayed with her in the hotel for three nights but could not continue her vigilance any longer, and called me for a solution. I suggested that my father's long term nurse fly out to accompany mother's return to Chicago. I found her telephone number and she agreed to come to California and take her home. The nurse remained for another four years until she passed away at 83. Meanwhile I took up my responsibilities to go to Chicago every few months to visit and we spoke regularly on the phone. Our relationship was chilly, proper, and acceptable. I am sure she thought I was doing it just to be included in the will and told me so, which I denied.

After one trip I hardly arrived home when the Doctor called regarding an operation that was pending and mother had refused to authorize. He said if it wasn't performed immediately she would die, "...would you talk to her?" I said I would try and convince her to proceed based upon his explanation of the procedure and the consequences of delay. He said that, "…time was running out."

I immediately placed a call to mother's bedside at the hospital. Her voice was weak and hard to understand but she listened to what I said, which was basically a repeat of the doctor's prognoses. She asked what I thought, indeed a rare occurrence, and of course I could only pass on what I was told, and the urgency in the doctor's voice.

She reluctantly agreed, and I told her that I would return to Chicago tomorrow, "…everything would be alright." Before I left for the airport the next day the doctor called and said that my mother's system could not absorb the physical trauma of the operation and she had died on the operating table. I now would proceed to Chicago, to bury her rather than visit at the bedside. The boys were there, the nurses, a few friends, and the Rabbi passed the cloth of interment over her in a short ceremony. Are the circumstances ironic? Could I be accused of making a vindictive and wrong decision to allow my Mother to die? I never once thought so.

The meeting with the boys at the attorney's office along with her financial manager was short and sweet, and certainly contained no surprises. Her estate was left to the three boys. I expected nothing less, and it has turned out for the best. They have had their inheritance, and I was not charged with any responsibility to pass along anything down the road. I have not had any guilt or second thoughts over this and I assume they did not either. It was now time to do something about my marriage to Sharon and I filed for divorce soon after. I also thought that it was time to take my chances with the boys that they would adapt and accept the decision although it may have left some scars for which I apologize.

It seemed like an appropriate time since even though at the beginning of our second separation I would sometimes return to the house and sit awkwardly with the family. Occasionally our get-togethers were augmented by Sharon's new paramour.

My greatest concern was to do as little damage as possible to the family, and I would financially sacrifice to do my best to accomplish this. I felt the burden of my decision, and confident that this was the right way to go. No more indecision, no more counseling, no more vacillating, it was time to man up. Even though it can take me a long time to make an important decision, once I do there is no turning back.

Sharon married the doctor who was courting her. She and the family received all of my joint financial holdings, some of my individual holdings, plus child support. It was not the normal division of assets and liabilities. In doing this I gave up my share of the house, a house we had purchased 15 years previously which was now worth 10 times more, plus all other joint accounts. She had an attorney in Beverly Hills, and I had a recommended lawyer in Orange County who thought I was certifiably nuts when I told him I wanted nothing from the marriage, just out. My legal fees for his services were less than $1,000.00, and the deal was signed, sealed and delivered.

I requested to keep my small coin collection and two wood statues from the Solomon Islands, a treasure of memories from our trip there 19 years earlier. I was not granted my statue request because Sharon had already given them to her sister in Chicago, while the coins remained on my side of the ledger.

My ex sold the house and moved with her new husband to the exclusive Rolling Hills Estates area on the Palos Verdes Peninsula, taking our son Michael with her, and into a new family. Robert was in college back east and Scott the oldest was starting Loyola Law School. I moved into an apartment to await the divorce decree to be issued.

Here comes the sun,

here comes the sun I say,
It's all right
By the Beetles

Divorce Decree

Eugene William Lassers....Sharon Banovitz Lassers being sworn do here by state the following statements are true and correct...This agreement serves as a full and final settlement of All matters of joint concern...

Wedding hold the date notices were sent out, *(set to music of Chattanooga Choo Choo by Glenn Miller)*

Pardon me boy is that the San Diego Choo-Choo?
Track 27, we're in se-venth hea-ven
I can afford to board the San Diego Choo-Choo –
I've got my bride and nothing to hide.
You leave the Santa Ana station 'bout a quarter to four.....

Linda and I desired to make our wedding something special, and we rented a private 'dome-liner, club car that once rode the Union Pacific rails from Portland to Chicago. It was hard to believe that the two of us finally were going to be married, a lapsed Baptist, and a wandering Jew, far removed from his heritage. It certainly was a very big step for both of us after a long relationship that went through hoops of indecision, doubt, perseverance, separation and reengagement.

The deluxe car, *Native Son,* would be attached to the rear of a regularly scheduled AMTRAC train from Los Angeles to San Diego, and then parked, awaiting the bridal party and guests to board for the trip back after the festivities. Linda and her Maid of Honor would board the train in Los Angeles and the rest of us did so in Santa Ana.

The guest list was limited since the car could hold only 50 people comfortably, and who to invite was a tricky road to navigate. There were some couples we had bonded with before our marriage, friends that went back further than that, in my case others who broke the other way, siding with Sharon and snubbing me. There were those who chose not to be close to either party until the air cleared, and lastly business associates. Looking back some of our best friends now were not invited due to the circumstances at the time.

Driving along the 405 Freeway through Irvine, Linda and I were in deep conversation about the wedding which still was in the planning stages. We were passing trucks, and cars seemed to be passing us, but I noticed in my rear view mirror that two of them were now pulling over to the side of the road. I wondered why? We were on our way to San Diego to meet with the Superior Court Judge who was to officiate at the ceremony on board the *Native Son*. After making the arrangements in his chambers we planned to stop for lunch and then speak with the catering department of the U.S. Grant Hotel where the wedding banquet was to be held.

A blaring siren interrupted our intense discussion and flashing red lights appeared in my rear view mirror. It was an uninvited guest to our wedding, the California Highway Patrol. How annoying, I did nothing wrong. I had not had a moving traffic violation for years.

"I never thought you were going to stop, and I had to use the siren," said the Motorcycle Officer. I never saw him and told him so. He had nailed three of us in one pinch for speeding, the guy was economical. After writing the ticket he left and advised us to be careful pulling back out into traffic. He was right on that, all the cars were doing over 75 mph. We received our first wedding gift, and we could not return it.

The Judge had been booking weddings on the side for years and already had two others scheduled for the same day, September 16, 1989. He earnestly promised he would come down and perform the ceremony for us on the train in front of our friends. The *Native Son* would be shunted to a siding in front of the station and reconnected to electricity. The plan was to have AMTRAC hitch it to the northbound train to Los Angeles that evening.

Meanwhile a sumptuous wedding dinner was planned up the street from the station at the historic U.S. Grant Hotel. We drove back to Long Beach and to our separate pads without attracting additional police attention. Now we needed to make a final selection of guests.

Our list looked like Heinz 57, it was so varied and different from where many of our friendships lie today. My three boys, Scott, Robert and Michael joined the festivities, and I was proud they were there. I am sure they had mixed emotions for which I do not blame them. Because Linda was part of my life for so long I hoped that they only wished the best, and glad our issues were finally resolved.

Of course my close friend Nina Rattner, and her husband Joel were definitely coming. Nina's advice and comfort during the divorce was monumental in helping my demeanor. Strong women can help get weak men over the wilderness of depression. Friends we knew from our participation with the Long Beach Youth Home, Paul and Lorrie Merrill along with Dr. Richard and Susan Bell, also joined us.

Mort and Susan Stuhlbarg accepted for which we were very pleased. They had been close friends with both Sharon and I, and it was a definite cross-over for us to welcome them. Susan as previously mentioned was in my house the night I moved into the back bedroom and started the long and tortured path of divorce after years of marriage.

The list reached 50 and included Bob and Mia Beglinger, who were known for always being late and they came through in style, missing the wedding train, and gave up chasing it at San Clemente. Our good friends Darwin and Debra Barrad were on board, and Robert and his recently new wife Yvette DiSteffano joined us for the event. Joann and John Carey played a pivotal roll. They had become good friends after Linda and I had become volunteers at the Long Beach Youth Home, and Joann was the 'Maid of Honor,' for Linda.

September 16th arrived in the glory of a California sunrise, and Linda and Joann were dropped off at the Los Angeles Union Station at mid-day and prepared to board the *Native Son"* dome car with private dressing accommodations which was attached as promised to the mid-afternoon train for San Diego. The distinctive yellow car stood out from the silver commuter coaches pulled by the train and it was the tail-end Charlie bringing up the rear. Linda and Joanne would both preen and dress in the deluxe bedroom suite on the ride down to Santa Ana where the train stopped for our wedding party and the other passengers to board.

Meanwhile my sons, the other invitees and I were standing on the platform at the Santa Ana Station with great expectation for the train to appear. The whistle sounded as it hit the curve at the street level crossing and pulled into the station. The *Native Son* was on the end and the girls were on the steps waving as the conductor hustled us on board at the opposite end of the car. This train was going to run on time.

"*...hurray up, all aboard*" yelled the conductor as our throng gathered to step up. It was a real surprise for nobody knew what to expect. Neither did the regular passengers as we disappeared into the mystery car at the end of the train. With a wave from the conductor, and a toot of the horn from the engineer we were on our way south singing Chattanooga Choo-Choo, and led by a professional performer we had hired to entertain on the way to San Diego.

The sixteenth of September must have been a lucky day for all went like clock-work. The car was put on a siding at the San Diego Station and plugged into a power supply, and voila, lights! The Judge was fashionably late and performed the ceremony at the front of the car, and my boys had arranged a carriage with horses for Linda and I along with the Careys to ride up to the Grant Hotel while the rest of the party transferred by bus.

Dinner was served, toasts were made, and wedding cake was generously cut and consumed, and we then transferred back to the station for the return trip. Our coach had now been reattached to the next departing train north, and it rocked gently taking the sleepy revelers back to Santa Ana, while the honeymoon couple got off at Dana Point, to spend the night. We watched the departing train continue on, the dim red running lights receding down the line. The next evening we left for Europe to begin our honeymoon.

A permanent record of the fantasy night was made by our friend Shirley Wild, the social columnist for the Long Beach Press Telegram. She took candid pictures, and filed a wonderful story about the wedding for the paper.

It was only by fate that I met Linda at all. In the early 1970's, I needed a part-time assistant to help with numerous odds and ends in my stressful business as the 'Good Humor' ice cream man. Once before I had tried a lady on a full time basis but it did not work out, maybe this time would be different.

My mechanic, Rex, suggested someone who might be interested. He had worked for me a number of years so I assumed he knew what I was looking for. Her name was Linda Johnson and she drove down to the plant from Los Angeles for the interview. I found her attitude, enthusiasm, and willingness to get her hands dirty refreshing, and I was convinced that hiring Linda was worth a try.

Ms. Johnson would handle everything from payroll to helping unload the semi-truck with the twice weekly load of ice cream products for my 60 trucks. She was an employee that once one job was finished asked, "....*what's next to do.*" Our relationship was as boss and employee, nothing more and nothing less when she worked at the plant.

Minted in Southern California, she was born at home in downtown Los Angeles, and was raised in a blue collar nomad family of five. Her folks were both 'Okies' who had migrated west to California in the late thirties, and may have been members of the "Dust Bowl" exodus from the plains.

The Bratton family moved around the country at the whim of her father Carl who always owned his own body shop business, and had the "have tools, will travel" disease. Linda and her brothers, Carl Junior, and Jimmy, were never in any one place for more than a year as the family moved from California to Oregon, Arizona, Texas, Iowa, Arkansas and Georgia. It was not an easy existence, yet Carl Sr., her dad, never lacked for anything he wanted, guns, boats, cars or airplanes. Linda never had any permanency in her life, close friends, or a loving mother. She married young, and bore one child who now resides in Oklahoma.

Linda, white as the driven snow, knew her family always claimed a small Cherokee Indian heritage with 'feathers' on both her father,s and mother,s side. Yet she physically looked English-Irish (her mother was a Glenn who had a bit of the Emerald Isle in her), and a small village In Wiltshire, England is called Bratton after her Dad's family name.

My half crazed mother in one of her non-coherent letters to me accused her of being an "Indian," which was proven by her high

327

cheekbones. This put Linda at least three grades lower than my folks country club set that they ran with.

My marriage to Sharon started to disintegrate in the early 1970's, yet the final decree was not issued until 1988, a time lapse of 14 years. We had failed to resurrect it, and I left and returned to the house twice over this time, not accepting the truth, and the flame of denial was kept alive by both of us. It would have been logical to end it then but neither of us wanted to pull the plug.

Linda was divorced, and there was nothing left for her in California once I closed the distributorship, so she decided to return to her family now living in Paducah, Kentucky. I wasn't making any effort to get divorced, even though I endured great unhappiness as did Sharon I am sure. By this time Linda's and my relationship had grown, and because our personalities are on the "prudish" side, our longtime friendship remained at that stage when she told me of her intentions, which was for the best since it would take a long time for me to get divorced. This revelation brought tears to my eyes something I hadn't experienced since childhood or any time since. It seemed that any happiness that might be in the future for me was leaving town on the 3:10, and was not going to return. There was no reason to. It would be two years in the wilderness for us both as Linda tried to pick up life in a southern town that she had never lived in but her family now did, and I tried once again to mend my marriage to no avail. One thing I know for sure she was not happy to be living in the south, family or not.

By 1982 Sharon and I were separated once again, and I was now in an apartment on the beach. I would see the boys as much as possible and during this period our last son Michael (born in 1975) and I spent some quality one on one time together at Sunset where I now lived. He had to tear up his roots in Lakewood and move to the Palos Verdes Peninsula with his mother which was hard since all his friends were in the Long Beach area. I am sure that there was some resentment, and it caused some scar tissue, but I hope no damage. He has proven himself in many ways as he now approaches his 38th birthday, and he, his wife Amy Jo, and two daughters now live in Littleton, Colorado..

In 1988 the divorce decree was final, and it wasn't until after the wedding the next year that I moved into our new town home we had purchased near Long Beach State College. It was hard to qualify for the loan because I had given up most of my assets in the divorce. I now was working as a Real Estate Broker, and lending institutions looked at my unverifiable income with a jaundiced eye, discounting my assets as they always do when you need a loan.

Our new home was a happy one and we enjoyed doing things together and being on the same page with our interests and inner clocks. We loved history, and politics, lived to travel, and had purchased a travel agency which gave us numerous opportunities to do this at discounted rates. Our money, though, remained tight, and we both worked the store-front putting in five and a half day weeks. Because of business irregularities by our partner, debit memos from the airlines, long hours, and other major problems it brought considerable stress, and we could only say it came with the territory.

Linda's father passed away in the early ninety's and even though there were siblings in Paducah, it became our responsibility to pay for the funeral, and the grave site. Receiving a loan from a friend we were able to shoulder the financial obligation. Yet it was hard to see how we would keep our remaining assets with our expenses escalating. Linda was a good financial manager, and bookkeeper, and the management of two apartment buildings on the side brought in some extra money. Her positive attitude kept me from brooding, she lived for the day, and now I do the same.

The assets that I was given by my Aunt Ellen sure saved our bacon since there was nothing more to turn to aside from our income. Part of the inheritance was given to Sharon, some allotted for the down payment on our townhouse, and part went into second trust deeds which at the time I considered a conservative investment, and which turned out not to be. Some paid off, one second trust deed went bad, another south. Later the LLC partnership decided to protect our interest on the latter and we paid off the first and retained title in a nine unit apartment building, eventually doubling our money. It put us on the road to financial recovery.

Our finances began to reverse themselves into positive territory, and prayers were being answered for fiscal salvation after many insecure years. The travel business was changing and it was financially impossible to front a brick and mortar store with employees once the airlines stopped paying commissions, and our path now led to some big decisions.

The housing market was booming and we had made money on our two story town home which had become physically harder to negotiate for persons in their sixties. Through our good friend, and realtor, Jill Rosenberg, we started to look at other options. She had found a one story small home on the Lakewood County Golf Course that could be fixed up for our senior years. It closed escrow in January of 2001 and we bought the new home for exactly the same amount, to the penny, that we sold our old home, a strange coincidence. While it was being rehabilitated our new friends Gordon and Judi Lentzner allowed us to stay in their house nearby while they were out of town.

We immediately closed down the agency store-front and brought the business into the house which provided a tremendous cost saving and Linda retained our outside agents in the process. Over the next few years our business grew and the cost of doing business plummeted.

ChildNet, a Southern California non-profit was another tangent to our financial recovery. Linda and I had been involved as volunteers for years, and over time were active with the Boosters, a fund raising arm of the organization, and with the Board of Directors.

Robert DiStephano, the CEO of ChildNet called me one day and asked if I would like to help out the organization by supervising their Maintenance Department for a period of time in that their present situation was in flux. I would not have to give up my current job (travel agent) to fill in for what would be needed. It sounded good to me so I accepted. For the first few weeks I was over-whelmed in trying to select new office copiers for their many locations. Also there was general maintenance to take care of with constant repairs especially at the Youth Home, and the non-public school. The children in our care had learning disabilities, emotional problems and some were wards from the Juvenile Court system. In addition I had a staff of two employees in the department.

I was turning in my time on an hourly consultant basis, but within two months it was obvious that this was a full time position and Robert asked me if I would continue on a permanent basis. I agreed to this in January of 2001, and while I thought I would just be passing through it has turned out that I have worked at Childnet for 12 years, a great place to be employed! I thank Robert, Allan Greenberg the CFO, and *bon ami* Kathy Hughes the new CEO for the opportunity and their friendship.

We were fortunate to be drawing social security, covered by Medi-Care, and a new reverse mortgage on the house was a God send. They paid us monthly rather than the reverse. So at the twilight of our lives we were blessed with financially security, and as I look back on the decision to have given away my assets in the divorce, I have received back double in return.

Linda and I have been a team, and it has kept our marriage alive, interesting and active. We enjoy each other's company and spending nights together at home. This is not to say that during our 24 year marriage that we have not been active in many different venues. Linda has excelled by being President of the Civic Light Opera, the Childnet Boosters, the Childnet Board of Directors and the Cancer League.

I also was President of the ChildNet Board and Young Horizons, another children affiliated agency. I still serve as the oldest member on the California State Headquarters Building Commission, and have volunteered in various other charities over the years. I have enjoyed my long time membership in our local Kiwanis Club, participating in the good things that they do. I arranged for our club to join others that put on Veterans bingo at the local V.A. hospital.

We have much to be thankful for especially the relations with the boys and their families. Sharon is more comfortable and our relationship is friendly. We have great friends that include Lewis and Jill Rosenberg, Mort and Susan Stuhlbarg, Gordon and Judi Lentzner, Steve and Linda Gordon, Joel and Lyn Epstein, Gerry and Sandy Facon, David and Jeri Goldstein, Darwin and Debra Barrad, and many others. Forgive me if I did not mention everyone by name.

Our family is most important to both of us. Scott and lisa live in Orange, Ca. and have two wonderful boys, Jordan and Matthew, who are as different as night and day and each will be successful in his own right. Robert and Pauline live in Long Beach with their very talented children, Sam and Erin, who, no doubt, will write their own chapters of success down the road.

As mentioned previously, Michael and Amy moved from Orange to Littleton, Colorado 3 years ago and love their new environment, and the friends they have made. Their daughters,

Amber and Madison, are definite comers and we look forward to watching them grow up.

Linda's son Mickey (Michael) lives in Broken Arrow, Oklahoma, and has raised one son Michael, who is now working full time. At present he is single, and we have taken them both in as part of our extended family.

Our opportunity to travel has been unprecedented, and we take full advantage of it as we advance further into our senior years. The philosophy is if we don't travel now, when will we? The opportunity to do so at reduced or complimentary rates has allowed both of us to enjoy life at a higher level than our wages and assets normally would allow.

As our lives are now being etched in 'stone' there is nothing that we want for and only pray that the days ahead will be kind health wise, and allow us time to see the grandchildren on their way. We both will keep working as long as we can, for it is the salvation of seniors to stay active. It lets us associate with younger people, and to have a purpose each day, and with that hopefully comes a peaceful night's sleep.

I believe that life is a circle, and from the beginning to the end it is based on the theory that everything is recycled, including us. At its expiration memories of a productive life, accomplishments, and family become our greatest assets. What you have on the walls, on the floor, in the garage or in the bank is not relative to the comfort of having a wall, a floor, four wheels, a garage to put it in, and a comfort zone in the bank, best yet, a wonderful wife to share this blessing with. A great life centers on being satisfied with what you have, and indeed we are.

What comes around, goes around they say. My life has come and is now going. It has been a *life of no regrets*. When I put the boys down at night in their beds we would sing Camp Nebagamon songs, and finish with this one to the tune of Taps.

Day is done.
Gone the Sun
From the lake, from the hill, from the sky.
All is well,
Safely kept,
God is nigh.

Gene and Linda pose at the 50th birthday luncheon for Linda.

One of the many articles written about the Touch of Travel T.V. show.

Wedding invitation.

Gene and Linda were married aboard the Native Son dome car shown here in San Diego, Ca.

The "boys". (L-R Michael, Scot and Robert at his wedding to Pauline).

SOCIETY / By SHIRLEY WILD

Wed on a train

■ **The party line:** Guests at the wedding of Gene Lassers and Linda Johnson were invited to board "The Native Son," a private railcar (Gene is a railroad buff) at the Santa Ana Amtrak station.

Champagne and hors d'oeuvres were served and the miles sped by. Jeffrey Polk, of the Long Beach Civic Light Opera, dressed in tuxedo and striped engineer's cap, led a group sing of "Chattanooga Choo Choo." Judge Norbert Ehrenfreund boarded in San Diego and performed the wedding ceremony, and guests took buses to the Grant Hotel for dinner. A white horse-drawn open carriage took Gene and Linda back to the train. On the way home guests had a traditional tiered wedding cake and a non-traditional chocolate cake in the form of a train. Linda and Gene got off at Dana Point station. Then they embarked on their honeymoon in England. On BritRail, of course.

■ **Head turners:** The bride, in a Rentillo-designed suit with peplum, of white lace on pink organza, with bodice overlaid with crystal sequins and pearls. A silk organza bow in her hair matched the one at her waist. Pearl-covered pumps and borrowed pearls completed the accessories. She carried white orchids and roses.

■ **Overheard:** "I do!"

■ **Spotted in the crowd:** Gene's three sons, who stood up for him, Scott (best man), Robert and Michael; Matron of Honor Joanne and John Carey; Carol and Walt Shaffer; Delores (she co-hosted a pre-nuptial shower) and Steve Morgan.

Photograph by Shirley Wild

Gene and Linda Lassers stop by Amtrak engine after their marriage in the private railcar "Native Son" in San Diego.

Article in the Press Telegram about the wedding.

Scott, Lisa, Jordan and Matthew Lassers

Erin, Robert, Pauline and Samuel Lassers Lassers.

In our seventies and still having fun

Linda & Gene

Michael, Amy, Amber and Madison Lassers